A HAND IN THE
DARKNESS

A HAND IN THE
DARKNESS

The Autobiography of a Refusenik

IDA NUDEL

TRANSLATED BY STEFANI HOFFMAN

WARNER BOOKS

A Time Warner Company

To my very dearest Lena, Leva and Yakov

Warner Books, Inc., 666 Fifth Avenue, New York, NY 10103
W A Time Warner Company

Printed in the United States of America
First Printing: November 1990
10 9 8 7 6 5 4 3 2 1

Library of Congress Cataloging-in-Publication Data

Nudel, Ida.
    A hand in the darkness : the autobiography of a refusenik / Ida
Nudel ; translated by Stefani Hoffman.
        p.   cm.
    Translated from the Russian.
    ISBN 0-446-51445-4
    1. Nudel, Ida. 2. Refuseniks—Biography. 3. Jews—Soviet Union—
Biography. I. Hoffman, Stefani. II. Title.
DS135.R95N825   1990
947'.00492402—dc20
    [B]   90-34378
                                                               CIP

Book design: H. Roberts

ACKNOWLEDGMENTS

AT MY DESK IN MY APARTMENT IN MOSCOW, OR IN THE COLD HUT in Siberia or in the sunny but alien Moldavian house, composing one letter after another to those imprisoned or in exile or in forgotten settlements thoughout that enormous land, I often thought that their fate carries a historic message. I was prepared to tell any writer everything I knew about the participants in the peaceful national movement that prompted the exodus of the Jews from the Soviet Union. Fate, however, decreed otherwise, and I was given the great honour and responsibility of telling our story—how ordinary people declared to a powerful punitive system that they no longer wanted to be its slaves.

My deep thanks to Dr. Armand Hammer and my literary agent Norman R. Brokaw, who during a dinner in Los Angeles easily and elegantly conducted negotiations with my publisher, Warner Books.

Stefani Hoffman was to me much more than just an objective translator. Her persistence helped to present events in their proper sequence. For that and for her involvement in my life story I am immeasurably grateful to her.

I want to express special, cordial gratitude to my first readers —Felix Kandel, Mara Subotsky, Channa Rabinowitz, Ehud Yaniv. They encouraged me in many ways.

My publisher, Nansey Neiman, read my original draft in Russian. Her remarks guided me during the first complicated stage of writing my narrative.

Susan Suffes, my editor at Warner Books, helped me overcome the doubts and diffidence of an inexperienced chronicler and made the manuscript a book, for which I am infinitely grateful.

I am deeply thankful for everyone who worked on the book. I am deeply thankful to members of Kibutz Negba who hosted me in the summer of 1988.

As always, my family—Lena, Leva and Yakov—patiently and lovingly tolerated the ups and downs of my mood during the long year of work on the manuscript. Their support was invaluable.

I believe that we all, participants and witnesses of great events, are blessed to live at a time when human history is turning its bright countenance toward us.

וַיִּוָּתֵר יַעֲקֹב לְבַדּוֹ וַיֵּאָבֵק אִישׁ עִמּוֹ עַד עֲלוֹת הַשָּׁחַר

בראשית לב:כה

And Jacob was left alone; and there wrestled a man with him until the breaking of the day.

—Genesis 32:25

כִּי שָׂרִיתָ עִם אֱלֹהִים וְעִם אֲנָשִׁים וַתּוּכָל

בראשית לב:כט

For thou hast striven with God and with men and has prevailed.

—Genesis 32:29

INTRODUCTION

IN FAIRY TALES, NOT IN REAL LIFE, GOOD CONQUERS EVIL. THE story of a Jewish woman who challenged the malevolent Soviet system ought to have ended tragically; after all, that's what had happened to so many before me. But the story of my struggle ended victoriously. Was it an accident or miracle?

It was both—and also something more. Something even greater than a miracle. It was the many new friends—people of good will—who followed in sympathy and in alarm the unequal duel of one against the many. These new friends appeared for demonstrations, demanding that their governments do something, wrote letters, organized conferences and traveled to the Soviet Union. This something more included those who came to me in exile or sent packages thus assuring my physical survival. Most of all, it was my sister, Lena, the first person to whom I turned every day with every request.

This story is proof that it is possible to carry out the most difficult of our people's ethical commandments—"Love thy neighbor as thyself." Each girl and boy, each woman and man who played a part in this victory—even if they remain nameless—are present in every event described in this book. And except for changing the names of a few people involved who did not want to be named or of people remaining in the Soviet Union, I am telling my story as I remember it.

All my actions were legal although I tried to let the secret police discover as little as possible about them. My position was open and honest and my motto was: "I don't want to live with you! Give me a visa to Israel. Let me and my people go!"

I decided to tell what happened to me, and what I felt and

thought during those long, hard difficult years of defeat and in those rare bright moments of victory. I do so in gratitude to all those who helped bring the wicked story to a happy ending. And I do so in amazement that in my life, which was no fairy tale, good conquered evil.

PROLOGUE

A very persistent knock forced me quickly to answer the door.

"Hurry, come down to my apartment, there's a war over there!"

No one had to tell me what "there" meant. Every Soviet Jew knew that "there" was Israel, a name, however, which none of us dared to say out loud, even in private.

"War—there! What's going to happen to them? What's going to happen to us?"

"Ida, hurry, war—there, how awful!"

My seventy-year-old neighbor and I hurried down the stairwell so as not to miss the Voice of Israel's transmission; we must not miss the latest news.

From that day in June 1967, as the latest news poured from the radio, my life acquired another meaning, another focus. Looking at the attentive Jewish faces around me, I felt that once again we were preparing for a meeting with destiny.

In the next days I dashed home from work in order to catch the latest broadcast. I wanted to hear with my own ears what was going on in the distant but now so dear "there." The first three days were torture, a nightmare of waiting for the war's end. On the fourth day my neighbor phoned me at work and said in a solemn voice that "auntie" felt much better.

I couldn't contain my joy. I ran to tell Jewish acquaintances working in another room. "Better; she's better," I whispered excitedly.

Their sad faces turned completely pale. "Why are you screaming?" they asked with barely concealed malice.

"What happened to you, Ida?" asked my non-Jewish colleagues.

I found it impossible to tell them the truth and said, "My elderly aunt got sick."

They did not even eye me suspiciously; nor did they show any empathy.

I understood my co-workers' reaction. They conserved their concern for themselves, which was only fair. They had become so tired from lack of money, from scandalous scenes in communal apartments, from the grayness and senselessness of their lives. I, too, was tired of the struggle for survival and of the work that failed to satisfy my restless nature.

Things were just as bad for me as for them, but those three days of my existence no longer circled around such problems, problems that wasted the soul. My life was no longer creeping like a snake; it was rushing in headlong flight, faster and faster. Truly fantastic things were happening "there." We were winning! Finally we Jews were defending ourselves with dignity. I no longer belonged to a nation of victims; I could proudly raise my head. I, that is we Jews were just like everyone else; if they beat us, we would retaliate.

What was the response to our triumph? Soviet society reacted with unanimous condemnation in the press, at work, in schools and on the street. The Jews, naturally, were aggressors, conquerors, always attacking other nations. How did it suddenly come to this? Why is it that in the past schoolchildren threw it up to me that all Jews were cowards, that the Nazis really murdered us to wipe all weaklings from the face of the earth?

What did it all mean?

CHAPTER 1

MY PARENTS, YAKOV NUDEL AND CHAYA FILANOVSKY, WERE barely twenty years old when I was born in 1931. Both had grown up in poor Jewish neighborhoods. As young people they had sincerely believed in the brotherhood of nations and the sanctity of the communist idea.

My father grew up in the city of Simferopol in the Crimea where he went to work at a very early age. As a boy of eight he strapped on a tray and went around selling pies that his mother had baked. Bullies would often take them away or beat him up. In tears he would go to his mother and fearfully await additional punishment for the lost wares.

My mother grew up in a little town of Belorussia called Nevel, populated mainly by poor Jews. Her father did not even have his own home. The revolution, flashing hopes and promises of universal brotherhood, brought joy to this impoverished family. My grandfather, Izrail Filanovsky, a poor shoemaker, became a member of the first Jewish collective farm, or *kolkhoz*. He resettled in the Crimea and for the first time in his life acquired his own home at Dzhankoy Station. Day and night he prayed for the safekeeping of his treasured possession.

As enthusiastic members of the Komsomol youth organization, my parents participated in the construction of a factory in Novorossiisk. However, the conditions were too harsh for raising a child, and when I was less than a year old my parents left me with my maternal grandparents. Already three years old before being brought back to my parents, now in Moscow, I met my younger sister, Lena, almost two years my junior. I could not play with the children in the courtyard since I did not speak Russian, but Lena and I studied the language together.

My parents were among millions of Soviet Jews determined to raise their children as Russians. Although both my parents spoke and read Yiddish, at home only Russian was spoken and my sister and I had to speak without a Jewish accent.

I grew up like all other Soviet children: day-care, kindergarten, school, communist youth organizations—first the Pioneers and then the Komsomol. But I knew that I was not like everyone else. I was a Jew.

When I was little and a young anti-Semite wouldn't play with me, he would say, "You're bad." Sometimes the other kids would scream at me, "You kike!"

Sometimes in meeting my gaze adults would say to me, "What are you looking at like that, Jew?" Something about me bothered these people. And from time to time the question, Why do they hate us so? tore me away from my daydreams.

I spent my adolescence in the physical and emotional darkness of World War II. On June 22, 1941, when Hitler invaded the Soviet Union, life showed us its black side. A day later my father, a reserve officer, left as a volunteer for the front. His few letters told us that Jewish officers were shot in the back by their own soldiers. I never saw him again; I was ten years old.

The Germans advanced at a headlong pace deep into the country, approaching the Crimea. Information began to leak out that the enemy was annihilating all Jews, old and young, healthy and sick. My desperate mother spent days and nights at the telegraph office sending telegrams to my grandparents, pleading that they come to her immediately in Moscow. She wired them money for the tickets but it was returned because the post office in Dzhankoy had already been evacuated.

Finally, she managed to find them by phone. "Papa," she implored, "all of you must come right away. Get a ticket to Moscow; here you'll understand what is happening."

"My darling daughter," he replied, "with whom will I leave

my house? I will pray to our God for you and for all of us; perhaps
he will save us."

"Give me Mama," she begged.

"Influence him, Mama, please; you will all die."

"Whatever your father says, will be," she replied.

"What can I do with you? Give me Lyuba!"

My aunt Lyuba took the receiver. "Lyuba, use your head.
After all, you're a mother! You'll build a new house. Lyuba, borrow
money from anyone and get here fast."

"No, I can't leave the old folks; Father can't abandon the
house."

"What can I do, how can I get you away, how can I save you?
I'll probably go crazy. Give me Isaac." And again she tried to
convince, imploring. "Isaac, at least send me the older children,"
she asked.

"No, we won't split up," her brother-in-law replied.

That night, after the phone call, she didn't sleep at all.

The enemy began to bomb Moscow. We learned to live in a
bomb shelter, to fill our canteens, to remember where the knapsack
lay. We learned to stay close to home in those rare hours when
children were allowed to run in the street. We learned not to fear
the dark and the thundering cannon that were meant to repel enemy
attacks. We learned all these things very quickly.

October 16, 1941, during an air raid warning, officers called
Mama from the shelter and ordered her to gather our things immediately; we were being evacuated to safety. Near the entrance
to the building, a truck stood that had been sent from my father's
place of work.

They gave us ten minutes. We raced up four flights to our
apartment, where another three families also resided. Mama filled
up our canteens with water, put winter hats on our heads even
though it was only September, stuck winter coats in our hands,
grabbed a pillow and blanket for each, tied it all in a big package,
and stuck a night pan, aluminum bowls, mugs and spoons inside
it.

We scrambled downstairs to the waiting truck. While Mama
crawled into the back, the driver managed to hoist up my sister and

me. Then he jumped into the cab and we sped off. It was the first time that I rode around Moscow in an open vehicle. The city seemed unreal, as if it were dead; without traffic or pedestrians the streets seemed unusually broad.

Mama hugged both of us as we rolled around like unwieldy balls when we hit bumps. The truck pulled up to the railroad station and, without stopping, we raced to the train standing on the tracks. Ahead of us, trucks continuously pulled up, unloaded women and children and quickly disappeared.

Someone pointed to a train car. Someone else seated Lena and me while Mama threw her bundle of things inside and climbed in beside us. It was an unusual car. Three tiers of wooden planks made it possible to load a lot of people into it, but you could only lie down or sit with your head slumped over.

"Bed down over there in that corner," said the man who had seated me and Lena. "Don't light matches and don't talk. Mothers, see that your children don't cry. Everything will be straightened out. Watch your children and keep them close to you. There will be water later."

Gradually the car was filled up with women and children.

After the train had started to move and had gathered speed, we realized that the train was being bombed. Dusk had just set in, and the long ribbon of cars made an excellent target. It had become a duel between the train engineer and the murderous pilot. The plane kept circling above us, releasing bombs. The train sped forward at a crazy pace, tossing us from side to side. Mothers clutched their children tightly, and feeling the terrible tension, even the very smallest of us was silent. The fascist bomber nevertheless struck his target, but luckily he hit the very last cars, which contained only equipment. The cars uncoupled while moving and the plane remained behind. When people realized that we were out of danger, the crying and whining really began. All at once everyone returned to life.

At night the train stopped at a small station. Although we were allowed to get out, find hot water and walk around, all were in shock from their harrowing experience and few dared to leave the car. During the day, at the next train stop, hot food was distributed—steaming porridge and stacked bowls of soup. We ate the porridge and saved the soup for supper. Life began to settle down. It was announced that all women and children from Moscow were being evacuated beyond the Urals. Our home on wheels moved east very slowly. Sometimes the train would stand in the same station for several days; sometimes it stood for several hours in the middle of nowhere. We didn't wash, got full of lice and grew savage from the inhuman life.

I was ten years old and I was already a bookworm. There were several books in the car. People read them aloud and to themselves, one after the other and reread them. Then they were exchanged with people in neighboring cars.

We were on the road for almost a month and finally arrived in a small Siberian town called Tyumen, where we were given a special bath to destroy the lice, which were literally eating us alive. Then we were scattered around town. Mama, my sister and I were settled in a little extension of a house that the owners had used previously as a storeroom. In winter the walls were covered with ice, in spring and fall with a green dampness. Nevertheless, it was a separate room and it had a stove.

Mama went to study agronomy and finished the course. Through the spring, summer and fall of that year she walked five miles to work each way. Serving as an agricultural adviser at a local farm, she spent the whole working day on her feet. Her reward for this labor, in addition to a meager wage, was some potatoes or turnips, or a few carrots that farmers let her take home. My sister and I didn't starve.

It was at this time that we received the news of our father's death. He had died near Stalingrad, a colonel and the political leader of his battalion. His friend wrote my mother: "You can be proud of your husband. If he were not a Jew, he would have been a Hero of the Soviet Union. He was the only officer in the battalion who led his soldiers into battle with the command 'follow me' as he went in front of them." This letter, heartfelt as it was, could not possibly soften the pain of the loss.

A few weeks later, we learned of the deaths of my grandparents' entire family in the Crimea. The Jews of the famous first Jewish *kolkhoz*, those who could not tear themselves away from their homes, had perished. Mother's father and mother, her only sister and her sister's husband and their five children were annihilated in a mobile gas chamber alongside the road leading to the dump where the Nazi murderers threw the corpses. The news of her family's agonizing death and the loss of her husband were terrible blows to my mother and for many years there were no songs or laughter in our home. She gave all her love and strength to preserving and educating us, her daughters.

In the beginning of 1943 we returned to Moscow to find that other people had illegally settled in our room. Although we succeeded in having them evicted, they made off with almost everything we had left during our flight. Now we found an empty room containing a bed, a bookcase and a closet. The only thing in the closet was my father's army uniform. So, we had to start life anew. Alone, without relatives and with two adolescent girls, my mother denied herself everything in order to give both of us a good education. She worked in a nursery school from seven in the morning until seven at night so that we had food and clothing and were able to attend school; nevertheless, our little family led a poor and secluded life. Only two other girls in my class had lost their fathers at the front, and aside from me, there was only one other girl who did not wear silk stockings and a school uniform. When the girls attended dances at the neighboring boys' school, I would stay home and memorize long poems of great Russian poets. I was a short, skinny girl, with a heavy dark braid that fell below my waist. A dreamer whose eyes reflected my imagined world, I fantasized about becoming an actress and would soulfully read heroic and tragic poems. During the midday recess the teachers would gather all the students in the school auditorium around a chair in the middle. Placing me on it so that all could see and hear, I would recite poetry by heart. The teachers would cry.

When I was fourteen years old, I learned to sew simple things on my own. I learned that by ripping out the seams of an old item, I could create something new from it, gradually moving on to more and more complicated things. After that, until my sister and I began to earn our own money, I sewed all the family's clothing. My mother bought me my first pretty dress when I had entered the tenth and last grade at school. I still remember the soft velvet material, the pleated skirt and rounded collar, the shiny belt buckle and buttons down the front.

My coat had been made from my father's overcoat. Although it was very heavy, I enjoyed the adult feel of it. Later on, when I was a student at the institute, the coat checker often said, while handing me my coat, "I know why you're so tiny—the heavy coat didn't let you grow."

CHAPTER 2

LIKE MANY OTHER STUDENTS AT THE MOSCOW INSTITUTE OF
Engineering and Economics, I participated in sports and in amateur
theatrical performing groups, went on excursions, attended the
theater and concerts. I had my friends and, valuing the traits of
honesty, kindness and devotion, I did not differentiate between
Jews and non-Jews. Rushing down the hall, I barely had time to
shake all the hands and respond to the many smiles.

Suddenly, everything changed. On one terrible day, January
13, 1953, the press labeled us "murderers in white robes." Stalin
decided to try to annihilate the Jewish community and concocted
a terrible tale about Jewish doctors murdering Soviet people. Thus
we were declared guilty. Friends no longer offered a handshake or
called out when I walked along the halls of the institute. And no
one smiled at me.

Silence reigned. I stopped going to sports practice, no longer
greeted acquaintances, didn't even smile. Then there were the
meetings where everyone branded the Jews as murderers. In my
student group I sat alone in the last row. No one wanted to sit near
me and I didn't want them to. Another Jewish girl sat in the first
row, demonstrating by her attitude that the proceedings had nothing to do with her personally. As the students pronounced the words
that shattered my innocent faith in people, I didn't look at their
faces and I couldn't lift my eyes. But I heard the sincerity in their
voices.

One girl, with whom I had shared a sleeping bag during a trip, said, "It's a shame that Hitler didn't finish the job and destroy them down to the last one."

"We shouldn't forgive them; they deserve death for such crimes," said another friend with whom I had occasionally skipped out on a boring lecture and had fun chasing each other around on ice skates.

"It's a pity that they didn't destroy them," the gathering decided.

I blotted them out of my life, right there, in the auditorium. At lectures I would enter the auditorium last, after the teacher, and I would leave it first, immediately after the teacher. I didn't address former friends or respond to their questions.

"What happened to you?" someone once asked me. "You act like an owl, ruffling your feathers and not saying a word."

"You betrayed me," I replied simply.

They whispered among themselves and left me alone. Perhaps they had not even associated me with those "murderers." But I had. I walked around with my head and shoulders bowed under the weight of the terrible accusation. It can't be, my heart screamed; I don't believe it, it can't be! This so-called doctors' plot completed my emotional development.

In 1954 I graduated from the institute with a speciality in the economics of construction. Young and still naive, I agreed to work in the Urals and landed in a small town named Kushva, where the entire population worked at one enterprise—a plant for the excavation of nonferrous materials.

Life in this town deep in the *taiga*, or forest, was isolated and quiet; the only amusement was a movie theater where the film was changed only twice a week. The food in the shops was monotonously constant—ham, bread, canned vegetables and fish in tomato sauce, barley and enormous amounts of alcohol. When the stores ran out of vodka, people would boil champagne and drink it like tea, getting drunk instantly. Often in the middle of the night I could hear the desperate screams of women and children as the besotted father of the family, roaring like a beast, would run with ax in hand after his offspring.

Having satisfied my desire for independence, I returned home after two and a half years and began to work as an economist for a construction firm in Moscow.

My life was typical for young educated people in the capital.

I and my friends, who were all Russians, avoided politics, attended all the theatrical openings, read popular novels and hiked around the country. With knapsacks on our backs, we covered thousands of miles, rowed and canoed on many rivers and climbed the mountains of our vast and beautiful country.

Sometimes, however, as I sat near a burning campfire, leaning against someone's warm back and listening to the sad songs, I would remember other faces, those of my former friends who had betrayed me a few years earlier.

"Why don't your eyes ever laugh?" my friends would sometimes ask.

What could I tell them? They would never understand. I was sure that they had either forgotten or had never even recognized the significance of those terrible events.

My mother became seriously ill with cancer in 1959, an operation followed by radiation treatment enabling her to live on for a few years. A bright moment during this time was my sister Lena's marriage to Leva, a young and likable young man. For us three women, unaccustomed to having a man in the house, his presence became a pleasant source of concerns and cares. We so much wanted him to feel at home with us.

When my sister became pregnant, we all were excited about it, but something went wrong. Having passed her due date, Lena was hospitalized when, suddenly and unexpectedly, Mama became very, very ill. The ambulance service did not respond to our entreaties over the phone. When, at last, they arrived, she had deteriorated to a state where she could no longer walk. I spent the whole night standing next to the stretcher on which she lay in the hospital waiting room, trying to ease her suffering as best I could.

The doctor on duty told me, "This is the end." I refused to believe him. Then they took her into the ward and told me to return in a few hours. When I rushed back, they announced that my mother had died. I couldn't comprehend it. The doctor had to repeat it several times.

Lena was lying in the hospital, past her due date. How could I tell her that Mama had died? What if the terrible news would suddenly affect her or her pregnancy? I decided not to say anything to my sister, and so she would not see my tears I stopped coming by the window of her ward in the daytime. I lied, telling her that

Mama was sick with the grippe and was not writing for fear of accidental infection. Finally she gave birth to a son, Yakov, in February 1963. Before giving Lena the baby, the doctor who released her from the hospital told her that Mother had died.

Time flew and our wounds healed. We all lived together in a tiny Moscow apartment where I had my own room, if one could call it that. Yakov—named after our papa—grew and he was put into a nursery school. One day it was my turn to pick him up. As we talked on the way home I failed to notice his unusual agitation. In the apartment, however, after I had changed into house clothes and had gone out to join him, he began running around the room with a red face and glowing eyes. He was crying and howling, "Tell me that I am not a Jew, tell me that I am a Soviet!"

My God, what have they done to the child to make him so crazy? Not even five years old and he is already full of such terrible pain! What had these beastly Soviet educators done to him to cause such rage? What could I do?

I pressed him tightly to me and told him, "We are all Jews; your father and your mother and I and your doctor, Abram Lvovich, we are all Jews—you, too." He resisted and burst out of my arms. I wrestled with him for some time until he became exhausted and quieted down.

In the middle of the night, I awakened and quietly, calmly thought everything through, turning over the possibilities in my mind. In the morning the three of us decided that Yakov would no longer go to the kindergarten. We would have to use one of our salaries to hire a nurse. I realized then that if suddenly there was the slightest opportunity to leave this "dear, beautiful country," if suddenly the tiniest little crack opened, I would try to squeeze through it.

It was no longer possible for all of us to live in one small apartment. I took out loans from friends, sold my few valuables and bought a one-room cooperative apartment with a small kitchen and moved into it in 1968. I was not far from my sister and we saw each other daily.

For my birthday in the spring of 1968 Lena gave me a radio, my life's dream. From then on I regularly listened to broadcasts from abroad. In June 1970 the Voice of Israel broadcast a report about the arrest of a large group of Jews in Leningrad. According to the report, they had wanted to emigrate to Israel, but the Soviet authorities refused to let them go. Allegedly, they were seized trying to hijack a plane and leave the Soviet Union illegally.

I was in shock over what I had heard. Others were doing something, but what about me? I had to go and find these others.

My neighbor could not help at all but he knew a Jew who, as he said, "maybe knows." But this other Jew, too, knew nothing. In frustration, I was practically ready to stop people on the street and ask.

I had already begun to despair, when Leva told me that his father might help. Boris Lvovich arranged to meet me in the subway where he told me that others regularly gathered near the Moscow synagogue every Saturday at nine in the morning.

"Boris Lvovich, I work in a planning institute," I said to him. "I have security clearance. If I start showing up near the synagogue, then I'll be fired for sure."

"You're right, I hadn't thought about that," he said. "I'll speak with someone and think about how to help you."

A few days later he called to arrange another meeting. Boris Lvovich gave me a note with the address and home telephone of Vladimir Prestin, a Jew who taught Hebrew. Boris Lvovich warned me to say nothing overt on the phone, not to use the word "Hebrew," and not to ask about lessons. Prestin would know why I was calling.

I couldn't believe my ears when the man who answered my call said cheerfully, "Yes, yes, I know you want to study Hebrew, come on Monday around six in the evening. If you have a pen, I'll give you the address!"

What's going on over there? I thought to myself. After all, they warned me to be careful, and he's blurting everything out over the phone.

My desire to find these other Jews was so strong that neither fear nor doubt arose in my mind.

I could hardly wait for the appointed time and almost flew to my first lesson.

Vladimir Prestin inherited his love of the Hebrew language from his grandfather, Felix Shapiro, the noted compiler of a Hebrew-Russian dictionary. He taught the Hebrew language to a group of ten that eventually dwindled to five people. Sometimes during a lesson someone would knock on the door. Prestin would quietly speak to the strangers in the tiny corridor where the piles of coats made it impossible to breathe. Then the strangers would leave and Vladimir would return to us, adopting a placid expression as he continued with the lesson, but dimples would play on his cheeks. He would tell us nothing. After all, I reasoned, he did not know what kind of people we were and why we had come nor what could be expected of us.

I let no day pass without listening to the latest news from Israel, both to hear what was happening there and what was happening to Jews at home. While the Israeli radio broadcasts reported names of Jews who had been arrested in the Soviet Union, the local media barely mentioned the cases before the trial. I felt more and more uneasy because it seemed that everyone was active. I didn't want to be left out.

Then there was the Leningrad trial in December 1970 of the Jews who had been arrested for attempting to hijack a plane the previous June. Eduard Kuznetsov and Mark Dymshits, the two chief organizers, received the death sentence for planning to leave the Soviet Union illegally. Eventually, the most "humane and just" court in the world—according to its own definition—commuted their death sentence to fifteen years' imprisonment.

During this time Vladimir Prestin was teaching me more than just Hebrew. Often during our lessons the telephone would ring in his kitchen, and the apartment being so tiny we could not fail to overhear his entire conversation. I thus came to learn how information was gathered from various cities of the Soviet Union and, on one occasion, I was present to eavesdrop on how this information was conveyed to Israel.

He quickly realized that he could trust me and one day I lingered in his apartment to ask him frankly, "Aren't you afraid?"

"I am doing nothing illegal," he replied.

"But in any case if I am summoned to the KGB, what should I say to them?" I asked.

He became very serious and said, "That is a very sensible question. You are not obligated to talk to them. Every citizen has rights as well as obligations. From childhood they indoctrinate us only about our responsibilities but they never speak about our rights. You have the right not to inform on a friend. You have the right *not* to speak with them at all. If they serve you a summons, officially, that's one thing, but if they do it unofficially, as they say, 'for a conversation,' you don't have to talk. You can say, 'I don't want to. I have the right.' "

On that day he opened a whole new world for me—the possibility of using Soviet legislation to defend my rights. This thought had never before entered my head; my Soviet upbringing had purposely denied it.

In the second half of the 1960's, I began working in a planning institute, where I made economic calculations for locating factories which would manufacture biological preparations to be used in agriculture and the food industry. My duties included designating sites where the planned enterprise would be most feasible. I liked my work because of its varied aspects—including travel to different parts of the country—but I was required to justify my calculations and conclusions before the directors of the institute. After Vasily Kucheryavy was appointed chief engineer of the institute in 1969, it became almost impossible to receive approval.

"You are not indigenous and you won't decide where we should build!" he told me scornfully in the midst of an argument we were having.

The first time he said this, I was dumbstruck. Later, going over the arguments and objections in my mind, I suddenly remembered those words. What had he said to me? What had he meant by the words "not indigenous"? That I'm Jewish? Too bad that I had remained silent.

Well, it wouldn't be the last time, I consoled myself; I would still have plenty of disputes ahead of me. There were several Jews at the institute who occupied managerial posts or were considered talented specialists, and they, too, silently swallowed such remarks. No one wanted a confrontation because it could mean his job.

Despite this, I once said to him, "Perhaps you are right, this project is not mine, but it's not yours personally either."

"We shall see," he said ominously.

A few months later the institute's bulletin board displayed a dismissal order. All those listed were Jews and my name was among them.

"Let's go together to the ministry and to the party regional committee," someone suggested. "We have nothing to lose; we're already out of work."

In our protest to the ministry we wrote of a "tendentious attitude toward us as Jews." At that time, in 1971, such a statement was a bold act. It was not acceptable to speak openly about the blatant anti-Semitism of Soviet society. Luckily for us, the ministry official was a young man who listened and accepted our petition.

We returned to work and at the end of the day it was announced that the order had been rescinded. My dreams, however, were very far away from ministries in Moscow. I continued my Hebrew studies and waited impatiently for the day when I would have assembled all the documents necessary to apply for emigration.

CHAPTER 3

THE ANNOUNCEMENT ON THE BULLETIN BOARD WAS WRITTEN in large letters: "On September 12, 1971, the personal case of Nudel, Ida Yakovlevna, will be heard. The attendance of union members is mandatory."

An evil mind, and one thoroughly familiar with human psychology, thought up this method of intimidation. Who would openly declare at work that he wants to emigrate to Israel? It is frightening to stand alone, under the gaze of an enormous hostile collective, to offer explanations and to withstand insults, threats and absurd accusations.

The tension was enormous. I had had no experience with such a situation. I knew from the unfortunate example of others that one could not speak about anti-Semitism in the U.S.S.R. That issue had to be avoided at all costs because such an accusation could result in a term in prison. I decided to declare that every ethnic group is equal and has its own history, its traditions and its culture. Each ethnic group, no matter how few in number, has its heroes, its poets, its writers. And each person on earth knows to which people he belongs, taking pride in their successes, sufferings and sorrows. I am a Jew; my people's motherland is Israel. The history of my people is full of proud and glorious moments. I wanted to live with my people.

The hall, which seated three hundred people, was filled to overflowing with more standing in the aisles and crowding in the corridors.

I arrived at the auditorium at the appointed hour. A large crowd standing near the door parted, letting me pass. Once inside, I stood alone and silent, next to the wall. The chairman declared the meeting open and read my application to the director of the institute for a character reference. Then I was summoned to a table on the podium.

I looked carefully around the hall in search of familiar faces. My friend Sonya, who was also Jewish, was slouched down, her head lowered.

But other Jews, or, to use the Soviet term, "individuals of Jewish nationality," were present in the hall. Russians, Armenians, Georgians, Tatars, Ukrainians and perhaps another hundred nationalities live in the Soviet Union. Quite naturally, they are called by their own names. Only the Jews are treated differently; we have a special privilege. In the press, radio and television we are "individuals of Jewish nationality." In the consciousness of the Soviet citizen the word "Jew" is automatically associated with "traitor, spy and enemy."

The administration tried to coax and persuade each of the institute's Jews to speak against me and to denounce my desire to emigrate to Israel. But using various pretexts they refused to speak, which was heroic because they were thus aligned with the traitorous Jew, Nudel.

(My fellow students who took the underground Hebrew lessons—we called it an ulpan after its model in Israel—did not dare to come. They were afraid.)

The administration nevertheless managed to find one to speak. "I, an individual of Jewish nationality, repudiate Nudel, Ida Yakovlevna, and hold her up to shame," he recited smoothly. And then he went on for another five minutes talking about the equality, brotherhood and friendship of all Soviet peoples.

I stared at the faces in the auditorium. Some showed scorn, others squeamishness. No matter how much they hated Jews, in their eyes this denouncer was a traitor. When he concluded there was no applause.

I had planned my speech over many days and nights, writing it down in advance, polishing it and weighing every word, until I believed in it with all my heart. Despite all this preparation, I still felt terrible—the psychological stress was enormous and I had no idea how it would end. Standing in front of the assembly I read:

I don't plan to find fault with Russia. I don't plan to find fault
with the Russian people. I was born here and lived here for
forty years and you can't deprive me of my childhood, youth or
adulthood. I am part of this land. But I am also part of another
land, which is the dream of my people—an ancient, wise and
furious people with a martyr's fate.

I shall not describe how we were persecuted, burned,
uprooted. I want to tell about something else, about how, having
now raised their heads, my people slowly but surely are joining
the ranks of the other peoples of the world. Not all want to
recognize us yet, not all are happy to see us in the ranks as
equals, but we are rising, despite everything. Because we have
no other way.

Jews are gathering together in their motherland from all
countries in the world . . .

Dead silence reigned in the hall. The secretary of the party
organization was the first to react. "This statement was written by
the head of a Zionist organization," she decreed. "Nudel cannot
write like that."

So that's it. My words had put them in a state of shock. I had
not imagined the force of my own statement. The meeting was
clearly not holding together. People were silent, thinking over my
words and ideas. The secretary of the party organization then began
to recite the traditional party speech, blaming worldwide Zionism
and the Jews for all of mankind's misfortunes. I couldn't control
myself and interrupted her, saying, "If you summoned me so you
could insult my people publicly, then there's nothing for me to do
here."

People in the audience began to shout, "Traitor, they ought
to drive them out of here. Hitler did the right thing in killing
them." Incensed, I turned to the director of the institute, "I repeat,
I do not intend to be present at a meeting where my national dignity
is insulted.

"Please explain to me and to all present how we shall pro-
ceed."

The director spoke firmly: "We have come to discuss the
personal case of Nudel, Ida Yakovlevna. Address yourselves only
to this issue. I shall permit no hooliganism."

His decisive remark convinced me that I had done the right

thing in speaking to him three days earlier. I told him then that
he had to conduct the meeting according to the constitution, which
prohibits inciting ethnic dissension.

But despite his warning, anti-Semitic slogans were shouted
out, yet they had not succeeded in turning the entire meeting into
a forum for bigotry.

This was my first victory; the meeting adopted the resolution
that if I implored them to take me back, they would never readmit
me to their country.

I was caught by surprise in November 1971, a month and a
half after I had submitted my application for an exit visa. The
officials at OVIR, the visa office, declared that for reasons of security
my departure was inexpedient. My conscience was completely
clear; I knew no secrets which could damage the Soviet Union. In
complete sincerity I couldn't believe or understand what the OVIR
workers were implying. What secrets did I possess—how many
tapeworms there are in a cow's stomach? That the Soviet Union
was a hundred years behind the West in the development of mi-
crobiology for peaceful uses?

"No," the OVIR worker told me, "you don't possess any
specific secrets, but you might have overheard something."

Overheard? But any person on the street could enter the institute! (In fact, those in urgent need of a bathroom often did
because there were no public facilities in the area.) Anyone could
freely walk the halls and overhear to his heart's content. What was
going on? Why wouldn't they let me go? What were they afraid of?

But this was complete nonsense! Even if some workers were
busy planning the most terrible means of destroying people, none
of them would run out into the halls and broadcast: "Listen to the
terrible secret that I was entrusted with!" No, I simply could not
accept such an obviously fabricated reason.

"You could have overheard something and it is in the state's
interest to detain you."

"For how long?" I asked softly.

"Possibly five to six years."

"Five to six years," I repeated, with horror creeping into my
voice. I can still picture myself sitting in the small Moscow OVIR
office on the first floor. There were two tables, each occupied by
a nonuniformed worker. I glanced at the window across from the

table, a first-floor window facing the street. It was covered by bars. From then on I was living my life behind bars. I was now a "re-fusenik," a Jew who had been denied an exit visa.

In January 1972 I was fired from my job. In traditional Soviet fashion it was called "personnel cuts" even though I was the only one let go. The trade union approved of the measure. I then applied for a job as an engineer on a building project. I filled out an application and was told to call back in two days.

"No," the head of the personnel department said later, "we don't need that kind of person." The pattern was simple; he phoned my former place of work and they told him that I intended to emigrate to Israel. Nobody would give me a qualified job.

At that time a new service which aided the infirm, aged and crippled who needed care in their own homes, started operating in Moscow. The pay for such work was low. I was taken without any questions because they desperately needed people. I was swept into the world of the sick and elderly who did not leave their homes for years on end, unfortunate people who had nobody or who had been abandoned by their relatives. I brought them food, medicine, linen from the laundry; I did everything that they could not do themselves. It was convenient because after I had finished my tasks, I had free time for my other activities. It was difficult, how-ever, because I came into contact with unending, agonizing suf-fering, but none of these people were willing to place themselves at the mercy of society or the state by going to a home for the ill or aged. "It's better to die from hunger in one's own bed than to live there and suffer indignities," a very old woman told me. I understood.

Once the head of the personnel department summoned me: "What caused you to drop such prestigious work?" I didn't want to get into any explanations involving the truth. I couldn't afford to lose this job, too.

"I have problems with my eyes, it's hard to work with num-bers," I told her.

A short time later I was called in again. "Someone from the police station came by and took an interest in you," the director informed me. "Submit an application for dismissal at your own request or I shall find a way of firing you." A few days later, feeling helpless, I submitted my letter of resignation and was immediately handed the necessary documents and wages.

Perhaps I had brought those unfortunate people a whiff of the healthy and normal world beyond the bounds of their imprisoning lives but my health care career was very brief.

My family submitted applications for visas in January 1972. We decided that everyone who could leave ought to do so.

I was delighted when my family received exit visas in March 1972 and I urged them on. "Listen, it's hard, but we must separate; leave without me. Finally, Yakov will grow up in a normal environment. That's the main thing." We would no longer have to explain to him that "Jews are also good people." We would no longer have to wipe the tears from his face when the other children in the courtyard taunted him for being a Jew and did not let him join in their games.

Everything seemed in a fog on April 14, 1972, when my dear family left. Like the frames in a movie, everything rushed past—running around to offices, assembling papers and documents, friends, farewells, tears. We stood near the last door to the airport as they were led away. I had no fear or doubts or apprehensions, for we were doing the right thing—freeing ourselves from captivity one by one.

My sister was crying when we exchanged the final kisses, but I was not. "Write me, my dears! Write! Who knows when we'll see each other again. I don't believe that it will take five or six years as they told me in OVIR. It's too absurd. I don't know even one secret. I believe that I'll come soon."

CHAPTER 4

IN THE SUMMER OF 1972 VLADIMIR PRESTIN ASKED ME TO HELP
the wife of Vladimir Markman, a recently arrested refusenik from
Sverdlovsk. She was coming to Moscow to find a lawyer for her
husband, who had been charged with slandering the Soviet system.
A short woman with a shock of red hair, Greta Markman was glib
and talkative. I began making the rounds with her from one legal
office and lawyer to another. This went on for two weeks. Some
shrugged their shoulders in embarrassment and said, "No, it's certainly awful—he's charged on a political article, but the case will
ruin my career, I'll lose my job."

The Jewish lawyers said, "You people are saints, but I have
a family, and I'm not planning to go anywhere. What could I do
in Israel? I'll never learn the language, or have another profession,
I'm the wrong age. No, I cannot take the case."

The very boldest would say, "Wait a minute, I'll ask the person
in charge whether he'll agree to assign me to a job in Sverdlovsk."
But he would return with a sad look and say no.

The chairman of the republic's collegium of lawyers told us
frankly, "Why should I waste money on a travel assignment when
there are good lawyers in Sverdlovsk? I trust them."

"But I don't," said Greta, "and the constitution guarantees
the right to a lawyer of our choice."

"Hire one then. I won't assign anyone."

Understandably, the Sverdlovsk KGB didn't want a relatively

more independent Moscow lawyer in on the case, and there is no force in the Soviet Union which can say no to the KGB.

Time was running out. If we didn't succeed in finding a lawyer by the following week, the investigative department would assign its own lawyer. He would be like a second prosecutor, on their side, not ours.

We decided to hold a hunger strike at the reception room of the Central Committee of the Communist Party of the Soviet Union (CPSU). Because almost all our acquaintances and friends had left Moscow for the summer, we were not sure we could count on others joining us, even one more person a day. Since we were afraid that Greta, who was not a Muscovite, could be expelled from Moscow, she did not participate in the actual hunger strike although she sat with us the whole time. On the designated morning, Greta and I were the first ones to arrive at the reception room. We were accompanied by Vladimir Zaslavsky. He had recently been refused an exit visa but was able to leave for Israel a few months after our hunger strike. We handed the secretary a statement in which we declared a protest in connection with the violation of the civil liberties of Vladimir Markman.

We waited for our turn. An hour passed, then two, but no one paid any attention to us. We asked that they connect us by telephone to one of the senior workers but we were refused. When the workday of the Central Committee came to an end, we went home.

The next day was a repetition of the first. In the middle of the day Vladimir Slepak, a refusenik and activist of the Jewish movement, arrived at the waiting room. He had just returned to town, learned of our protest and hurried over to support us.

"No, no, Volodya, you can be of more help by not staying with us now," I told him. "The most important thing is to find people who would agree to join us. We don't have a guarantee even for tomorrow. We are very tired. A whole day with almost no water in this stuffy room, with our nerves on edge all the time. Find people." He left.

Volodya was successful and on the next day there were five of us. The Central Committee continued to ignore us completely. They will get bored sitting there and starving, they will go away on their own—that was probably what the KGB thought, watching the growing group of protesters. We did not plan, however, to give in and we even hoped to muster people for another week of protest.

My personal situation at the time was rapidly deteriorating. I was not working at the moment and officially could be charged with parasitism. The Soviet regime often used this "criminal" charge to arrest those who had been dismissed from their jobs after applying for emigration to Israel. In unusual cases such as my public protest, the police could go after me in a serious way. Moreover, it turned out that the hunger strike and the impossibility of resting for several consecutive days had gotten me into such a state that I needed medicine to correct a heart problem which had surfaced in recent years at times of intense physical or emotional stress.

What would happen to me if the KGB did not halt our protest? I did not see how I could get out of the situation and save face. I clearly could not go on a hunger strike for two weeks.

On the fourth day we numbered seven people. Near us I noticed another small group of three men and one woman. From their appearance they seemed Jewish. I went up to the woman and asked her, "Are you Jews?"

"Yes," she replied, looking at me carefully. "Are you Jews, too?"

I told her about our protest action and suggested that they join us. They conferred among themselves and then agreed. We wrote a new statement and affixed eleven signatures to it, including the four Jews from Kishinev we had just met. Around noon, we learned that soldiers dressed in plain jogging suits were being bused to the Central Committee building. A police general surrounded by a bevy of officers entered the Central Committee waiting room.

"Citizens, I suggest that you leave this waiting room and do not reappear here tomorrow. If you do, we shall arrest all of you. You are disturbing public order and obstructing the work of the Central Committee." Although there were many policemen surrounding the building, they detained no one. What were they planning to do? There were eleven of us, including two women— me and one from Kishinev.

At one o'clock another general arrived, threatened us with arrest and demanded that we leave the reception room.

"We have not violated the law. The reception office is open until six o'clock and we shall wait until they respond to our complaint."

He left but the soldiers remained. The working day ended and they did not arrest us. I decided to invite the four Jews from Kishinev to come home with me because they were in an unfamiliar place and afraid of being separated from one another. Since I was alone, I was willing to put them up in my small apartment.

We had barely entered the apartment when the doorbell rang. It was very clear from the long, very peremptory, even authoritative ring that it was a policeman. I signaled everyone to be quiet. I figured that I had to stall him by not letting him in while I decided what to do.

After ringing several times, whoever it was left. Back then the Soviet police were not yet equipped with walkie-talkies and a policeman would be forced to return to the station, appear before the head of the operative section and tell him what he had done, receive new instructions and then go and carry them out. It would not have occurred to any officer of the operative section of the Moscow police force that a woman would dare to disobey a police order.

When the doorbell of my apartment rang again, it was completely dark outside and I decided not to open the door. I felt confused and anxious. Clearly, the police were now furious about my earlier disobedience and would certainly vent their anger on the others in my apartment.

The ringing switched to knocking. "Open up, the police, a document check, there are outsiders with you," cried the policeman from the other side of the door. I remained silent. In frustrated anger, he banged his feet against the door.

"Do you have a search warrant?" I asked finally.

"Open up immediately, I am Major Zagladin, deputy police chief. General Zvyagintsev, the on-duty Moscow chief, ordered that your guests be sent away. Open the door at once, I am carrying out an order."

"I won't open it, it's too late. The constitution guarantees the inviolability of one's residence after ten o'clock in the evening."

"What constitution?" he retorted. "The general gave me an order and I must carry it out."

I was silent. My guests called me to the window. The building was surrounded by KGB agents, or chekists as we called them, using their original name from Lenin's time. In the hot summer darkness their white shirts shone like beacons. There were so many of them!

Brainless fools! We three men and two women locked in this apartment wanted only one thing—that a man be given the legally guaranteed opportunity to hire a Moscow lawyer.

There was another knock at the door. A quavering, senile voice said, "Darling, please open up." The bastards had gotten the cooperative's elderly chairman out of bed. After all, he was the officially elected representative of all the tenants. I vividly imagined that his sick heart was palpitating in fear, remembering the Stalinist Gulag. "Darling," he moaned, "open up for them."

"Tell the major that he's a beast, making you get out of your bed! This business is not for your sick heart. I know what I'm doing," I yelled back.

The policeman again kicked the door hard. Then a door slammed down the hall and it became quiet. It was eleven o'clock. I sat down on the couch and wanted only one thing—silence—but my apartment was full of people I had to take care of. ·

"Let's settle down for the night," I said to the Kishinev group. I set up a folding cot for one man in the kitchen, put another two on the floor in sleeping bags and the lone woman shared my bed. "The attack has been repulsed. As they say, morning is wiser than the night." But I could not sleep. I thought about my strange life. Where was this situation leading me? What had I achieved? Would they let me out of the Soviet Union, and if not, could I adapt to my unsettled situation or would I seek a solution through other means?

In the overcast dawn hours I tried to ascertain from my side of the apartment house whether there were any policemen or chekists around the building. Perhaps they were near the entrance?

It was already seven, then eight. No one was coming after us. Time was dragging on. A few hours ago we had been under siege; were we now free? At least we would have time for breakfast in peace while they were thinking about what to do with us. No one knew what to expect. One thing was definite though: there was no food in the house, only hot tea.

At nine the doorbell rang. I opened the door almost joyfully. It meant the end of uncertainty. A policeman entered the apartment and calmly asked us to present our documents. He checked the passports and told all the non-Muscovites to follow him. I went also. It would not have occurred to anyone watching us that only ten hours before passions had seethed in this group of people now walking so calmly behind the policeman. On this clear, warm morning it was impossible to understand the reason for the entire fracas of the night before. At the police station the Kishinevans were interrogated and forced to sign an order expelling them from the city. They left by the evening train.

Once a week, on Saturday morning, Jews would gather around the synagogue on Arkhipov Street. Here it was possible to meet Hebrew teachers, to arrange for studies and to meet foreign tourists. Here both the young and old struck up acquaintances and became friends or lovers. Those who were planning to emigrate and were contemplating their next move came to learn from the experience of others: "What answer did you get from OVIR?" "What did your colleagues say at the meeting to discuss your character reference?" "Should I write a complaint?" Among the large crowd of Jews one could also see Russians who wanted to leave their homeland.

So many problems were dealt with here. Victor Polsky would let people know when there would be another phone conversation with the West to discuss issues of emigration. Mark Nashpitz would help gather food to bring to prisoners. Older men or women alone about to leave for a visit knew they could find help in carrying their huge suitcases laden with food for a prisoner. Yakov Rakhlenko, a good-natured young bachelor, or Valery Kryzhak, another young refusenik, was always willing to undertake such a trip. Every year I tried to get a dozen of the Jewish calendars issued by the synagogue in order to send them to the prisoners. With my reputation as a troublemaker, no synagogue official would give them to me, but I received them from Volodya Shakhnovsky, a Hebrew teacher who was on better terms with the elders of the synagogue. Information had to be conveyed to the West. It was necessary to meet with tourists from England and America in order to have them understand what was happening and how they could help us. In addition to working on education and publicity, we had to arrange for material help for those who had lost their jobs as a result of applying for exit visas.

In spite of the watchful surveillance of the chekists, people would get together and set dates for demonstrations and solve pressing issues. If someone needed to speak confidentially, he would walk a few feet off to the side.

We were neither revolutionaries nor subversives. People expressed their feelings openly. The information practically flowed on its own into the hands of the KGB, which had no dearth of cassettes for recording phone conversations.

Having appraised the strength of the oncoming wave of emigration, the authorities began exerting all their efforts to stifle it. An education tax was imposed only on those who wanted to emigrate to Israel, forcing each person who had received a higher education to pay several thousand rubles to compensate the state for its expenses in educating him. Only a very successful person was likely to have acquired such a sum of money; consequently for many it represented the end of their hopes to emigrate.

I was among those who protested actively against this discriminatory order. A large group of us went to the Presidium of the Supreme Soviet to protest. We demanded that someone talk to us but got no response.

On the following day, we intended to repeat our protest. Unsuspecting, I left my house and briskly approached the subway.

"Ida Yakovlevna, wait," a male voice called after me casually.

Assuming it was an acquaintance, I slowed down, and then an athletically built young man approached me. "Get into the car," he said firmly. A car immediately stopped next to us and I silently obeyed. Why, I asked myself later time and again, did I get into the car? It hadn't occurred to me that my meeting with the KGB would happen just like that. My involuntary Soviet instinct dictated that if somebody gave an order, it meant that he had the right to do so. And if he had the right, then I had to submit.

The car drove us to the police station. "Get out," he commanded. I did and was immediately surrounded by policemen. I spent the entire day in the office of Major Zagladin, the deputy police chief. At first he threatened, "Instead of the Middle East, we'll send you to the Far East."

I stood my ground, demanding a visa to Israel. Then he began to praise me and at the same time tell me nasty stories about my friends. I cut him off immediately, "That doesn't interest me. Give me what I deserve, give me a visa!"

Several hours later, when it was dark out, he asked me, "What are you going to do tomorrow, Ida Yakovlevna? Don't return to the Presidium again."

"That depends on what you did with my friends today," I replied.

Furious he began to yell. After he had worn himself out, I said quietly, "I'm ashamed of you. You are a man. You are backed up by the entire police force with their pistols and dogs. You are threatening me, but I don't even know whether I'll be leaving here today or not."

He turned red as if he had been stung and charged out of the office. A few minutes later I was released.

The most active in gathering information about other refuseniks was Dina Beilin. She found out which people were in need, drew up lists and organized help for them. Volodya Slepak was the main figure who met with tourists. Not only did he speak English, he also lived in the center of town, which was convenient for meetings. Aleksander Lerner, a respected Soviet scientist, was another person who met with foreign visitors. Mark Nashpitz was our trader; he knew how to get hold of all the goods that were constantly in short supply and he put together packages for those going to meet prisoners.

Once when Vladimir Prestin told us students at the Hebrew ulpan that he was having trouble maintaining his contact with other cities because the KGB had disconnected his telephone, I offered the use of mine. From then on it rang day and night and information streamed in from many cities about those who had been dismissed from their jobs or threatened by the KGB or had been refused exit visas. I became acquainted with remarkable people and my apartment turned into a kind of transit point for many Soviet Jews on their way to Israel.

As the saying goes, "You can't dance at all weddings at the same time." I therefore decided that my special contribution would be to concentrate on helping the prisoners and those who were harassed by the KGB. The fact that I was living in Moscow made this task easier. I found out the addresses of several relatives of prisoners and wrote them, inviting them to stop by my place on their way to the prison zone. Long before that, I had begun to write directly to those prisoners themselves. Some responded good-naturedly and with gratitude, while others became suspicious, wondering what personal advantages I could derive from my actions. Gradually the various sympathies and antipathies were clarified.

Moisei Mendelevich, whose son Yosif had been sentenced to thirteen years of strict regime for trying to leave the Soviet Union illegally, was my most active assistant. Once he sat down at my table and together we drew up a list of all those who had been arrested in 1970. We then supplemented the list with the addresses of the places of detention and of relatives. My list included information about medical problems and the date and place of birth of each prisoner so that I could send them postcards (sometimes with scenes of their native areas) on their birthdays. I was constantly adding new names and addresses as the KGB throughout the country kept on arresting people who were active in the emigration movement.

Dealing with so many people was so exhausting that I asked acquaintances among the refuseniks to help but no one was willing to do so. "I don't want to go to prison. What you are doing is very dangerous. I have children," were among the excuses. I also did not want to land in jail. But I didn't have to stand for hours at the window waiting for the return of a child, trembling with fear that the chekists had beaten him up; I did not have to spend sleepless nights with pangs of conscience for fear that as a result of my activity a son would be expelled from an institute and conscripted into the army. Only I alone had to answer for the consequences of my risky activity. This was both my strength and weakness.

I was approaching the prime of my life—just over forty years old, free and physically strong. I liked to go hiking in the mountains, swimming in the rivers and walking in the swamps and taiga. At times I had gotten into dangerous situations, but I had self-confidence and knew that I could do a lot that others couldn't.

After I had been fired in January 1972, I had tried to find an equivalent job elsewhere. When that did not work out, I found a compromise by performing menial jobs. I earned modest sums of money, which gave me the free time to devote to my cause. Someone had to tell the world about the sacrifice and suffering of my brethren who were fighting for their sacred right to live with their people. Why shouldn't I be this someone?

CHAPTER 5

MY SPECIAL INTEREST IN THE FATE OF PRISONERS OF ZION WAS evoked partly by a feeling of gratitude to them. Those Jews who had been arrested and imprisoned for their activity on behalf of the Jewish emigration movement had led the way. I was one of hundreds of thousands who had taken up their cry "Homeward!" but I had not managed to leave, and they were still in prison. Indeed, I was motivated not only by a feeling of compassion, but also by some guilt. After all, I could speak with whomever I wanted, choose my own books to read and shop freely in any store; I could also lie in bed and have a good cry without anyone else seeing my weakness. Their life, however, was a daily battle for their existence and their dignity.

I felt obligated to do everything within my power to ease their burden. By applying for a visa to Israel, I had been branded a traitor, but also I had been freed from much of the usual Soviet bondage, so I no longer had to lie or feel like a hypocrite. I no longer had to engage in humiliating and senseless games for fear of losing my job. Part of my motivation derived from the tragedy of my own family in World War II. Their deaths in a portable gas chamber made me think about individual responsibility. If only someone nearby had stretched out a hand and said, "Follow me, you must not remain here or you'll perish!" perhaps they would have believed a neighbor rather than my mother and they would have been saved. No one, however, did.

Subconsciously, I harbored a faint hope that the Soviet authorities would act rationally. Placing myself in their position, I wondered why they would want to keep a person who maintains contact with prisoners and conveys information about them to the West. Wouldn't it be better to be rid of a thorn in their side? My logic was supported by the fact that at the time I had submitted documents to emigrate in 1971, a large group of active refuseniks had received exit visas and left for Israel.

In fact, during the early 1970's the authorities employed a two-pronged attack to deprive the growing Jewish national movement of its natural leaders: granting exit visas to prominent refuseniks was one way, and arresting the most active Jews was another. This duality reflected the authorities' contradictory interests. On one hand, they did not want a rise in Jewish self-consciousness with its subsequent reinforcement of the emigration movement; on the other hand, they wanted western goods, but they had no exchange commodity to offer the West other than Soviet Jews.

This contradictory official approach occurred in one case after another. For example, a head of a section might receive a visa whereas an engineer working under him might be refused on the pretext of knowing state secrets. Having lost their orientation, uprooted from their usual routine, people went around in confusion. After breaking with their past, many who unexpectedly received a refusal became outcasts, literally sitting on their suitcases as they fell into a deep depression.

The critical circumstances brought unusual people to the fore, those who had an appetite for social activism or perhaps those whose social potential had not been satisfied because of the abnormality of the Soviet system. These people began to transform their personal energies into the dynamism of a new social group—the Jewish refuseniks. I'll never forget my excitement when I first attended a meeting with a group of American congressmen at Volodya Slepak's apartment. I was astonished by the fact that many of the congressmen not only knew the names of activists in the movement but were also well acquainted with their stories. For the first time it struck me that western politicians took seriously what was happening in the Soviet Union and were actively trying to help. This knowledge gave me hope and inspired faith that I had a chance to win my personal war against the KGB. I also learned that if one's name is known in the West, one greatly increases the chances of surviving his or her conflict with the Soviet government.

At the time that I decided on my course of action, however, I was not aware of it at all. It didn't occur to me to calculate in advance how many years I could continue in such a difficult situation and whether, indeed, I would survive the KGB with any dignity. I did what was natural for me—what I had to do—and lived in peace with my conscience.

I took upon myself the duty of informing people about what was going on behind the walls of Soviet prisons, behind the doors of Soviet psychiatric hospitals. I had to tell about those who could not speak for themselves or who were afraid to do so. How many were there who suffered anonymously? Thousands? Each had his or her own story and own pain.

Based on information from relatives, friends and people of good will, I had compiled a list of forty-six names. Until late at night I would work at the task of composing letters to people I did not know, whom I had never even seen and who were often half my age. It was not easy trying to figure out how to write a standard letter that would be interesting to people of different ages, intellect and tastes. The regime deliberately isolated dissidents, religious believers or would-be emigrants from their accustomed milieu and placed these people together with primitive criminals. Deprived of normal communication with equals, these prisoners developed an agonizing need for social contact. Their discomfort would become so acute and their inner tension so high that finally they would speak with anyone of even moderate intellect.

In order to relieve some of the prisoners' anxiety and to provide them with some fuel for their imagination, I decided to write about what was going on in the world outside the prison zone. For example, I copied information for them from an Israeli calendar which Vladimir Prestin had given me. In the letter I wrote that this was from a recently published geography book. Being absolutely sure that the censor would never know whether such a book had been published or not, I wrote sixteen copies of my letter and sent it to the various zones. Two weeks later the majority of them returned with the stamp, "not permitted."

What could be not permitted in a text on the geography of Israel? The word "Israel"? I decided that I would not give in so easily. I wrote a complaint to the Gulag administration and appended the complete text of my letter. I asked them to underline in a red, blue, green or yellow pencil which information was not permitted to be conveyed to a prisoner. Although I never received an answer from the Gulag, my subsequent letters began to make it through.

I would also collect at the synagogue signatures for telegrams for them and send them on holidays. The first time I collected 106 names. Having written out sixteen copies I went to the post office. My heart was trembling in fear that at the post office they would phone the KGB and arrest me on the spot. To my surprise, the telegraph operator was happy to get some work; my telegrams alone fulfilled her daily quota. The people on line, however, complained indignantly that they had to wait so long. I did not acknowledge their remarks but I was glad that no one knew that the telegrams were going to "criminals" in the prison zone. And then a woman standing behind me began to defend me. When I had finished paying, she quietly said to my back, "Don't leave, wait for me." She turned out to be the mother of David Chernoglaz, arrested on the same day as the Leningrad group, and charged with anti-Soviet activity for illegally promoting Jewish culture. Seeing the address of her son's camp on the form, she had guessed that I was involved in the case.

Once a mischievous idea popped into my head. Jewish family names sound like abracadabra to a Russian ear. I could possibly insert a few words of Hebrew in between the signatures on the telegram and no one would suspect. It would be a pleasant surprise for the fellows in the zone. The next time I wrote a few words of greeting and encouragement between the names. From then on each telegram carried a special greeting which escaped the scrutinizing eyes of the censor. For example, one message told of the visit of Israeli athletes; a later one announced the early release in August 1974 of Silva Zalmanson, who had been arrested along with her husband, Eduard Kuznetsov, and her brothers Vulf and Izrail for participating in the Leningrad hijacking attempt.

Those who had been released told me how prisoners and the administration in the political and ordinary criminal zones reacted to my telegrams. The first time that one arrived containing over a hundred signatures, the entire zone, Jews and non-Jews, were so excited that, as an eyewitness told me, it "shook" the zone.

Isolated from society, the prisoners were leading monotonous, dull lives. Meetings with relatives were rare and were poisoned by all the indignities which both the prisoners and their relatives suffered in the course of the meeting. Everything around them, including the faces, were painted in the same gray hue. The very same faces for years, the same watch towers, fences. Suddenly there was a surprise—a telegram arrived from the free zone. A hundred people who know about you, think about you, and care about you! They were not afraid to affix their names to words of greeting and even to send it to this godforsaken place.

I was sure that it was important to communicate to the prisoners how the emigration issue was progressing. When I had written openly, the letters had been confiscated. I then decided to use telegrams. In order to evade the censor's suspicions, I would send telegrams with signatures in a fixed sequence but I did not include signatures of those who had received exit visas. Having grown accustomed to a certain order of names, the prisoners immediately noted the ones that had disappeared. This information helped them get a picture of the scale of the emigration movement. The fact that a large number of names reappeared from year to year helped them understand that they were in the front ranks but that there were others behind them. When one of the prisoners was released, I included his name, too, among the signatures.

My correspondence with prisoners in political camps was mainly "one-way traffic," because of restrictions on their mail privileges. I wrote frequently and in quantity and occasionally they sent greetings via their relatives. When Anatoly Altman's mother died, he began to write to me. When Hesya Penson emigrated to Israel, her son Boris began to correspond with me. When Greta Markman left, her husband Vladimir began writing to me. This pattern continued for many years with Jewish political prisoners throughout the Soviet Union.

My life was full of constant worries about "my" prisoners. I collected everything and anything that could be useful for them or for their relatives who traveled to the zone to meet them. Knowing about my efforts, Jews began to bring useful items to the synagogue on Saturdays. For example, American tourists brought remarkable Japanese 3-D postcards of winking half-naked girls, which were as valuable as money because they could be bartered for tea or food or given in exchange for having a letter sent out; vitamins in the shape of candy and energy-giving white chocolate, which the guards mistook for sugar, American jeans and other clothing all came in handy.

*   *   *

I spent an enormous amount of time and effort talking with
hordes of people until I found the key to affecting a prisoner's
lot. I started by getting to know lawyers who defended my
"clients." I spent hours waiting in their offices; some refused to
speak with me. Perhaps they were afraid of a setup or perhaps
they did not understand why this outsider was interfering in such
a delicate situation. I looked for arguments to convince them.
Possibly, my sincerity won them over and they consented to speak
with me. Then I would gain their sympathy and trust. For many
years I turned to them with requests and would receive the most
expert advice while none took money from me. I did not form
this kind of relationship with all lawyers, of course, but I did with
many. My experience taught me, however, that no one, especially
a lawyer, could really influence the situation in camp. The penal
system did not permit outside control. The Soviet legal system
has an unique element, the *procurator's office*, which is theoreti-
cally supposed to see that the laws are correctly applied and that
justice is administered. In reality, however, the procurator's office
is part of the penal apparatus itself, thus rendering the prisoner
defenseless and without rights. Nevertheless, I found the vulnerable points in the penal system and developed a tactic for dealing
with it.

Not only did I use my system successfully, but I also explained
its effectiveness to others, including those outside of the Jewish
movement. Once when I was listening to a broadcast of Radio
Liberty I was shocked by an appeal of Nina Ivanovna Bukovsky
in defense of her son Vladimir Bukovsky, a political prisoner who
had spoken out against psychiatric abuses in the Soviet Union. She
had tried everything; even Andrei Sakharov had gone on a hunger
strike in defense of Bukovsky. The desperate mother appealed to
those who tormented her son, "If you must have a victim, take
me instead of my son!"

The next morning I went to her home. "Nina Ivanovna, believe me, and do what I will tell you and don't listen to the
skeptics."

I searched for the words to convince her. "I don't promise that
you will get him released, but I can guarantee that he will remain
alive. The key is steady complaining. You will have constant, official, and new information about Vladimir which you can convey

to the West. If they do not reply, you begin to complain about a violation of the decree of the Presidium of the Supreme Soviet."

Nina Ivanovna listened skeptically to my fiery speech. "What do you have to lose if it doesn't work?" I asked, having almost lost hope of convincing her. In dissident circles many considered it immoral to turn to the authorities. Nina Ivanovna adopted my system and turned out to be a marvelous pupil, who far exceeded her teacher in the results that she achieved. Several years later her son was exchanged for a Chilean communist leader, Luis Carvalan.

November 1972

My Dearest Ones!

After a two-week gap, I finally received a pile of letters. I sat for almost three hours straight reading them, talking and communicating with you. Will this really be our only method of communication?

Lena, it has become a tradition for us to discuss my altruism from letter to letter. You contend that if I continue to be so active, the KGB will never let me go. How can I explain it to you? Recently, when I myself was feeling very low, I received a card from Volodya Markman in which he wrote, "Ida, why are you silent? I can't go on without your letters!" His words ring in my head. Perhaps I'm wrong; my problem is that I don't know how to do things halfway. I either do it right or not at all.

Michael Sherbourne, an English Jew who speaks Russian and has been in constant contact with refuseniks since 1972, let me know via friends that he hopes to see me—that is, get me out of here—around New Year's, but he already promised me several times and each time he did not come through. I thus receive this information with hopeful feelings mixed with doubts.

Lena, there's no point in your reacting so strongly to the letter in which I wrote about possible complications. I'm not even sure whether I ought to warn you or not. I consciously chose this life. It's my decision. Please accept it as a given. Please.

All my love,

Ida

CHAPTER 6

ONLY AN EVIL MIND COULD THINK UP THE TORTURE OF UN-
certainty. The authorities generally did not specify, even vaguely,
how long restrictions on emigration would exist. When they did
suggest a time limit, as they had in my case, then it was such a
fantastically distant date that the mind would refuse to accept it as
real.

People facing extreme situations divide into two clear
categories—passive and active, or cautious and incautious. The
cautious ones take their bearings, weigh the risk and organize their
lives anew, retaining their former lifestyle as much as possible. The
incautious ones part with friends, quarrel with relatives, pack their
suitcases and begin to pound at all doors with the hope that one
will open. The lucky ones found the right door and it opened a
new world for them. So far I had not had the luck to find the right
door.

At the end of December 1972 a group of such incautious individuals decided to declare a protest hunger strike in order to
attract the attention of Soviet authorities. We chose the central
telegraph office, as the building was open all night and if the
chekists did not interfere, we could remain there as long as we had
the strength to hold out. A certain danger existed that the KGB
would find out about our plan and would try to disrupt it in advance
by arresting participants in their apartments or near their homes.

To prevent this from happening, our contingent of thirty men
and women divided into small groups and arrived at the telegraph

office very early, before the subway had started running. We sent telegrams to Soviet leaders demanding exit visas for each of us, the release of those convicted as a result of their desire to emigrate and the adoption of a fair law on emigration. Some of us assumed that we would have to end our hunger strike in jail.

We settled down at two large tables in the open hall of the central telegraph office on Gorky Street, Moscow's main street. Friends and relatives dropped by, keeping things lively.

Then the head of the Moscow OVIR came up to us. Circling the tables, he nodded to each one of us and promised a visa immediately to whoever would stop his hunger strike; but no one believed him. We knew that the KGB, not he, decided our fate.

The chekists were also in the room. They were nervous but for some reason dared not arrest us in broad daylight. Late at night, when the building had emptied out, a police unit arrived and offered us two options—we would be removed by force or we would leave on our own. We left on our own and they led us through service doors to a side street where police cars were waiting. They piled us into a waiting intercity bus that took us a long way through the nighttime streets of Moscow. We finally came to a stop and waited in front of closed gates.

For most of the others it was their first open demonstration of resistance to the authorities. For many it was also a victory over their fears, doubts and conformist behavior. We had spent a week preparing the demonstration, constantly weighing and reweighing the arguments for and against it. What if they were to arrest us and give us a sentence? Or have those of us who still had jobs fired? Or abuse our children at school and incite other children against them? There was no end to the doubts and fears. Yet how long would we have to wait for an exit visa if we sat quietly and let our fate be decided? We were determined to find a way out.

In the time that we had been brought to the locked gates, our excitement had begun to fade. We were tired and cold in the unheated bus. We all wanted a speedy conclusion to uncertainty and waiting. We had long since stopped talking among ourselves; the only sounds were those of people breathing and tapping their frozen feet. I was dreaming of only one thing—being able to lie down, close my eyes and get lost in blessed sleep. The order "Get out!" brought me back to reality. We found ourselves in front of a long one-story building with black, barred windows. Above the door was a sign: "District Detoxifier of the Lenin District of the City of Moscow—Ministry of the Interior of the RSFSR [Russian Soviet Federated Socialist Republic]." What did it mean?

Inside, men and women were put into separate cells containing only bare metal beds and having small thick-barred windows. I took off my coat, put it on the bed and lay down, hugging my shoulders for warmth. The edges of the coat covered my feet but it was impossible to warm up: the ice-cold building was almost unheated.

I put on my coat and began to pace in the small area between the beds. This was futile, as the hunger, tiredness and stress all produced chills. How long would they torture us here? We began to knock on the doors of the cells and demanded a procurator. Instead, three plainclothesmen arrived, who summoned us one after the other and kept us busy throughout the night with interrogations and filling out forms.

Early in the morning we were loaded into cars and taken to "The People's Court of the Lenin District of Moscow." One after another we were summoned to the courtroom. When I was led in, I confronted a judge and a policeman with his back to me. The one who led me in sat near the door. The judge read a charge alleging that I had insulted the honor and dignity of a policeman.

"What policeman?" I asked in all sincerity. While we had been demonstrating at the telegraph office, not one policeman had appeared before the arrival of the arresting unit. "There weren't any police there."

"That policeman over there," said the judge and pointed to the policeman standing near the window, who now turned his face toward me.

"I don't understand."

"You insulted his honor and dignity," the judge reiterated.

"What did I do—pull off his pants? I don't understand your charge."

"Citizen Nudel, you are insulting the court and will be strictly punished." My sentence read: fifteen days in isolation. "Sign here that you are informed about the sentence."

"This is not a court, it's a farce. I did not break the law; an outrage was committed against me and you are furthering it. Who will judge you for this?"

"Remove her immediately!" ordered the judge.

The policeman who had brought me in took me by the shoulder and by the arm above the elbow and forcefully shoved me out of the courtroom.

They led Nora Kornblum and myself out of the court building. I understood what they were doing to me—they wanted to test my endurance, but why were they doing this to peaceful, inconspicuous Nora? How could she have annoyed them?

Nora, a slight woman of medium height with fair hair, a little over thirty, became my cell mate. We went together through the standard prison admission procedure. They took our fingerprints, photographed us facing straight ahead and in profile, with our ears completely exposed and with our ears covered by our hair. They forced us to strip completely and carefully searched our underwear for unimaginable hidden things. For a very long time they led us from cell to cell, from a small one to an even smaller one. Sometimes they took us into separate cells, then suddenly brought us together in the same cell.

Finally a policeman came and led the both of us down long corridors, constantly clanging his keys. We went up and down, up and down, and eventually in some dead end, he unlocked a cell and ordered us to go inside. I barely crossed the threshold when I stopped short; in surprise, Nora bumped into my back. The cell seemed like a long crypt with its dark walls, small lamp in the ceiling and a tiny, barred and dirty window that barely let in any light. Along the walls on the right and left were two rows of bare, metallic, two-story bunks. In the corner was a toilet and sink with a water tap. A long table flanked by two benches ran down the center of the room. Everything was black, dirty and stinking. The guard shoved Nora and she went past me, leaving me by the door.

I looked up, and near the ceiling I caught sight of a hand-scrawled "Shalom." A black veil seemed to fall from my eyes and the room no longer seemed like a tomb.

"Nora, look, someone was here before us."

The door clanged shut.

Nora did not share my enthusiasm. Her mother had refused to give her the permission form to leave the country (which was a necessary part of the visa application) and she had taken part in the demonstration in order to defend her right to decide her own fate. Not expecting to wind up in prison, she had not told her parents about the demonstration. The news of their daughter's arrest would be a terrible blow to the old, sick couple. In addition, she had taken only two days' leave from her job. No one, however, was expecting me at home, and like the boy Motl in Shalom Aleichem's tale I could say, "I feel good, I'm an orphan."

I knew, however, that we were not completely abandoned and, with the help of the activists on the outside, foreign correspondents would send information to the West about the hunger strike and the names of those who had been arrested. Concerned people in the West would sit by their phones in the hope of obtaining more details. My poor sister Lena would find out the next day from Israeli papers that her stubborn sister had again wound up in an "incident." She would weep over my fate and over her own helplessness as she anxiously awaited the latest news.

While sitting in our cell, we heard noise, then male voices, the patter of feet, the sound of keys and the clang of the heavy iron doors. The first minutes had been so silent that it seemed Nora, the guard and I were the only people left in the world. Someone yelled through the prison window and we recognized the voice of one of our friends. The guard had warned us that it was forbidden to call through the little window or speak to anyone outside. Moreover it was forbidden to stand on the table, approach the window or stand next to it. This inspired us to climb on the table and begin to shout out the window so that our friends would know that we were nearby.

Instantly the guard burst into the cell. We jumped off the table, pleased that our friends knew about us. As soon as the guard reclosed the heavy, squeaky door, we were by the little window again.

"How many of us are being held here?" we asked through the window.

"Everyone they picked up at the telegraph office, but we didn't know that they had also arrested women," they replied from the neighboring cell.

"There are two of us," I told them while Nora argued with the guard. "Nora Kornblum and I."

"Hold on, don't despair, we're nearby."

Except for the wooden table and two benches, everything else in the cell was metal; even the planks on the bunks were made of iron. There was no blanket, pillow or mattress. How could I sleep on this cold metal?

"Nora, let's try to sleep on the bench; at least it's wooden," I suggested. The bench, however, was very narrow and uncomfortable and one always ran the risk of tumbling off.

"You must not lie on the bench; sit up now. You are violating cell discipline. You'll go to the punishment cell," the guard barked through the food opening.

"Hey guys, everything's metal in here, how is it in yours?" Nora asked at the window.

"The same. Let's demand a wooden plank for sleeping." We agreed.

"Call the chief!" we demanded.

"The chief," they seconded us from the neighboring cells as we began kicking the doors, the din of our blows echoing back to us.

"Don't carry on, you'll be put in the punishment cell," warned the guard. Then a few more guards arrived to help him. Evidently, they were apprehensive about us.

The block supervisor was summoned and we explained our indignation. "Tell our relatives to bring us towels, soap, toothbrushes and toothpaste. Give us something to sleep on. We're not animals."

The block supervisor left and a few hours later we were given wooden boards, towels and soap. As soon as the door of the cell would close, the peephole would continuously open and close. This ever-watchful eye and the click of the door bolt were the most annoying things. We reacted violently to each new sound. Nora began to argue and protest, demanding that they stop their incessant spying but it had no effect. They were deliberately toying with us and when we became especially irritated they left the peephole open all the time.

That first night in prison was agonizing. Fully clothed, we lay on a bare wooden plank, our clothes catching between the cracks, a lamp shining directly into our eyes. Engulfed in sad thoughts about relatives and myself, I finally fell asleep.

I was awakened by the sounds of loud and familiar music. Damn it, I thought, even here they play the hymn of the Soviet Union! While shouting at us, the guards forced us to get up.

"Don't violate daily discipline, get up, the block supervisor is coming," said the guard, bustling behind the closed door. "If you don't get up, you'll get the punishment cell," he hissed.

The key clanged in the lock and we decided to get up. Four men in police uniforms entered the cell. We refused to talk to them in protest against the fabricated charges. Then somebody gave us a piece of damp bread and two small lumps of sugar and warned us that that was our food for the entire day.

The day passed under constant, intolerable observation. We heard nonstop remarks on the other side of the door. I asked for a sheet of paper and a pencil to write a complaint to the head of the prison, and much to my surprise, I received them. I wrote briefly, "I know that prison is not a zoo nor am I an exotic animal. I therefore request that immediate measures be taken to stop the stream of spectators." Unexpectedly, my complaint worked. The following day no one whispered behind the door.

We fell into the prison routine but that did not make it any easier—every night was as painful as the first and every awakening was just as rude. The guards, however, became more accustomed to us and began to talk to us and even to help us. Our friends in the neighboring cell sent us gifts—two tiny lumps of sugar they had saved from their own meager rations. Even though the guards were forbidden by law to have any contact with the prisoners, they themselves passed along this generous gift. Moreover, when we shouted our thanks to our friends through the tiny window the guards ignored our disruption.

In addition, the petty criminals who remained in prison filling the relatively easy service jobs such as kitchen work or serving food showed us their solidarity. Once when they were handing out food, they even covertly gave us two cigarettes. Although we did not smoke, we appreciated their generosity. A few days later, they gave us an extra lump of sugar.

It's most unpleasant to catch unexpectedly the eye of your vigilant guard while sitting on the john with your pants down. It's even worse to be unable to wash. I began to demand that they take us to the bath but this was denied. "A bath is against the rules for those serving fifteen-day terms." "Against the rules" was the magic formula used to excuse every indignity and there was no way of fighting it.

Once I asked Nora to hold my scarf in front of the peephole while I washed a little in our cold drinking water. The guard threatened us with every earthly punishment imaginable and demanded that we remove the scarf from the peephole. By now we knew that he was not authorized to enter the cell alone. I washed myself quickly, the cold water pleasantly stinging my dirty body. I had barely managed to dry myself and pull on some clothing when the bolt clanged and the iron door opened wide.

The block supervisor rushed in. "What's going on here?"

"I was washing and didn't want the overseer to look at me."

"Who's an overseer?" he asked uncomprehendingly.

"The one who's looking at us around the clock."

He finally understood what I was talking about. "Why are you washing in the cell?"

"I already wrote to you about that. You ought to give us an opportunity to wash."

He probably never had such prisoners before. Indeed, a guard explained to us before that we had been put in the male sector of the prison.

Never in my life had I ever eaten such awful bread. It contained everything that it shouldn't, including sawdust. When squeezed hard, it left a brown moisture stain on my hand. It suffered from an almost total lack of flour but its smell gave us the feeling that its contents included plenty of industrial oil. Neither Nora nor I could eat it. We broke it and laid the pieces out in thin layers on the table in order to make rusks, which we then ate dry or soaked in water. On days when we were given no food, we ate the "bread" that we had produced. According to the conditions of our punishment, we were given food only every other day, and the slops they served us then were terrible. And every day they brought us tepid water which they called "boiling."

In a few days I began to notice something strange happening to us. We were sleeping both during the day and at night, a heavy slumber that left us weak and sluggish. Suspecting they were slipping drugs into our food or most likely into that "boiling" water, I stopped drinking it. In a few days I returned to my normal state and told everyone about my discovery. Nora and I suspected that there were also drugs in the soup and decided to eat less; we even refused it twice. We were, however, weak and exhausted by the lack of proper food, air and space as well as by the prison's dirt and stench. Eventually, dizziness forced us to eat. As disgusting as the slops were, cooked from old, unwashed barley, it contained the calories necessary for life and we began to wait for it with the impatience, even excitement, of starving people. On Saturday we received holiday fare—a small white roll and a tablespoon of salad with real vegetables! The days stretched from hungry day to feeding day.

We had one distraction: we were taken daily to a little exercise yard for a forty-five-minute walk. They took us out one cell at a time, and despite the guards' threats, we managed to exchange some remarks with our friends. When they let us women out first, we would pass by the men's cells and our friends would stand by the food trap in order to yell encouraging words to us. The exercise yard differed from a cell in that instead of a ceiling, we had several layers of barbed wire above our heads. An armed guard walked alongside this "sky," carefully watching everything that we did during the walk. At his command the exercise could be halted at any moment.

Still, it was a walk, a meeting with the sun and sky. It was rest for our eyes, tortured by the constant glare of the twenty-four-hour light bulb. It also gave us a change from the all-pervasive gray around us and the locked space which suffocated us. In reflection it amazes me that we regarded this as a new, exciting experience. When we returned to our cell, we would notice that in our absence they had carried out a search. Were they looking for transmitters, tape recorders or video cameras in our wooden beds? They had already confiscated all our possessions.

Every morning we were given our daily allotment of one small square sheet of paper "for hygienic purposes."

The hours dragged on in the prison cell, the days passed even more slowly and the weeks simply did not move. Nora and I had exhausted every personal and social topic. We had worked out all the arguments Nora needed to convince her mother to attach her written permission to Nora's visa application. At this point we didn't mind anymore if the guards were listening in. It was harder for Nora to be with me because I preferred to remain silent and think about my affairs, problems and dreams, whereas she needed companionship. Eventually she began to weep and I tried to speak with her more often but she still cried silently, without sobs, the tears flowing down her cheeks. I felt responsible for her tears to some extent because if I had talked with her more, she would have spent less time alone with her sad thoughts. But I was very tired and lacked the strength to speak for several hours a day. I needed silence in order to regain my mental strength.

Despite our different temperaments, we were in strong agreement that each must make her own contribution in the struggle for freedom to make it a more meaningful and complete liberty. I pointed out that in that respect her prison stay was not in vain:

"Who knows, Nora, perhaps you will soon receive a visa and leave. The days in prison and the suffering you endured in order to acquire your freedom will be a cherished memory, the pride of your life."

The days crept along slowly, but at least each one brought us closer to the end. The morning that we were supposed to be released we tensely kept walking to the door and listening to the sounds outside the cell. The guards also became nervous because we escaped from their field of vision when we leaned against the cell door, and for that they showered us with threats. On the first day they had taken away our watches so we did not know the time. Moreover it was a hungry day with just water, a slice of bread and two lumps of sugar.

Probably around mid-morning the guard opened the door, called Nora's name and said, "With your belongings!"

Nora left quickly—she had no belongings. We parted hurriedly. Even though we had been waiting for this moment all morning, the order caught us by surprise. Already beyond the cell door, Nora shouted something to me. I then heard noise in the hall as they evidently were taking people out of the neighboring cells. I tapped the next cell but no one responded; it was empty. All kinds of thoughts about why I was left behind began to flash through my mind—was it an arrest, an extension of the sentence or had they just forgotten about me? No, this is not 1937! I thought. I stood by the door pressing my face up to it as I had been doing when they took Nora away.

I resolved to pull myself together and get used to the idea that they might not release me that day. Removing the coat which I had been wearing all morning, I spread it on the bunk and lay down, trying unsuccessfully to erase the thought that they probably had given me another sentence. As I contemplated the horrors of interrogations, trial and camp, I listened to the measured steps of the guard outside—back and forth, a stop to check the peephole, and back and forth again. How could a person do such boring work, voluntarily agree to be both captor and captive? After all, he was a captive just as I was except that he spent the night at home in his bed. All his life was passing here, next to the cell, pacing, spying.

Suddenly I heard a metallic ring as the key chain hit the door. I remained lying down. Why should I hurry if it was a sentence?

"Why are you lying down?"

I remained silent.

"Take your belongings and follow me!"

I followed him submissively, without asking any questions. I knew that the only answer I might receive was "It's against the rules to know." He led me through long halls with endless numbered doors. In the cells behind those iron doors were thousands of people—some criminals, some innocent. Had I really been one of them? Clinking the keys as he went, he led me to a small room with one little window. A man extended a document toward me.

"Sign right here," the man told me.

I choked up and asked, "What kind of document is this?"

"A form for release."

A stone seemed to slide off my chest. This time I got away with it, I thought joyfully. They gave me back my purse and apartment keys. The guard led me into another room and opened the metal door. How great I felt to be alive again!

While I was riding the trolley to the nearest subway and then almost automatically following the subterranean passages to my line, my thoughts focused on one thing only—how should I go on living? I had been given a glimpse of life behind bars. Now more than ever I did not want to serve a long prison term; this kind of exotic experience did not attract me. But who would grant me freedom if I remained silent? Who would speak instead of me? Many of those who might have done so were already in prison; they were isolated behind innumerable locks and their voices were almost inaudible. I had to speak for them as well as for myself as long as I was able to. I wanted so much to avoid landing in prison again, but that fate now seemed inevitable.

Back at home I entered my apartment and closed the door behind me. In the past a homecoming from business trips meant the warm reacquaintance with friends, my books, my favorite objects, but this return was something inexplicably and irrevocably different. After I had shut the door, I felt a strange sense of security, relief that I was freed from those watchful, alien eyes. After all, I was free to close the door and stay home as long as I wished. I could lie down, sit, do anything. What a blessing to lie in a clean, comfortable bed. What pleasure to put on a bathrobe and sit by the table, to pick up a book, or turn on some music! And a bath, that greatest invention of civilization! There I could relax, cleansing my mind of all thoughts.

In the bath I discovered that my body was covered with vertical blue stripes. I soaped and scrubbed but it did not help. I went to the bedroom mirror and carefully looked at the stripes. They were just ordinary black and blue marks! No one had beaten me; where could they have come from? I then realized that they were the result of lying on the planks. While sleeping my body had slipped into the spaces between the planks, thus forming the marks.

In the morning, when I put on my shoes, I discovered that they had gotten very big. When my cousin arrived she said, "Ida, you look terribly thin; you're all skin and bones."

I hadn't even thought about it; that explained why the shoes were so big.

"Why are there pieces of plaster on the floor?" she asked. "Where could they have fallen from?"

I looked up at the ceiling and discovered a small hole. While they had kept me in the lockup, they had broken through the ceiling!

"The bastards. They're so brazen that they didn't even clean up the plaster. As if to tell me, 'we can do anything.' "

For a long time I had known that they could do whatever entered their infantile heads, stuffed as they were with scenes from detective stories. After I had lived awhile with my broken ceiling, I understood why they had done it so blatantly. In a few days I developed the unsettling feeling as if I were walking stark naked through the streets. It seemed that every sound I made was transmitted to the KGB. Just thinking about it drove me crazy but I kept on telling myself that I had to put it out of my mind and learn to live as if there were no hole in the ceiling, no bugging and no KGB.

February 1973

My Dear Ones!

You are dissatisfied with my letters, but in them you can see my soul and mind. What more can you expect from letters? Everyday details are not interesting. Moreover, I cannot always write openly. We must always keep in mind that the letters pass through very careful censorship. You can even find out the personal number of the censor. He leaves his mark on the inner side of the envelope, on the line which glues together the two parts.

For almost a week I was busy with Margarita Suslensky. She left for a meeting with her husband, Yakov, who had been charged with anti-Soviet activity and sent to a prison camp. She returned in hysterics. They searched her for eight hours. They stripped her naked and felt through her hair. They called in some man and said that he was a gynecologist. Without surgical gloves, using his dirty bare hands, he made a gynecological inspection.

"Why did you agree?" I asked indignantly.

"They threatened not to let me out of the zone. I was alone and afraid of their outrageous treatment. I was forced to agree."

"What were they looking for?"

"Letters," replied Margarita and she handed me two tiny little tubes.

"Well, Margarita, you deserve a special medal," I said.

She smiled weakly and sadly.

Yesterday I attended a seminar at the Lerners'. There were a lot of people and the room was stuffy. At least for a while I was among people who are occupied with other problems. I listened to them and found it interesting to be in another world. Some simply live a normal human life. Sometimes I envy them . . . sometimes.

Today I have chest pains, but they will go away. I need to walk in the forest, breathe in the air and enjoy nature.

All my love to all of you,
Ida

CHAPTER 7

From the time that I offered my telephone for gathering information about the Jewish movement in other cities, people who had no place to stay while visiting the capital would drop in on me for a day or two. Some were on their way to Israel and had to get their papers in order at the embassy; others were delivering complaints about persecution by the authorities; and there were the relatives of prisoners of Zion, who were on the way to or returning from a meeting.

People would come at all hours, day and night. Many did not even warn me in advance and often I had never met them nor knew their names. And, of course, I couldn't be sure of what had really brought them to me. Having responded to the doorbell and answering affirmatively to the question "Are you Ida Nudel?" I faced a dilemma. Who, indeed, was standing in front of me, someone in need of help or a chekist? I tried to discover the answer in the course of the conversation. I asked quite detailed questions about the life of refuseniks in his city so that a possible lie would surface. Throughout this time, though, it seemed the KGB never exploited my openness for their own purposes.

One day I was sitting at my desk and copying information I had received in a letter from Israel that would interest the fellows in the prison zones. The statistics on Israel would give them food for thought and discussion. I could not, however, focus on what I was writing. I had not left the house the entire day or talked with anyone and was overcome by a feeling of overwhelming loneliness and unease. I had to go outside and phone someone to find out what was going on in the world; my own phone had been disconnected. I left my apartment building but made a sharp about-face at the telephone booth because a passerby had taken a sudden interest in a nearby sign and I recognized him for what he was— a tail. To make sure I was not wrong, I almost ran in the direction of the subway stop, turned the corner by an enormous apartment house, stopped abruptly, and looked around. The stranger turned the corner just as quickly and, carried forward by his momentum, moved ahead of me. And he knew it! He immediately slowed down and continued at an unhurried, even leisurely pace. Well, I said to myself, it is unpleasant, but it's inevitable.

In later days, whenever I discovered that the KGB was watching me as I left the house, I would try to think of a reason. Had something happened to someone? Perhaps they were planning to arrest me or conduct a search? As a result I developed a keen awareness of danger. I can't explain how, but I learned to sense it when they were trailing me. I was fearful that the constant tension of detecting my tails would give me a persecution complex. I therefore often told myself not to think about them, and to detach myself from them if there were people around.

In order to live and to win out, I could not permit myself to fear those trailing me. It was some task to train myself to be that way. I had to look them straight in the eye. Indeed whenever a confrontation arose in the street, they were always the ones to turn their gaze away first. I felt the barely restrained fury, which made their faces turn pale. I saw their hatred, which trickled with sweat down their faces. How they would have loved to torture me, to tear me apart and to destroy me right there on the spot! They knew however, "Today we still can't do it." We stood facing each other, they in impotent fury and I in horror from the knowledge of how great their hatred was. My God, I thought in such moments, how I would like to be far from this hatred! Will I ever know such good fortune?

One Saturday near the synagogue Dina Beilin introduced me to two short, plump women who looked like sisters. They were the wife and daughter of prisoner Simyen Marinov. The daughter, a very young, pregnant woman, had large dark brown perpetually questioning eyes. Marinov had been arrested in 1970 and while serving his term in a labor camp, he had been arrested for a second time and was facing a trial set for September 1972.

I invited them to come home to talk. Their story was a familiar one. They had decided to emigrate, had received an invitation from Israel, and had begun making the rounds of offices. He came to Moscow to apply for help at the Dutch embassy, which represented Israeli interests in Moscow. Outside the embassy, police encircled him, beat him severely until he lost consciousness, then arrested him on a charge of hooliganism and sentenced him to two and a half years' imprisonment.

To his second trial, Marinov was brought in on a stretcher; his spine had been so severely bruised that he could not even stand. In addition, his body was covered with horrible welts. The man was a physical and mental wreck; when his wife was allowed to see him for a few minutes, he whispered, "I don't want to live any longer; I can't."

After his wife and daughter returned home I began to spend many hours sitting at the intercity telephone office in expectation of a conversation with them, but they did not show up for the telephone calls which I had ordered. I then began to write complaints on my own and would send the text to them for their approval, but they remained uncooperative. They would hold on to my letters containing the text of an official complaint until I had to remind them of it by a telegram. I finally became tired of this situation and asked their permission to write my complaints directly. They agreed with relief and from then on I assumed the role of Marinov's "relative" and defender. I started a correspondence with him but it took several months before he understood my motives.

I usually made an agreement with those prisoners I was trying to help that they would write me regularly on specific, agreed-upon dates. The precise system enabled me to discover rather quickly whether anyone had landed in a punishment cell or was otherwise in trouble. If I did not receive a letter on time, I would send a telegram of inquiry to the head of the camp. At first the administration would ignore my telegrams but the very fact that someone was carefully following the case of a prisoner gave them pause. Recognizing my stubborn nature, the majority of camp administrators preferred answering my inquiries to facing an involved correspondence with their superiors, which could only lead to trouble.

My connection with prisoners was maintained basically by letters. Sometimes they managed to send me a letter that bypassed the censors, but all of my correspondence passed through the censor's hands. I wrote about events in the refusenik world, in Israel and the world at large but sometimes the censor would expunge a section of the letter.

I tried many ways to relieve the Marinovs' suffering, putting in much effort to reveal his story to the world. That was not enough, however, to save a person's life. I made the rounds of lawyers but none would give me any specific advice. In a state of distress I sat in a small park near my house and painfully sought the answer to just one question: what could I sink my teeth into in order to save this man?

The simple answer I found, of course, was medicine. Like everything else in the Soviet Union, medicine was supposed to be the "most humane in the world." The next morning I was at the medical board of the Gulag and succeeded in being received by the chief doctor. The elderly, balding and corpulent man listened attentively to my story. "Leave me a statement; I'll arrange for it to be checked," he said.

Without a moment's pause I handed him the required statement.

"It can't wait; he is dying. Tell me to whom you will give my statement."

He pressed a button and a man entered the office. The chief doctor handed him my statement and said, "Take this under your personal supervision."

As we left the office I was told I would receive an answer in a month.

"That's no good. He is paralyzed and dying. I can assure you that I shall put the blame on the medical service. Please phone the zone now, I'll wait in the hall. Please ask for a summary of his medical record because I know that the officers are beating him."

"Call me in two days, I'll phone the zone. I promise to send you a written reply in two weeks, including a diagnosis." He gave me his phone number.

Two days later I spoke to him and understood from the conversation, although he did not say so directly, that everything that I knew about the condition of Marinov was correct. He assured me that Marinov's life was not in danger and I trusted him. I imagined what was happening in the zone: a call from the Moscow chief physician of the ministry frightened not only the doctor but also the head of the zone. They probably put Marinov in the infirmary, washed him, fed him, administered medicine and began to figure out how to save themselves from a commission of investigation. Both the doctor and the head of the zone realized that they had to answer for this prisoner. I had accomplished my first task: Marinov would not die. Moreover they would no longer dare to beat him because both the doctor and the head of the zone understood that someone influential stood behind this prisoner.

I had to know what in fact was happening to him. I asked him for any information. Sometimes he would send a short letter, but then there would be a long silence. His wife told me that she also did not receive letters; or that's what she told me. Then I would receive a postcard written in uneven handwriting in which he complained that his feet were not functioning; he was not given crutches and was being humiliated.

I was living under extreme tension because Marinov was far from being the only prisoner I was helping at that time. Something extraordinary was always happening to one of the prisoners or to me. Sometimes, after recovering from another bout of stress I would remember that I had not received news from Simyen. I had only one alternative, to write a letter to the head of the zone and to ask what was happening. Once I received the following reply: "With regard to your complaint a conversation was held with the convict Marinov. He said that he had no relatives in Moscow and would not write any more letters."

I thought this was a lie but then reconsidered—what if it isn't? Rummaging through my desk drawer, where I kept all the postcards and letters from prisoners, I found several from him. Reading them over, I tried to create a picture of the person behind them; in addition, I reviewed my impressions of the family, his story, official documents, the charge and sentence. I was struck by the strange regularity of his correspondence, the gap between letters was almost always two and a half months. Was this an interval between being stirred up? A case of schizophrenia with its ups and downs? Or a conscious tactic to stimulate my campaigns in his defense by means of periodically suspending his correspondence?

Subsequently it even became difficult to force myself to write to this person. Although it was disgusting to think he might be manipulating me, he was, nevertheless, an innocent victim of senseless cruelty. I had taken it upon myself to help him and I would carry this matter through to the end. I was no longer tormented by doubts.

In my efforts on behalf of Marinov I received unexpected help. One morning the doorbell rang at an unusually early hour. Wondering who could be there, I opened the door to encounter a tall, young man with a shaven head. I could tell from his emaciated look that he had just been released from a labor camp; the deep pain in his eyes and a certain expression on his gray face identified him as someone who had come from the criminal zone.

"I would like to see Ida Nudel," he said.

"I am Ida Nudel."

His eyes lit up. "Simyen Marinov asked me to drop in," he said.

"Simyen! Please come in." I invited him into the kitchen and saw how his hungry eyes devoured everything.

"I'm Boris Shilkrot," he introduced himself and told me his story. As a student he had written and posted leaflets calling on Soviet students to fight for democratic changes. The KGB figured out soon enough who the author was and Boris was arrested and sentenced to three years for anti-Soviet activity. After he had completed his term, he was kept under police surveillance and after a short time arrested for violating the conditions of his supervision. He had met Marinov in one of the camps and the mere fact that both were Jews had brought them together.

I put a plate of apples on the table. He ate one, seeds and all. "May I take another?" he asked.

"Of course, I put them here for you."

He ate another in the same thorough manner yet still could not take his eyes off the fruit.

"Let's take a little break," I said. "You could get a stomach-ache."

"No," he said, "nothing will happen. I have been dreaming of apples for a long time."

Eventually Boris ate all the apples that I had in the house and while he was eating, he told me about Marinov, the zone and himself.

Marinov was indeed different from the others. Innocently convicted, he refused to take his punishment submissively or to try to adapt to the realities of his predicament. He protested in every way possible; he declared hunger strikes and sent off innumerable written complaints. His protests were sharp and denunciatory. He considered the Soviet system fascist and the camp administration Gestapo.

When Marinov would emerge from another stay in the punishment cell, he would again send complaints and protests. The more they tortured him, the more desperate he became. Boris told me that his legs were partially paralyzed and he could not straighten them at the knees. He could move only by crawling, leaning on his arms, and he was forced to cover long distances in rain or snow. "While he crawls, the officers kick him," Boris said.

"I'll take this amusement away from them," I promised Boris. "It will take a lot of effort and time, but I'll wage such a campaign that the administration will remember this outrage."

We wrote out telegrams to the government of the Soviet Union, the American President, the UN, the Central Committee of the Communist Party and various Soviet officials, in all about two dozen telegrams. Boris and I signed them all.

The head of the telegraph office refused to accept "such a text." Waving my passport in front of his face, I cited the demagogic slogans about the just and humane Soviet society which had been drummed into both our brains since our childhood. Finally he accepted the telegrams. When I had the opportunity, I dictated a copy of the telegram to Michael Sherbourne, our contact in London.

On the basis of my numerous battles with the Soviet penal system, I knew that as soon as my telegram would reach the camp chief's desk, Marinov's situation would change.

The eventual results were unexpected. Suddenly I got a telegram from Marinov's wife that she and her children were offered immediate visas to leave the Soviet Union. In October 1973 his family left for Israel.

After they had left, in an effort to get a broader perspective on Marinov's situation, I decided to check again with Michael Sherbourne.

"Michael, could you tell me what's happening now with regard to Soviet Jewry?" I asked him.

"Why do you ask?"

"I need information in order to decide what I should do."

"My dear," said Michael, "the superpowers are talking about the problem of Soviet Jewry all the time. I don't know whether there is greater interest now. You can probably sense this better than we can."

Our phone conversation took place in the home of a person who was departing for Israel that night. Scheduled to leave in a few hours, he was unafraid of the KGB.

I returned home by subway after this conversation. The long trip, the late hour and the regular rocking of the half-empty car put me in a reflective mood. If I understand it correctly, I thought to myself, the KGB is purposely getting me worked up so that I, in turn, will arouse our friends in the West. Perhaps I should not take the bait? If you want me to make a fuss now, then I won't! I reasoned with myself. But then my vision turned to a man with paralyzed feet creeping along the ground while criminals and officers laughed cheerfully and kicked him. No, damn them—I cannot silently wait for his release.

In my next phone conversation with Michael, I told him everything that Boris Shilkrot had told me about Marinov. Every conversation with Michael cost me an enormous amount of physical and emotional energy. I was afraid they would suddenly cut me off and I would not succeed in telling him everything I wanted to. I would grow nervous and hurry Michael along, always asking him to do something—whether to stage a protest demonstration, send a telegram or make a phone call.

"Don't get upset, Ida," he would calm me, "we'll do everything we can."

When I had already been in prison for several months, I suddenly received a postcard from a woman who signed it Ida. I had been subconsciously expecting this because when I was arrested, a lot of people knew that I was planning to refuse to serve in the army. I had just turned eighteen when I applied to emigrate to Israel, and many knew that I would go to prison rather than the army because after army service you can't leave Russia for many long years, whereas after prison . . .

When I received the postcard, I did not know how old she was or who she was, but it was immediately clear that this was a person who also wanted to go to Israel and who wanted to help me. It was, perhaps, my happiest day. We began to correspond, and I began to receive Israeli postcards from her! Even when I had been at liberty, I had never seen Israeli postcards; I saw things made in Israel for the first time when I was in prison. Then I began to receive telegrams from Moscow with sixty signatures—on Passover, Purim and my birthday. This was very supportive. In camp the main thing is support from outside, that is, letters. Only someone who has been in prison can appreciate the significance of letters—it is the greatest happiness in camp to receive letters and there is nothing greater. Prisoners prize letters more than vodka, hashish and cigarettes. And I received many letters from her. It is really satisfying to work toward a goal and to know that someone is thinking about you, and if it were not for Ida, I would not have felt this.

The main thing that kept me going was Ida's letters, and in many cases when I had to make some decision I consulted with her. I had no one else. My friends were criminals and I came in contact only with them, but I had different goals and a different path to follow. Even my *mother could not help me; indeed, I was more likely to give her advice than to receive it. Therefore Ida was the sole person who could evaluate my situation and make suggestions. I needed a person like that in order to endure my sentence and she seemed to sense this; she appeared just in time.*

*Mark Slogin**

*Mark Slogin is the fictitious name of a man who refused to be conscripted into the Soviet army and had been arrested in 1974 at the age of nineteen.

CHAPTER 8

MANY PEOPLE FROM ABROAD WERE ACTIVELY CONCERNED with many refuseniks' cases and some even came to the Soviet Union to learn more. Once a tourist, a man who had taken part in the French resistance, came to visit me. We spoke about my problems, and as an illustration I pointed toward my ceiling.

"Look carefully at the spot where the wall meets the ceiling. Do you see the hole? The chekists broke through there while I was in prison."

"Why?"

"In order to overhear my conversations and perhaps to complicate my life."

He turned pale and asked, "Do you think they are listening to us now?"

"I'm sure they are."

"How can you live that way? It's awful. I would go crazy in such an apartment."

"You're right. But then I convinced myself that I had to continue my life this way. A healthy person must adapt to any situation. Sometimes I begin to get frantic, but it passes."

"I advise you, Ida, go away someplace. You can go crazy!"

"There's no place to go. People are fearful of me. Almost no one speaks to me—only people who live like I do—people with a broken ceiling.

"The road I follow is like a narrow tunnel, the width of which is equal to the width of my shoulders and it's impossible for me to turn to the right or the left. Only forward. Otherwise I will have lost and will have to give in to the mercy of the KGB."

"Perhaps it's not so categorical? Perhaps there is a middle way?"

"Perhaps, but not for me. You can never escape from yourself."

I would often sit on the sofa and catch myself glancing upward toward the hole. I would think about my life, its failures, my solitude and my self-imposed isolation. I dreamed about victory, arriving in Israel and meeting my sister and family. I thought about those isolated and lonely prisoners I had helped. In planning my actions in their defense, I often turned my eyes toward the hole, which embodied the dark force of the KGB, trying to figure out how it would respond to my every move.

Once I found out how it worked when an elderly Jew from the Ukraine dropped in to explain that he had been refused an exit visa. We spoke for some time and before he left I gave him a Hebrew textbook and a book on the history of the Jews. Perhaps I dropped some phrase about books in our conversation.

I soon received a telegram informing me that he would phone me at the post office in three days, earlier than we had agreed upon. The Jew told me that when he left my building, a policeman stopped and took him to the police station. There he was carefully searched, as if in prison, down to the seams and folds of his clothing. They took away the books I had given him and warned him that if he were to maintain contact with me he would never leave the U.S.S.R.

Only outdoors could I speak with someone openly. For hours we would walk in any kind of weather, talking all the time. Even on the street, however, I was not always sure they were not trailing me with their ultramodern bugging equipment. It was like a game for idiots involving bugging, surveillance, tails at my back, cars. I could never accept that it was important for the state to know about my conversations and thoughts. They knew that we never planned any violence.

The chest pains I suffered from became more frequent and I decided to go to the district clinic. In the fall of 1973 a young doctor examined me carefully and when the nurse had left the office, she asked me directly, "Why are the police interested in you? I see according to the stamp on your medical record that it was sent to the interior ministry." I looked into her eyes to see whether I could trust her and briefly told her my story.

"Are you working?" she asked me.

"I have a problem. I usually get fired from a job within a few months."

"I'm looking for someone to take care of my son," she said. "If I'm insulting you with this suggestion, forgive me. I need help for four hours a day."

I happily accepted her offer under the condition that our work relations be officially arranged through an employment agency. A different branch of the same agency that cared for the old and sick accepted me without any discussion because they, too, needed people.

When I came to meet the boy, the woman warned me that he was unusual. His father was a black from Nigeria. The mother and child had recently returned from there. Large for his age, the boy was four and a half, well built, slender and graceful. His grandfather called him Aba, and his mother called him Abong. "Do you like me? Are we going to be friends?" I asked him with a smile. He became shy and hid behind his grandfather's back.

The next morning I went out with him to the woods near his home but the little boy did not walk beside me. As soon as he saw someone in the distance, he would run away. He would crouch on the ground, putting his head between his feet, and remain in this doleful position and I could not budge him. When he thought passersby were looking at him the wrong way he would grab a stone and fling it at them. In the evening I asked the mother, "Is your son's mental health all right? His behavior seems disturbed to me."

"No," she replied, "don't worry, he's all right. I warned you that he's not like everyone else. He's black."

Indeed, he was black and different and lonely! Even the people closest to him, his mother and grandfather, were not like him. He was unique.

"Did you ever introduce him to black people?" I asked his mother.

"I work a lot. I'm the only breadwinner," she replied.

He needed to see people just like himself, but where could I find them in Moscow? I made inquiries and it turned out that many black people were studying in a veterinarians' school not far away. Explaining to him that he was not alone in the world, I took him for a walk near the gates of the school and promised to show him people just like himself. Two men finally came along but they stopped reluctantly when I called out. I explained why I was butting into their conversation and asked them to speak with the boy. Instead they merely asked him his name.

"I know the story of this couple. So this is the child?" one of them said with mild curiosity.

This approach ultimately proved unsatisfactory as, even though I hopefully took the boy several times to meet black people, rarely would anyone, even the women, show any interest in him.

Gradually, however, the child began to get used to me and would calmly give me his hand when we crossed the street. He began to run to me when he saw unfamiliar people and he would take my hand when he thought people were looking at him. Eventually he stopped sitting on the ground in his pose of universal sorrow or throwing stones at passersby.

One warm summer day I decided to get a suntan. I took off my dress and lay down in my slip in the woods. He began throwing stones at me. "Why are you doing that, Abong?"

"What are you doing!" he demanded.

Hasn't he ever seen his mother undressed, I wondered to myself. "I'm tanning myself."

"What's that?"

"I want my skin to be like yours."

He was silent for a long time. Finally he asked quietly, "Is that really pretty?"

"Of course it is."

Hiding behind a mound of stones he remained quiet for a long time.

Abong began to show me more trust and sympathy. He would smile at me voluntarily, not just in response to mine, and he would tell me about himself. I was very proud that I had found my way into the heart of this lone soul. Once I overheard him speaking on the phone with his father and I heard him shout, "Papa, I have Ida, she is also black!" My jaw dropped in astonishment. Why did he think that? It was true in a certain sense; like him, my people lived among others as if we were just like everyone else, but we had a different mentality. But why had he decided that I was black? I recalled the incident in the forest when I had explained to him that the color of his skin was good. Apparently he had understood that in his own way, deciding that I was like him. It was strange; he could see the color of my skin, but in his eyes it was black. The more I knew about the suffering of this child, the more I compared his fate to that of my own people.

After we had become better acquainted, his mother told me the following story: she worked long hours and when he was a baby could not take care of him at home and therefore decided to put him in an ordinary Soviet nursery. The child went very happily for a few days, but suddenly he obstinately refused to go. She had no choice—he was forced to go until one day the mother found out that the children and the nursery teacher had been beating him. The children would pounce upon the poor child, and as the teacher helped them hold him down, they would beat him as hard as they could. The baby's public Soviet education ended at that point. Left alone in the house with his elderly grandfather, he grew up isolated, alien, different, becoming wilder and wilder. My involvement with his upbringing somewhat slowed down the development of his antisocial behavior and led him to realize that he could be accepted as he was.

Of course it was an interesting challenge to help raise such an unusual child but at that time my life was filled by another passion—to do everything possible to get to Israel. Insofar as the authorities continued to place obstacles in the way of my emigration I devoted my energies to the movement in the Soviet Union. As a result, my life was filled with such a whirl of events that in retrospect it seems hard to reconstruct them in sequential order. I was always engrossed in so many problems at once that it left me little time for introspection.

September 1973

My Dearest Lena, Leva and Yakov!

I again got mixed up in numbering my letters to you. The frenzied pace of my daily struggle sometimes confuses me.

I don't want Lena to think that I disapprove of her personality and her principles. On the contrary, if all people were like Lena, there would be neither wars nor fights. I value you very highly, my dear sister, but this inhuman situation requires another quality— stubbornness. Otherwise it's impossible to break through these stone walls.

I am against your standing in front of the UN and carrying on a hunger strike to the death. I am happy that my case has been placed before Soviet representatives in America. That's one more uncomfortable situation for them!

Lena, I reread your letter and think that it's completely senseless to appeal to Soviet officials. Write only to Ambassador Dobrynin and to him alone; he'll send it on to the KGB in any case. But Dobrynin lives in the West where one can demand a reply from him; the others are hidden and invisible to the world.

My dears, goodbye. I wish all of us a speedy victory. Hugs and kisses to all.

Fall arrived just now. Yesterday at ten o'clock the weather changed abruptly and my body is having trouble adjusting. That's why my handwriting is so uneven today.

I again send you kisses.
Ida

CHAPTER 9

IN THE FALL OF 1973 THE REFUSENIK COMMUNITY WAS PAR-
ticularly concerned about the health of Silva Zalmanson, the only
woman at the first Leningrad trial, who had been arrested on June
15, 1970, and sentenced to ten years of imprisonment for trying to
hijack a Soviet plane. At that time her father, Yosif, reported that
she was not well and was losing her hearing. We had been acutely
sensitive to the issue of health conditions in the camps ever since
the human rights activist, Yuri Galanskov, had died in November
1972 in the Mordovian men's camp. Although he had been seriously
ill for a long time, the KGB cruelly deprived him of adequate
medical help and they let him die. In view of Silva's illness a group
of Jews decided to go to the Presidium of the Supreme Soviet to
demand an early release for her and those who had been convicted
at the Leningrad trials.

Late in the evening on the day before the protest, my doorbell
rang.

"Who's there?" I asked.

"The police. Open up!"

I stood indecisively behind the door. If I opened it, they would
take me away and I would be unable to join the demonstration the
following day

"Open it, I insist. This is the deputy police chief of the Seventy-second precinct."

Yes, I recognized that voice. It was Major Zagladin, the man who had banged on my door and threatened me with arrest and all sorts of punishments on that night in the summer of 1972 when the KGB had decided to end our hunger strike at the offices of the Central Committee. I opened the door.

Two men stood there. One was in plainclothes. "May I come in?" asked the one in a police uniform.

"Who's the other one with you?"

"I'll explain in the apartment."

"No," I answered, "explain now, it will be too late once you're in the apartment."

"I insist, Ida Yakovlevna, that you let us into the apartment."

"Since you are in uniform and I know you personally, you may come in, but the other person must remain outside or he must identify himself."

"Let us in, Ida Yakovlevna, we'll explain everything inside the apartment."

"It will be too late once you're inside," I repeated. "Who's with you? I won't permit him to come in."

"Nevertheless, I insist that you let us in."

The standoff seemed endless. The three of us could barely control our emotions. I had to leave the house early the next morning. My stubbornness could lead me to the police station ahead of time.

Finally I let Major Zagladin enter the apartment. He closed the door behind him and hissed, "Please let him in, I beg you. Don't forget, Ida Yakovlevna, that you still have not received an exit visa."

"Who is this man and what does he want from me?"

"He is the deputy director of the district KGB department. Tomorrow you must not go to the demonstration. I beg you, don't get me in trouble."

"My apartment is bugged; the KGB is now listening to your every word." He turned pale and changed the tone of the conversation immediately.

"Let him in or tomorrow it will be very unpleasant for you."

Tomorrow I certainly didn't need any unpleasantness, since I wanted to get to the Presidium of the Supreme Soviet.

"All right," I said. The major rushed to open the door. Standing in the doorway, the man in plainclothes entered and announced,

"If you dare to leave your house tomorrow morning, you'll be arrested," and turning, he walked out of the apartment, with the major right behind.

I spent a fitful night trying to decide whether to leave the house or stay put. I was sure that the KGB would carry out its threat. If I left the house, I would get fifteen days. But it seemed to me that things had been calmer in the past few weeks. Possibly some kind of superpower talks were going on. What if the Soviet authorities suddenly were preparing to hand us over to Israel? If I obeyed and didn't go out, the chekists, sensing that they could intimidate me, would begin to break me so badly that I would be unable to gather up the bones. No, it was impossible to remain home. No matter how much I feared prison, I must ignore these intimidations. Tomorrow I would leave the house.

In the morning I tremblingly opened the door of my apartment. No one was there. The landing was also empty. I took the elevator to the first floor. All was quiet. Now I had to open the front door. "Well," I told myself, "forward!" I looked around carefully as I opened the door. Nothing seemed suspicious as I went calmly along the road.

Suddenly a male voice called out, "Ida!"

I quickened my pace, a little faster and I was running—hurrying to get to the road, next to people. A man was racing after me. Suddenly I saw another one coming toward me from the other side. They surrounded me. I screamed, although no one was around; it was like being on a deserted island. "See what they're doing! Help! Help!" I changed direction, trying to run away from them. One of them quickly caught up with me. I saw a car approach from behind on the asphalt road, and then, feeling a blow, I started to fall. One jumped me. I tried to break away but my attempts were pitiful. I couldn't move under the weight of his heavy body. Someone grabbed me by the feet. The man who had pinned me stood up, grabbed me by the arms and dragged me along the ground. I resisted, thrashing with my feet and arms but I couldn't pull loose.

They dragged me to a car. A man jumped out, quickly opened the door, and they literally threw me in; the driver covered me with the weight of his body. Both kidnappers hopped into the car, slamming the door behind them. The driver returned to his seat and the car raced off.

I was squeezed in between two thugs. A third, in the front seat next to the driver, had turned to face me. All four were breathing heavily but were not speaking.

I was taken to some police station where I wandered around a room cluttered with tables and chairs. I could not calm down because they had treated me so outrageously. The telephone was immediately taken out of the office.

They brought me a roll, bread and a cutlet from the cafeteria across the way. They also gave me a pitcher of water. Hours passed. My tormentors grew tired and more frequently left me alone.

Near the window was a broad, low sill which it was possible to stand on. Glancing around that vantage, I saw that the room was on a high first floor; the window led onto a roof above the entrance. It wasn't that high; it was possible to jump from the window down to the roof. If the roof faced an inner police courtyard below, then I could not get away, but if it led to a side street, with luck I might escape. But where could I go? Home? They would be looking for me there. I couldn't go to any acquaintances; they would get in trouble with the police.

I jumped back down as a policeman came in and ordered me out. A second one appeared instantly by the door. That was a bad sign.

"Follow me!"

They took me out of the police station and led me to a Black Maria, the notorious police car used to transport arrestees. They led me into a very narrow boxlike compartment and locked the door. It was uncomfortable to sit or stand, even for a short person like me. I had the feeling we were traveling for hours, and my feet grew numb. The car stopped but I remained inside for what seemed like an eternity. I couldn't think. I was so tired; all I wanted was to be able to lie down in peace, close my eyes and be silent.

Finally the metal door opened. "Come out." It was not clear whether this building was a prison or a police station. They led me to the far corner of a room where several policemen were seated at tables.

"Give me your passport."

"I don't have my passport with me."

"How come?"

"I'm not in the habit of carrying it."

They filled in a police form. "Sign."

"I won't. This arrest is illegal; what is the charge?"

"No one said that you were arrested. You were planning on disturbing public order. The civil militia detained you."

"Not the militia—thugs. They jumped me, knocked me down and dragged me along by the hands and feet."

"Wrong," said the policeman. "They were very polite. Members of the people's civil militia detained you. You will be strictly punished for slander. Call in the witnesses; she refuses to sign the protocol."

The "witnesses" entered and silently signed their names where they were told to. No one told them anything and they asked no questions.

"Sit over there and wait."

I sat down on a bench, with a policeman standing nearby.

Then a sloppily dressed fat and dirty old hag entered the room. It was hard to associate this creature with the word "woman."

The policeman said, "Go with this woman into that corner." I went; who knows, maybe we would have to sit in a cell together.

She turned to me, "Get undressed, there will be a personal search."

The policemen were standing behind me. She said, "They will turn around."

I began to comprehend. "What does this mean?" I asked. "Am I arrested? Where is the order? You have no right to ask this of me."

"They found an intellectual," said the policeman. "Undress or we'll do it by force."

"My arrest is illegal, I refuse to undress."

"Undress her," ordered the man sitting at the table.

Two strapping policemen grabbed me and twisted my hands behind me. That pestilent hag with her disgustingly filthy hands unbuttoned my coat and blouse and began fumbling around my chest.

"My God, why this?"

Finding nothing, her vile hands tugged at my skirt, pulled down my pants and again ranged over my bare skin.

I was seething but remained silent. They let me rearrange my clothes, took away my glasses and all my personal items and led me half blind down some stairs that kept winding down lower and lower. As I started to fall behind, the man behind me would shove me in the back, saying, "Hurry." I grabbed on to the railing with all my strength and groped at the steps with my feet. I endured his shoves in silence, praying I wouldn't fall and tumble down the steps.

We finally stopped; they unlocked a door and shoved me inside. A woman was sitting on the floor of a tiny, almost dark cell. The door closed and the lock jangled. Part of the floor was covered by a wooden plank, probably for sleeping. At one end of the plank was a small elevation, apparently a headrest instead of a pillow.

I could hear men's voices and the measured steps of the guards on the other side of the door.

"What are you here for?" asked the woman. I couldn't see her face, only a bright spot from where her voice emanated. "They picked me up at the train station," she said. "What about you?"

"I was going to a demonstration. I'm a Jew, and I want to emigrate to Israel."

"Stop talking in the cell," ordered the policeman, "or I won't take you out."

Damn them. There was no toilet in the cell and I needed to be taken out.

I took off my coat, lay down on the boards and covered myself with it. I was choking with tears. No, I would not sob. But I did not have the strength to hold them back. I covered my head so they wouldn't hear my suffering. A little later the door opened and they led the woman away, leaving me alone to contemplate my full bladder.

I couldn't sleep and desperately needed to go to the bathroom, but to do so I had to speak to them, and doing that was like putting myself on their level.

I finally decided that it couldn't go on this way; I kicked the cell door with my foot. "Take me to the toilet." The door opened slowly and I went out.

"Come here," said the policeman.

"I can't see; they took away my glasses."

He came up to me and turned me in the right direction. Slowly, carefully groping my way along the floor, I finally reached my goal.

What good fortune it is when you're not pressured and your bladder is empty! I gulped water from the faucet; I had not had anything in my mouth since the morning.

The policeman led me back to the cell. I lay down on the wooden floor and tried to sleep. Time dragged on endlessly in this basement. I had no contact with the outside world. They brought cafeteria-like food, which meant that it was not a prison. It also meant that it was probably morning.

I was alone in the cell. Indeed, I did not want companionship; any conversation would have been torture. Only silence could cure me of yesterday's pain. Again they brought food. That meant that it was probably already evening. How long would I be here? What was awaiting me beyond these cell walls? What kind of revenge was the KGB planning for me? From time to time I drifted off, half dozing, half sleeping. I was indifferent to everything; my thoughts, what few I had, stirred very slowly. I was existing, but not living.

For several days my routine consisted of being led to the bathroom and receiving food twice a day; I couldn't think, or perhaps I did not want to.

I did not know how many days had passed in that way when the door opened and I was given the order, "Get out, follow me."

This time it was easier—we were going up. I was led into a large, very bright room.

A policeman behind the table ordered, "Come here."

My eyeglasses, watch and purse were lying on the table. He let me take them all. I put on my glasses, greatly relieved to be able to see what was going on around me.

The policeman said, "You are free." They told me they would phone the employment agency for which I worked at the time and explain that I was absent for a valid reason.

I left the police yard and started walking briskly. I did not know where I was or where I was going, the main thing was to get as far away as possible from that dreaded place.

When I hesitantly asked a passerby the day of the week he looked at me strangely and said, "Saturday."

The Sabbath! I could go to the synagogue and find out the Jewish news. But first I would go home, climb into the tub and wash myself of the dirt and horrors of the past days.

Many people had assembled near the synagogue on that day and I discovered that I had not been the only one abducted. The police had grabbed over twenty people. A woman pounced on me,

"At a time like this, they're arresting people, and you can't phone and say where you are!"

"There was no phone in my cell," I replied. She must have bit her tongue.

Many refuseniks had long ago cut themselves off from Soviet life; they no longer read local papers or celebrated local holidays. Accidentally our attempt to draw attention to the situation of prisoners of Zion—in particular to the ailing Silva Zalmanson—coincided with a joyful Soviet "festivity"—a peace conference in Moscow. The KGB feared that the emissaries of peace would see our demonstration and have their naive faith in the most just society on earth clouded by doubt. They therefore seized each of us within a few feet of our homes and concealed us in various basements so no one would hear a peep from us.

"It only seems that way to you," the chekists often told me, when I accused them of violating my elementary rights. Then why do I still shudder when I recall how that hag's dirty hands poked all over my bare body?

Ida was the highest authority for me on any issue, and she always answered my questions seriously, even the trifling ones. I knew that I could speak to her on any topic because she would never laugh at me.

Not one letter got lost; Ida followed each one so that there would not be a break in the correspondence, which would then be difficult to overcome. I did the same, writing to her, even without waiting for a reply. When her letters stopped arriving, I declared a hunger strike. Because we numbered them, I knew that they had been confiscating her letters. If letter number seven came after number five, then I knew that six was missing. I wrote to the head of the camp that I would fast until they gave me her letters and they gave them to me. I also received a teach-yourself Hebrew book in the mail.

It was funny, but the camp administration was afraid of her. The chief camp security officer said to me in annoyance, "Who is this woman? Why does she write? Tell her not to write anymore and to stop bothering people. She writes to the Central Committee and then I have to explain things."

Ida really wrote and complained. She knew where to write in order to make an impression on the camp administration—to the Central Committee, the Presidium, the procurator general—and the security officer had to answer every letter. He therefore tried to see that everything was all right with me so he would not be bothered with a new complaint from her which he would have to answer. Her letters forced them to follow their own rules, which they perpetually violated.

The security officer wanted to know why she meddled, but I was not surprised. I thought that it ought to be that way. We are Jews and share a common fate. We must help each other.

Ida was an unusually sensitive person. She wrote, "I can tell from your letters whether you're in a good or bad mood," and she was right. Once something unpleasant happened but I wrote her the most ordinary letter at the time and she immediately responded, "What happened to you?"

When she heard that I was being transferred she traveled to meet the train, but they kept moving me from one prison to another and she kept missing my train. I was no longer under a prison regime and was being sent to what is called chemistry—low-paid work at some chemical or other large enterprise. Finally we arrived at the city where we were supposed to live—and did not have the right to leave—and they brought us in buses from the station to a five-story dormitory building. I would have to observe a nightly curfew but would have some free hours during the day. I immediately headed for the shower room; I wanted a shower more than anything else after all those awful, stinking mattresses which had probably been slept on by hundreds of people, even dead people and who knows who else . . .

After the shower I wanted to go to my room but they told me someone was waiting for me; I couldn't even imagine who it could be. Who could be waiting for me in this unfamiliar city only a few hours after my arrival?

I went out and saw a woman. I looked at her—I had a photograph—and asked, "Ida?"

She said, "Yes, Ida."

I was very happy that she had come to meet me and she immediately said, "Let's go to a restaurant now; you need to be fed."

I said, "No, Ida. The first thing I need is shoes, because I have nothing to walk in." I bought shoes and then we went to a restaurant. I had a bald head and unshaved face, was exhausted from the transit and was wearing a torn jacket and simple wrinkled pants although my shoes were new. In short, I looked rather strange and she doubted whether they would let us into the restaurant, but I said, "With a woman like you, they'll surely let us in."

In the restaurant she ordered fish for me but said that I must not drink because there would be an inspection in the evening and they could send me straight back to the camp. I didn't even look at the fish. I had just come out of the camp and was almost at liberty and I talked and talked and talked. She told me, "Eat, first eat." The fish was very tasty and I praised it and felt good in the restaurant. After I ate, I started talking again.

On the bus back to the dormitory I continued to talk and talk and tell her about the camp. She listened and encouraged me to continue. We returned to the dormitory of the chemistry works and Ida said, "Well, that's all. I'm going back to Moscow, but write regularly and phone;

I'll also call you." She accompanied me to the door and we parted for the first time.

She helped me in so many ways! She forced me to study English in my spare time and sent me money to study with a teacher for a month and a half. She sent packages regularly with various things including a tape recorder and books on Jewish history and culture.

Mark Slogin

CHAPTER 10

I HAD KNOWN THE ARTIST ARON BAZUCHOV FOR SEVERAL
years and he certainly was a strange person. He told me that he
was sometimes bothered by nightmares which would arouse him
from sleep and he would then work for long hours on his paintings.
His works spoke of Jewish suffering, pain and tragedy. It was
impossible to view his paintings without a spiritual or even physical
shudder. Death—corpses, mountains of skeletons—were drawn so
that you could almost hear each of them screaming about its fate.
His tiny room, which he solemnly referred to as his studio, was
filled with images of human misery.

Aron did not try to exhibit officially because his paintings,
unlike the art approved by the authorities, did not reflect the
"happy life of the Soviet people" and he was gravely apprehensive
that he might be sent to a psychiatric hospital. Although we remained in contact during the first half of the 1970's I told him
honestly that the chekists would never let me or my contacts out
of their sight. Sometimes Aron noticed that he was being trailed
for several days after a meeting with me. Occasionally he enjoyed
it, as an adventure that stimulated his nerves or, as he said, that
"attached significance to oneself." Afterward, however, he would
become afraid and turn his fear into anger at me. He was open
about the reason for remaining in touch. "If I decide to emigrate
someday, then you are the only one that I can count on. I won't
go without my paintings."

"I probably won't be able to create any longer," he would tell me. "Here they don't exhibit me but at least I paint. Over there no one will bother me, but I probably won't be able to paint anymore. I'm old already; I'm thirty-five. For an artist that's the end."

"I don't understand you; why are you afraid of your shadow here, yet you paint, but there, where you could paint what you want, you won't be able. What kind of strange logic is that?"

"You'll never understand. You're a fighter. You have a different mentality."

"Stay here, enjoy your fears and work. What sense is there in leaving if you know you're dooming yourself?"

"I must bring out my paintings. Without me they'll perish. If I don't bring them out, the world will never know about the existence of an artist named Aron Bazuchov, influenced by Soutine and just as talented."

"Perhaps you overestimate yourself?"

"I am a genius of Jewish suffering."

Concerned that the authorities might try to arrest me because of my activities, I felt it time to have my teeth checked. My friends who had been released from labor camps had told me that toothaches could be a serious problem there. In the zone they did not treat problems, even dental ones.

I told Abong's mother that I needed a dentist. As she was a doctor, I figured she could help me. "Fine," she said, "I'll get you an appointment."

Several nights later the boy's mother was standing at the door, looking pale and frightened. "Ida, I must tell you something very important." Although she told me not to be frightened, she was trembling herself.

"Did something awful happen to the child?"

"No. It's something to do with you."

At first I could not make sense out of what she was saying. "I never saw such a thing," she said. "We make every effort not to let other doctors know so their treatment won't be prejudiced; I never saw such a thing, written out that way . . ."

"Tell me clearly, what's going on?"

She composed herself and began more or less to make sense. Having taken a form for an appointment with the best dentist, she consulted my patient's file. To her horror she discovered that there were two folders in my name—a normal thick one with years of information and a second, new shiny one, the likes of which she had never seen in all her years of medical practice. On the first page of both was a warning to doctors: alcoholic. On the old records it appeared in the upper right-hand corner; on the new it was written in large letters. The new folder contained several documents dated at various times, testimony of witnesses and of doctors that I had been brought to the clinic in an intoxicated state. The conclusion was that I was a chronic alcoholic who needed compulsory treatment. So there it was—ready-made vengeance.

I asked her not to act on this disinformation. I would think about it overnight. I promised her that her name would not be mentioned and that I would not say a word about what I knew. She could rely on me; I promised her I had enough time to avoid reacting in panic.

By morning I had my plan ready. I went out early for my eight o'clock appointment and without waiting to explain things to the dentist, who clearly did not want to see me, I went into the office of the chief doctor and asked him to receive me. A woman in a white medical robe was sitting in the office. I asked the chief doctor, "Please look at me carefully, do I look like an alcoholic?"

He replied, "No, why do you ask?"

"On my medical file, on the upper right corner it's written that I'm an alcoholic. Please explain to me what that means."

"That can't be," said the doctor. "We never write on the cover of the medical record, even if the person is sick."

"Please ask your colleagues to bring my medical file, I was just now with the dentist in office number eight."

I was astonished to see him obediently dial a number, check on my name and ask that my file be brought to him immediately. A few minutes later, it was on his desk.

"Yes, you are right, there is a note, but what does this mean?"

"It means that you are being used in the struggle against an activist of the Jewish national movement."

"What nonsense," he said. "What's going on?"

"You are a tool in the hands of the KGB and will pass judgment on me, declaring me an alcoholic."

The woman who was sitting at the table lost her patience and said, "Yes, you are an alcoholic. I myself received you several times. You were so dirty and drunk that it was disgusting to touch you."

"So you're the author of this work," I said. "Penal medicine in action."

The chief doctor jumped at these words. "What are you talking about? What penal medicine? How dare you say such a thing in my office?"

"Yes, but you see for yourself what's written on my card. Please look at my medical history, there can't be any incriminating notes there." There could not be because each doctor starts his comments on the following line, without leaving any free space, as I knew from past experience. The chief doctor patiently looked at the entire record and said, "Yes, there are no such entries here."

I was dying to say to him, "Please, ask them to bring the other, false file and there you'll see everything very clearly and will figure it out," but then I would endanger Abong's mother, destroying her career in the Soviet Union. I therefore remained silent. When he had finished reading the file, I said to him:

"I am a Jew and I want to emigrate to Israel; KGB people are not letting me leave. I come into conflict with society, I go to demonstrations and I protest. Phone the deputy police chief Zagladin and he'll tell you who I am."

He dialed Zagladin and introduced himself, "This is the chief doctor of the clinic. Nudel, Ida Yakovlevna, is in my office. She insists that you know her and that she is registered with you. I would like to know, is she registered as an alcoholic?"

Zagladin explained something and he said, "I'm not interested in her political convictions. I'm a doctor. Is she registered as an alcoholic or not?"

Zagladin continued to explain something to him.

"Thank you. Goodbye.

"You see, I am erasing this note. Are you satisfied?"

What good was that erasure, when in the registry there was a clean shiny file, drawn up according to the last word in Soviet punitive medicine and asserting that I was a chronic alcoholic? But what could I say? I remained silent.

"Are you satisfied?" the doctor asked.

"We'll see," I said, "how events develop further."

"Only I can't understand how this could have happened."

"You don't understand? Even after your colleague's lies? This is already a matter for your conscience."

Crying inside and wondering about my future, I left.

* * *

When I went to care for Abong that day, he carried on and didn't listen to me; perhaps he sensed my tension and was responding to it.

Anxious about him, I dropped by again late in the afternoon to find out how he was. The boy was all right, but his mother told me the medical part of my story which affected her.

She herself had ignored my request not to mention the falsified documents and had taken her own steps. Apparently she had gone to the dentist and said in the presence of other doctors that she knew me as a patient and she simply could not understand where that note had come from, and that I was a completely healthy person mentally. The consequences were revealed quickly enough—in the middle of the day she was summoned to the chief doctor's office and was given a reprimand with an entry in her personal file for violating Soviet medical ethics because she had told a patient, that is, me, the diagnosis of my "illness."

That evening, Aron Bazuchov came to take me to a farewell gathering for a family who was leaving for Israel in a few days. I had arranged that when they would submit their documents the next morning at the Dutch embassy, where the consul who represented Israel's interests was located, they would include colored slides of Semyen's work among them. When we left the house, I suddenly tensed up as I opened the front door of the building. In the gathering dusk I caught sight of several policemen and cars around the building, and even some plainclothesmen. I slowed down and said to Aron without turning my head, "They're after me, you'd better get away; it will be unpleasant."

"No, I won't leave you in such a situation," he said.

"Then keep going, don't move away from me."

Aron took my arm as we walked along a very narrow road. Suddenly a familiar, large figure loomed ominously ahead of us; it was the same person who had once come to me with the deputy police chief Zagladin and announced that they would arrest me the next day.

We were heading directly toward him. At the last moment he took one step to the side, letting us pass, and turned and followed us closely, breathing heavily down my neck. He was so tall and bulky that his head and breath hung directly over me. The three of us continued this way in silence until we approached the subway entrance. Suddenly he stepped off the sidewalk, drew even with me, roughly bumped my shoulder and turned to the subway.

"Aron, what should we do?" I asked.

"You should know better than I," he replied. "I don't like this business at all. What will happen to my paintings now?"

Since it was a Thursday, the day when Michael Sherbourne usually called from London, I decided to call Yuli Kosharovsky, the refusenik who would receive Sherbourne's call. I briefly told him the whole story and he promised to report everything to Michael.

We continued on to the building where the party was and where we were supposed to hand over Aron's slides. I started out calm, but when we entered the elevator, goose pimples suddenly ran down my back, my whole body trembled and I could not control myself. "Aron, let's get out of the elevator, I can't go on." We went out and stood silently on the stairs for a while.

"Well, did it pass? Perhaps we should return, I'll take you home?"

"No, let's do what we came for. Let me rest a few more minutes; I need to take myself in hand and stop trembling." We went up to the apartment, gave them his slides and wrote down Sherbourne's address in London. I found it too difficult to mention what had just happened.

Aron took me home and promised to come by again on the following day. The next day I felt conflicted—on the one hand, I was terrified of leaving the house without Aron, but on the other, I knew that I could not remain at home indefinitely. The KGB would conclude that it had finally intimidated me and would press on until I could no longer bear it. My God, was I scared! Ida, I told myself, there is no other way but proceeding straight ahead no matter how frightening it is.

When Aron arrived in the middle of the next day, I suggested, "Let's go to a restaurant, I can't stay home any longer."

Downstairs on the street my eyes, like those of a frightened animal, took in everything around me; my back stiffened and my body tensed up as if about to go into a spasm. There was no one suspicious.

Aron took me home from the restaurant and promised to come again the following evening.

"Don't go out alone. Stay in the house and wait for me."

What kind of life was this? I had to overcome my fear and leave the house on my own. "No," I told him, "don't come tomorrow, I'll go out alone. Take the addresses and phone numbers of my friends in case they hide me in a loony bin. Phone right away and tell everyone what happened," I requested.

"Let's hope," he said, "that the worst is already behind."

But the worst was going outside into the uncertainty of the courtyard. While I was going down in the elevator and then on the stairs I drove myself on with the mental order, "Forward, Ida, forward!"

In the meantime the news flew around Moscow and the West that the KGB was planning to confine me to a psychiatric hospital. In a telephone conversation Michael Sherbourne convinced me that "they wouldn't dare do that," and he informed me that official representatives in England were trying to clarify my situation. "Ida, don't be afraid," he shouted into the receiver. "Don't be afraid, they won't dare."

I wasn't so sure.

Early one morning my doorbell rang. I opened the door and found an elderly man standing there. I had seen his face someplace, but I couldn't remember where.

"May I come in?" he asked.

"Please."

"Ida," he said, "I brought you some money from the synagogue. Some people think that you will be arrested soon. You need to think about your health and get a little stronger. This money is for you; spend it on fruit." He put one hundred rubles on the table.

Oh, how hard it was for me at that moment. Ever since my sister had left, no one had asked how I was doing and what I was living on. I myself avoided bringing up my personal affairs with others.

I no longer had friends in the real sense of the word. Those from my past life were somewhere very far away. I did not allow myself to even call them, never mind meet them. Many worked at closed enterprises and to maintain friendly relations would have been dangerous for both of us. Those who worked with me in the movement were fellow thinkers but not close friends.

Seeing the storm of emotions churning inside me, the man hastened to leave the apartment. Embarrassed by the situation, I did not even manage to ask him his name. (Indeed, it would have been a bad idea in my bugged apartment.)

His presentiments coincided with my own. After all, I had chosen a path, consciously and voluntarily, and had to be aware that this might happen. One day they would ring the bell or grab me on the street and say, "Ida Yakovlevna, you're under arrest!"

My Dear Ones,

I very unexpectedly had an opportunity to send you a letter that will bypass the censor and decided to answer your request to tell about my daily life. My letters, as you know, are carefully scrutinized. As soon as I begin a new protest campaign the censor gives me all my mail, even letters he had detained, so as to distract me. After each meeting with correspondents or influential people from the West or after demonstrations they deprive me of letters for some time. They found my sole weak spot and punish me by depriving me of my mail. As soon as I begin to complain loudly, the censor quickly reacts; the next day I receive a heap of mail. It's like in prison or camp where the first punishment is to cut off correspondence.

I am the kind of individual who is "internally disciplined" and I follow a rather strict daily regime. I usually get up at seven in the morning and go to bed exactly at eleven. Until midnight I listen to the radio or rather I try to listen to free world transmissions despite the jamming. Often they do not jam the first three minutes of the news. Sometimes they stop jamming for a few minutes during a broadcast and I succeed in catching something. Sometimes they don't jam the Voice of America so strongly. If I switch from one station to another, then some information seeps through.

I usually go every week to the market to buy fruits and vegetables unless I am too emotionally exhausted—the retribution for solitude. When I need to restore my balance, I wander in the woods for a while.

My apartment, as you can imagine, is always very clean; I eat simply and enjoy preparing my food myself. My clothing is unattractive and poor but comfortable and warm. I still have some more or less attractive fall clothing but the summer and winter is another story! It's not a matter of principle but just of circumstance. It's very time-consuming to shop for something nice. It's better to have an acquaintance who works in a store but I have neither the time nor the acquaintance. I consider it senseless to waste hours in stores and, besides that, I can't stand the stuffiness. It costs me several hours of sleep and destroys my daily regimen, which I don't like.

I often get up in the middle of the night and travel to another city if I have to.

I don't tell others because I'm convinced that people don't know how to respect others' secrets and there's no sense in writing about it even in this letter. I don't commit any crimes or violate the laws of the country, but I don't want to inform on myself, and how I manage financially is a delicate topic. I earn literally pennies taking care of invalids or others—not enough to live on. It was really difficult and I counted every penny until Lena helped organize matters and, like other refuseniks, I received remittances from abroad which enabled me to live. When the family of Eric Moonman from London adopted me, then things got even better. Then they were joined by a group of women from Liverpool and I began helping others with little or no support of their own. Fortunately, I am not greedy for money or material things.

I write letters or complaints for four hours a day and sometimes I am busy organizing and preparing for demonstrations and so forth. I never go to the movies, theater or concerts—I can't stand this censored culture—nor do I listen to Soviet radio, read the papers or participate in elections; I don't even read books in Russian. I have totally excluded myself from this society; unfortunately, however, I am still here physically. Although the conflict torments me, I feel completely emancipated. I do not depend on anyone financially or in any other way. What a fantastic life! And many others feel the same. No one believes it! I am completely free in spirit; I do what I want. Sometimes I am put in jail for this or beaten up a bit or punished in some other way, but everything has a price. You have to pay for your pleasures!

Are you satisfied with my account?

All my love and kisses

Ida

A FEW MONTHS AFTER THE KGB HAD TRIED TO TRAP ME BY falsifying my medical papers, one morning I went to my mailbox and discovered a large gray envelope without a stamp or postmark or even a return address, just my name. I opened the envelope right away but it was too dark in the entrance so I went outside, eager to see what it was about. The following was written on official KGB stationery: "In connection with your declaration, please appear on January 17 at eleven o'clock at 23 Volodarsky Square." The signature was illegible.

What declaration, I wondered. Perhaps it's the one that I had sent two years ago when I tried to explain that I did not possess any secrets? Had they remembered it now, two years later? I didn't know whether I should go or not. Clearly they had thought everything out—they knew I was home and had put it in my box, leaving me little time to decide. It was ten o'clock and I needed forty-five minutes to reach that address. Probably I shouldn't go—they couldn't have remembered my declaration after two years. But what if they had suddenly decided to speak to me about the heart of the matter? If it meant a visa I should go. Perhaps they were willing to release me and wanted to speak with me beforehand? How they tormented me! But then again, I shouldn't go; I had nothing to say to them and they would surely twist my words. Anyway I called David Azbel, a fellow refusenik, who was very active from 1973 to 1974, and I told him about the invitation.

"I have only an hour left and I need forty-five minutes to get there. If I don't call you, you know what it means."

"Maybe I should go with you?" he suggested.

"No, there's no point. I'll take only my passport. Goodbye."

"Ida, don't get so upset, this is not 1937." But I was very upset.

At the entrance I handed the letter to the person on duty. "Your passport," he said. I gave it to him. Suddenly a man appeared from somewhere saying, "That's for me." He took my passport and the letter and told me, "Follow me. I am very surprised. We did not think that you would come." I kept silent. He led me along endless corridors, up and down narrow, winding staircases. In my imagination floated pictures of the tortures and interrogations that I had read about in books.

Finally he led me into a large room with small windows high up in the wall, a large table and another long one perpendicular to it. High-backed chairs were placed near the long table. At his suggestion I hung my coat on an empty rack near the entrance to the office.

"Sit down," he said. I sat somewhere in the middle of the long table. During a silence he read something or pretended that he was reading. "You want to emigrate?" he asked suddenly.

"You surely know that very well; I appealed to you numerous times. Please tell me your name and title," I said calmly.

"I'm the one who asks the questions here," he replied.

"How should I address you? Citizen Chief?" I asked, using the particular form of address of prisoners to prison authorities.

"No, because you're not under arrest," he said.

"Then tell me your name and title," I repeated. "Perhaps you're ashamed of your name?" I suggested impudently.

"Don't forget, Ida Yakovlevna, that I summoned you." Nevertheless he relented. "I am the adviser on Jewish affairs, Krymov, Vadim Pavlovich." Working himself up, he continued loudly, "What liberties you are taking! You organize demonstrations, write protests, stir up people. You appeal to people abroad, meet with foreigners and slander your motherland," he said loudly, stirring himself up.

"I speak only the truth and you know it. You choke us and at the same time don't want us to scream? Let us go!"

"Have you forgotten where you are?"

"Yes, I know where I am." Each inch of this room is covered with gallons of human blood. Its walls guard terrible secrets, which mankind will never know.

"We don't intend to tolerate you any longer."

"It's all in your hands; perhaps I won't leave this room."

"You'll get out of here. Sit quietly and wait until you are given a visa. And don't stir up your friends in the West. Who do you think you are, trampling on the head of the Soviet government?"

I was silent. After all, I have never asked myself by what right I undertook to speak in the name of many. No one had authorized me or ordered me or asked me to stand up for another's rights. I did it of my own free will. I saw it as my duty.

"Where did you get the idea that there are plans to put you in a psychiatric hospital?" he asked calmly.

"So that's it! Now I understand everything." And I told him the whole story from beginning to end.

"That's all a fabrication. We checked it. Nothing of the sort has ever happened. The chief doctor does not confirm your story. There was no inscription at all on your medical record. That's slander and you will be punished for that on a criminal basis," he announced.

"Everything that I told you is the absolute truth."

Suddenly he took a sheet of paper out of the desk drawer and, glancing at me, said, "Here is the chief doctor of the clinic's explanation. You mean to say that he lied?"

I wanted to say, "Every word of yours a minute ago was a lie, yet you're indignant if someone else dares to do it to you," but this time I had the good sense to remain silent.

"The chief doctor already told you that the incident is closed. You can tell your friends that it's over," he said.

"Time will tell whether or not it's closed," I responded.

"Do you have any questions for me?"

I still had not grasped what was happening to me.

"Aren't you interested in when you will emigrate?" he provoked me.

"You won't tell me the truth," I answered.

"You think very poorly of us!"

"Then when will I go?"

"You must understand, Ida Yakovlevna, that everything depends on the international situation. Your departure lies in the indefinite future." After a silence he then remarked, as if to himself, "But perhaps tomorrow, who knows?"

I got up and headed for the coat rack, which we reached simultaneously. He reached out for my coat but in my imagination I suddenly saw him helping me put it on and I shuddered. I looked him in the eye; he understood my meaning and silently turned away. I grabbed my coat and without putting it on went out to the hall. He followed me and said, "To the left," and he started walking briskly, without looking back. In a short while he led me to the exit, gave me back my passport, and said, "Let her out," and I quickly left that fearful building.

My watch showed that I had spent forty-five minutes there. I phoned David Azbel and recounted the conversation. "They want to consider the incident closed. Tell this to Michael Sherbourne if he calls," I said.

It was here that I made a horrible mistake. I fell into the KGB's trap.

On February 22, 1974, I declared a hunger strike and joined a group of men who had started one a week before me. Four men were on strike in David Azbel's apartment and I was in mine. I explained my reason for joining the hunger strike in the following statement to the Presidium of the Supreme Soviet, which officially decides issues of emigration.

> The small pink sheet of paper called a visa costs 900 rubles, but no one ever measured the suffering which one must endure in order to receive this paper. It has been over two and a half years since I declared my desire to emigrate to Israel. What haven't they done to me in these years! They placed me in a prison punishment cell when I turned to the Presidium of the Supreme Soviet; there they starved me and created unbearable conditions, they baited me like a wild beast during the hunt. Several times they grabbed me off the street and threw me into dirty and stinking cellars which are called preliminary detention cells and I wallowed there next to criminals, wiping up the dirty floors with my body. They broke through the ceiling in my apartment, which is regularly bugged. Every word, every groan and every sigh of mine is recorded on tape. But that's not all.

The threat of being placed in a psychiatric hospital hangs over me; whether sitting at home or going outside, I am aware that this threat can be carried out at any moment. When will my tormentors be sated? Hasn't enough blood been sucked in payment for my desire to live in Israel? On January 17 I was summoned to the KGB where I was told very definitely that my departure lies in the indefinite future, but maybe tomorrow, depending on the international situation. Led to desperation by the hopelessness of my situation and having no other means of expressing my protest against tyranny, I resort to the sole method available to me—I declare a hunger strike.

I took this desperate move without the protection of family or friends; my name was known only to a narrow circle of people both in the Soviet Union and in the West. I therefore had no illusions of succeeding in obtaining a visa. Moreover, knowing my heart condition, I was not sure that it would be easy for me to fast. In the past I had successfully managed three-day hunger strikes but this one was supposed to be open-ended—until victory or death and defeat. The prospect of hunger did not intimidate me. I knew that one wants to eat only on the first two days; after that one becomes indifferent to food and feels some kind of inexplicable lightness and excitement, or perhaps it would be more correctly called a calming.

Seven days later Azbel's wife came and suggested that I continue my hunger strike at their apartment. "At our place the telephone rings constantly; people call from all over the world. Correspondents, refuseniks and even guests from distant countries drop by."

Her proposal was not just attractive but downright tempting. I accepted. I had not left the house for a week and was beginning quietly to go crazy from the solitude. Moreover, in extreme situations it's much safer to be with people because the presence of live witnesses excludes the possibility of a provocation or falsification by the KGB.

In Azbel's apartment I truly understood the meaning of the words "We are concerned about your fate." The telephone rang incessantly; it seemed as if the whole world was sleepless and indefatigable in our support. Phone conversations in English exhausted David even more than the hunger strike itself.

The hunger strikers were being supervised by a doctor, Sanya

Lipavsky. Reliable and obliging, he was always ready to help the most active refuseniks. He endeared himself to everyone by his ability to get hold of all the unavailable goods and medicines. He never asked anything for himself. When asked whether he had applied for a visa, Sanya would answer that he had not because his father was serving a term in a labor camp for economic crimes.

On the sixteenth day of his hunger strike, Azbel was summoned to OVIR where he was told that he and his entire family would receive visas within a month. Friends in the West confirmed the information and, on the seventeenth day, a victorious David stopped his hunger strike.

I stopped mine, too, because it no longer made sense to continue. The authorities completely ignored me. I did gain something, though, because my name became known in the international community. But I paid the tremendous price of creating a problem with my heart; it would hurt with every physical effort. A doctor I knew took a cardiogram and said, "I don't know what's the matter; the muscle is strong."

I lay quietly and sadly in my own apartment for weeks, then months, telling myself that I must be patient and stubborn and not panic, since my heart muscle is strong and will certainly recover. The radio was my only link with the world. I knew what was happening outside but the world did not know what was happening to me. I rarely received Lena's letters and she received mine even less frequently, the KGB punished me for the hunger strike. My rebellious spirit did not want to accept my physical weakness. Just lying in bed and staring at the broken ceiling was torture; therefore, as soon as I became a little stronger, I dug into the English language as if it were my salvation. Everything I had in English lay on the chair near my bed.

I did not even have the mental energy to reply to the letters from the camps. Once I received a postcard with the brief text: "Ida, I haven't received letters from you for a long time. What happened? I can't do without your letters. Vladimir Markman." That sentence echoed in my head, but I simply couldn't manage to write. Each letter was a piece of my soul and with each letter I tore away another particle of myself. I had finally torn off so many there were no more! Totally empty, I did not know what to write. I did not have the physical strength to describe my hunger strike or to relive it by putting it into words. I lay in bed daydreaming or reading, with the smallest tasks taking hours to accomplish.

The promised recovery was slow in coming. I knew that with patience I would eventually be up and around—but writing all those letters to the zone was, for the first time, too much for me.

My Dear Ones!

When you spend all your time in the apartment, muscular energy transforms into malice. That's probably why I've begun a series of open letters to everyone—to the left and right and center, to presidents and simple people. Only a visa or a recovered heart will stop me.

You have the greatest responsibility—to publish my fiery appeals, if not in the newspapers, then at least in leaflets so that I won't feel that all my fire and suffering is in vain. If by the end of this year the world won't shudder at the sound of my name, then I'm worth no more than a penny on market day. Of course, that is a joke, but in every joke there is a bit of truth, that is, if I am silent, then no one will hear. I decided not to be silent—for myself and for others. Perhaps it would be more interesting if instead of "laments" I would write a book, but the problem is that the more I write, the more angry I become. The more angry I become, the more the truth comes to the tip of my tongue and it's simply impossible to refrain from anti-Soviet remarks. I wanted to refrain from them but what else is there to speak about?

Lena wants to speak to me over the phone. I think that's impossible; the chekists won't allow such a gift. Maybe we should speak on Nixon's hot line? It's busy all the time, but unfortunately not because of me!

You write that in the list for emigration I am now somewhere near the top. Someone important recently inquired personally after Mark Nashpitz, who, two weeks later, was stuck with five years of exile. Therefore I am a pessimist. They say that a pessimist is a well-informed optimist and that's me. But I'll keep on fighting—"a drop hollows out the stone." That's what I'll do in my remaining time here.

At one time Senators Jackson and Kennedy fasted in defense of David Azbel and me. Please write them that you requested a meeting with Dobrynin and also give my cordial greetings to both of them. Remembering my own personal experience, I am against Lena's planned hunger strike because it will undermine her health. Again and again I beg you to remain as calm as possible despite the fact that the situation around me is dramatic. Remember, I shall do everything that I consider necessary at the specific moment.

Don't cry and we shall yet celebrate together.

I recently appealed to Queen Elizabeth of Great Britain for help. I must tell you in confidence that those who read my first "laments" really wept but I can no longer find the words to stir them. I am exhausted.

And now an appeal to Yakov. My dear boy! I hope that during these months when the entire family is working to help me, you will also participate in this important cause. Help Mama by doing all the domestic chores that you can.

> *Love and kisses, my dears,*
> *I wait for letters and news,*
> *Ida*

CHAPTER 12

INVARIABLY, AFTER I HAD JUST BEEN FIRED FROM ANOTHER job, a moment would come when I could no longer absorb someone else's pain nor maintain the pace I had set for myself. I would stop writing my letters to the zones, my complaints to the procurators and Soviet authorities, and I would send only brief letters to Lena (so there would not be a long interval between our communication), and I would pick up one of the books which tourists had brought in. In general I read books on Jewish topics—history, tradition, philosophy or life in Israel. My favorite book was Saul Bellow's *To Jerusalem and Back*. Stretching my legs out on the couch, I read for two or three days straight until I had finished the book. I also read everything that I could get ahold of by Elie Wiesel, Chaim Potok, I. B. Singer or Cecil Roth, and the book *O Jerusalem* by Collins and Lapierre I reread many times.

No one would disturb me; my telephone had been disconnected long ago and I no longer had any close friends. I insisted that my friends from my past life not drop in—it was too dangerous. I did not seek out any new friends and if I did not phone anyone, no one would know where I was or what was happening.

Such a situation had its advantages as well as disadvantages. On the one hand, if I did not want companionship, no one forced it on me. On the other hand, if something happened to me, no one would know about it.

Even though I preferred being on my own most of the time, at those times when I felt I lacked conversation or laughter I would attend one of the many seminars organized by refuseniks in Moscow in those years. Judith and Aleksander Lerner hosted scientific seminars which sometimes featured guests from abroad. Grigori Rozenshtein's seminar on the Phenomenon of Man covered topics in sociology, theology and other fields. The seminars provided an opportunity to talk with people who were experiencing similar problems.

In addition, the meetings on Saturday near the synagogue helped restore my mental equilibrium. Often, particularly in the cold months when our faces and hands were freezing from the hours spent on the sidewalk near the synagogue, the Lerners would invite some people to their house and over a cup of tea or bowl of soup we would get rid of the tension of the preceding days.

I don't know how some inquisitive people got hold of it, but Dina Beilin gave me the telephone number of Albert Ivanov, deputy director of the administrative department of the Central Committee of the CPSU, and said that he sometimes talked with people. His position was a very high one and the fact that he would talk with people was surprising. I don't remember the specific reason I phoned him the first time in 1973, but there was no response. I began to ring more and more frequently and finally one day he answered. I introduced myself and told him a little about my situation. He replied that he was familiar with my name and story. Our telephone discussions became frequent and continued until the early spring of 1978, when Ivanov went away somewhere for half a year.

At the very start of my one-sided dialogue with this high-placed Soviet official, I asked to meet him personally and to discuss a series of important problems, the most pressing of which to my mind was the release of prisoners.

"No," he declared emphatically, "there will be no personal meeting. It's enough that I am talking to you on the telephone."

"Listen, Albert Ivanovich, right now it's minus five degrees Fahrenheit outside and I'm standing in a telephone booth because long ago my phone was illegally and forcibly removed. I am trying to help not only my people but also you. Not because I love you so much, no more than you love me, but because it is in my interests that your assistants will release another innocent victim."

"Citizen Nudel, I don't have time; be specific," he said, interrupting my pathos-filled speech.

I began then to tell him the events and facts that caused me to turn to him. Ivanov was not our friend but when I managed to convince him that the situation was becoming senselessly cruel and making waves abroad, he promised to help. There was one issue, however, on which he would not budge and that was the case of the Leningrad hijacking group. Whenever I would try to steer the conversation to them, Albert Ivanov would interrupt me curtly, "These people committed a crime and must suffer the punishment. There will be no pardon for them."

Why did Albert Ivanov himself endure my sharp criticism? In the beginning of our acquaintance he would throw down the receiver when I went "too far" as he said. Over the years he became accustomed to my explosive manner, the way I expressed my thoughts and feelings. Numerous times he was able to comprehend that I was not lying and he acknowledged this frankly.

I told him about the KGB's tricks of which he most likely was unaware and about the reaction of western public opinion to our efforts. I sensed that this information interested him.

"Do you listen to western broadcasts?" I once asked him.

"What are you talking about, Ida Yakovlevna, why should I listen to slander?" he replied.

"Too bad, you could find out a lot of useful information; in any case write down the wavelengths and the times of broadcasts," and I dictated the broadcasting schedule of the Voice of America and the BBC.

I don't want to give the impression that at the drop of a hat Albert Ivanov solved our problems and handed out visas right and left because that was not the case. Many times I would return from a conversation feeling completely drained. I would lie motionless on the couch for hours, worn out by the recent debate. I paid a high price for every victory, no matter how small. Although I was stubborn and persistent, my demands were moderate and reasonable—and I would present the benefits to the Soviet Union as a basic reason for accommodating our requests.

"What do you gain from it," I would ask him, "if this man dies? The whole world speaks about your senseless cruelty. You claim to belong to the family of civilized nations but you act like primitive barbarians. What do you gain from that? Where is your reason, your common sense?"

He would hang up and I would continue dialing his number until his patience wore thin and he lifted the receiver.

"You promised not to hang up, Albert Ivanovich, you are not keeping your word," I reproached him.

He would lie and twist things around and the conversation would continue until he promised to interfere in the case. Most often he kept his promise and if he didn't solve a problem, at least he became familiar with it and I could use it as an argument in my next verbal battle with him. It was difficult for me to argue with him, particularly since I had very little knowledge about the developments in the West which determined East-West relations even though I eagerly seized upon any information from foreign broadcasts.

My barrage of telegrams, protests and complaints exposed the hypocrisy of the legal and penal system and forced officials to respond to them. I thus succeeded in helping almost every prisoner whose problems came to my attention. Although I could not obtain their release or save them from conflict with other prisoners and the administration, I learned how to get them assigned to a hospital, receive a better diet, regain the right to correspond with family and friends and sometimes I even managed to get someone out of the punishment cell, protect another one from rape or surround a third with a wall of immunity. Often the administration preferred not to enter into a dialogue with me and I managed to get those who could not adapt to the criminal milieu out of the zone alive and in relatively decent health. I did not, however, understand why the chekists, who followed my every move, allowed me to continue doing what I did.

Whenever the time came for the release of a prisoner whom I had helped, I would look forward to meeting him with great excitement. Life had taught me, however, that such a meeting might not take place. Some of them were afraid of jeopardizing their future situation, which was so uncertain anyway after release. Some supposed that a meeting with me could lessen their chances for an exit visa. Indeed, there can be no end to the real and imaginary fears that might enter a frightened person's mind.

Simyen Marinov, whose family had left the Soviet Union, was scheduled to be released in March 1974. The procurator's office assured me that indeed he would be released on time. Boris Shilkrot, who had become friendly with Marinov in the labor camp, traveled especially from Leningrad to Moscow to meet with Marinov upon his release. A person who has been isolated for years in a camp loses contact with the everyday realities of life on the outside. After his release he is both dazzled by the wealth of sensations—the variety of colors and smells, the presence of women and children—and overwhelmed by the need to readapt to normal. To prevent the prisoner from drowning in this new world, I regularly tried to have him met outside the camp gates by a sympathetic person. This time it could not be arranged nor could I ask Boris to go since he had been released from this zone just a few months earlier.

In a letter to Marinov, I asked him to inform me as soon as he was released. I advised him to send a telegram from the post office at the railroad station.

On the eve of Marinov's release, Boris arrived in Moscow from Leningrad. We received Simyen's telegram in time and Boris went to the train station. An hour passed, then three and four but there was still no Boris or Simyen.

Boris arrived in the evening and told me that when he had come out of the subway a policeman had detained him. The police kept him in the station for five hours.

"That's it," I said. "They don't want us to meet."

A few days later I received a letter from Marinov with a few crookedly scribbled lines of rapture and gratitude.

A few weeks later when I picked up my mail I noticed a long telegram in the pile of letters. I saw the signature, "Simyen." Marinov had received an exit visa, would be in Moscow on such-and-such a date to arrange his papers at the Dutch embassy and he planned to visit me in the morning. I relayed the telegram to Boris in Leningrad, who hastened to see the man with whom he had spent the most difficult and bitter period of his life.

"If I understand the chekists correctly," I said to Boris, "he won't show up at my apartment."

"Let's steal him away from them," he suggested.

"What?"

"Listen, I figured out how to do it!"

The next morning we went down to the courtyard to phone

the Dutch embassy. Very casually, I asked whether a man on crutches named Marinov happened to be there.

"Yes," the secretary replied, "he's waiting for the consul."

"Will he be there much longer?" I asked.

"Not more than forty-five minutes," was the answer.

Boris and I almost ran, taking a shortcut through the columned passageway under a building on our route. Probably I had gone this way a thousand times. Just as we entered the passageway, a large wooden board flew down behind, barely missing us. I quickly glanced back and saw that it was covered with nails. Boris went back to lift it, looking around carefully.

It was not instinct that had saved us but mere chance. I glanced up but saw no one. I went around the building and looked at the windows and balconies. Where could it have been thrown from? According to my calculations it came from the balcony of the apartment on the third floor above the passageway. I suddenly recalled another incident which had occurred several months earlier at the very same spot. At that time an enormous clump of snow had fallen, almost hitting me. Then I had turned in the direction of the noise and caught sight of an officer who had also reacted to the sound. I saw his eyes; they were directed upward, estimating the place from which it could have fallen. Then he looked at me very carefully, turned and left. The officer's eyes seemed to tell the truth. Halting my rapid pace for a moment, I realized that a hunt was in progress and that I was the prey.

Quickly returning to the present, I urged Boris, "We'll still manage to catch him." A taxi took us directly to the gates of the embassy.

"There he is," said Boris, leaping from the taxi to intercept Marinov, who was just leaving the embassy. He pushed Simyen into the taxi, and we drove off before he had time to react. When Boris turned his smiling face toward him from the front seat, Marinov understood and his face lit up.

At my home Marinov sat on the edge of the couch, constantly turning his head, first toward Boris and then toward me. But in front of my eyes I kept seeing the shadow of the board with the enormous nails flying toward me.

I was tired and wanted peace and quiet, but Marinov kept on talking. For two and a half years he had been my banner and my sorrow. Now a free man was sitting in my apartment. Free. He and his children, his grandchildren and his grandchildren's grandchildren. Either seriously or joking, he said that he wanted to have another son.

"Why not," I said, "that's what we fought for, you and I, so that you would be happy." He mumbled something, and I could see from his pose that he alone was the victor. Well, I said to myself, I congratulate you, Ida. It was worth fighting with those beasts to save this handsome man. You did not traverse this difficult path with him in order to get words of gratitude. Only now, sitting across from him did I understand why the KGB had tried so furiously to prevent my meeting with him. It was my triumph over them. Sitting in front of me was a man I had helped transform from a victim into a hero, having given meaning to his suffering. He was, without a doubt, a conqueror.

They left together, Boris back to Leningrad, Marinov to Israel. I remained alone in the quiet apartment, with only one thought: Why didn't the KGB let me go?

September 1974

My Dears,

    Aron, the artist I told you about, just ran here to tell me he has received an exit visa and I decided to write you at once although, realistically, he will not arrive before October. He is arriving absolutely alone. He constantly asked me what will happen to him, and I really don't know. When I ask this very question about myself, I know that the same thing will happen to me as happens to the rest. But with him it is different. His soul-rending paintings constitute his world.

    When I asked whether he would consider living in a kibbutz as a first alternative, he almost fell off the chair in fear that someone would limit his freedom and force him to do something other than paint.

    When I "evacuate" him, it will be my last attempt to export an artist. I have no intention of enduring such a temperamental person again.

    To tell the truth, I am tired of myself, too. Now I must study languages.

Love,

Ida

P.S. Please don't be angry at me for constantly troubling you with such problems.

CHAPTER 13

WHEN ARON RECEIVED AN EXIT VISA, IT SEEMED THAT THE most difficult work had just begun. All his enormous paintings had to be brought to the Tretyakovsky Gallery for an inspection. We arrived early at the gallery, and he brought in some of the canvases and placed them facing the wall.

The chairman arrived and asked, "Whose paintings are these? Turn them around."

Running from one canvas to the other, the chairman of the art commission said rapidly, "Show me what's here!" While scurrying between the paintings he would stop first by one and then another. The enormous canvases displayed bones and skeletons performing a dance of death of the living and the victory of evil. Seeing his reaction, Aron perked up.

"Where were you hiding for so many years? This is genuine art," he said. He went off to phone the ministry of culture, returned and again began to look at the paintings.

"Genuine painting, genuine," and again darted out to make another call.

He came back looking very serious and said, "I am very sorry, I cannot give permission to export them. But don't put them away; I want to look again."

Aron, however, no longer heard anything. He quickly took away the canvases. We finally decided to appeal to Ekaterina Furtseva, the minister of culture. We were received by some director who asked us what we wanted.

"But the commission has already refused you," he stated.

"These are my personal paintings, I myself painted them," said Aron.

"That doesn't matter; they belong to the people," he replied.

"They are my paintings; first they belong to me," said Aron, beginning to boil over.

"Don't leave and you will have them."

"No, I want to leave together with the paintings."

"The paintings must remain but you received a visa and can leave."

"I would rather burn them."

"Leave me everything, I'll hand it over to the department and you'll receive an answer," the director pronounced.

The following evening I heard over the radio that the authorities had disrupted another unofficial exhibition of Moscow artists with bulldozers. I called Aron, who proposed that we see what was happening there.

The next morning, we met several people who had witnessed the previous day's rampage. The artists decided to organize the exhibition anew. I began to urge Aron to take part in the new exhibition.

"My friends agreed to help you and we decided how to organize it," I told him.

I was very nervous because, as usual, everything seemed to be happening at once. At the end of August Shimon Grilius was supposed to be released from a labor camp and I was not the least bit ready to receive him. Grilius had been convicted for participating in a Jewish nationalist group at the Ryazan Polytechnical Institute. While in a labor camp, he had developed serious problems with his arm. Once I had intervened on his behalf and was eager to know what had happened afterward.

Shimon arrived late in the evening, looking out of place in his black prisoner's jacket with his name sewn on the front. He told me that the police had run after him, thinking he had escaped. We started talking and I asked him to tell me the whole story about his arm.

"That was a curious story," he said. Once he had been summoned to the doctor, but he was very wary because any contact with the administration usually boded ill. The doctor's extraordinary politeness only made him warier. And then he unexpectedly made Shimon promise that rather than complain he would turn to him at once with any possible problem. Shimon had no idea what was going on, but he did get medical help and was released from heavy work.

"You didn't know that I wrote a complaint?" I asked.

"Did you really? Thanks! My arm felt so bad, I was in total agony and they had me assigned to very heavy work. I could have wound up with a crippled arm."

By the time we had spoken of his plans and feelings, about those who remained imprisoned and about matters in general, it was already late into the night. I suggested that he take a shower and I began to prepare his bedding.

Suddenly the doorbell rang and, figuring that it was the police, I became very angry, muttering, "They don't give a moment's rest; as soon as a man is released, they're already at the door."

The bell rang again and I decided that there was no way I would open it. "Who's there?"

A male voice with a typical Ashkenazic accent asked, "Does Ida Nudel live here?"

I recognized the voice of Yosif Davydovich Zalmanson, the father of Silva, Vulf and Izrail all of whom had been imprisoned for their role in the Leningrad hijacking attempt. Entering the apartment, he told me that in the morning the Riga OVIR had phoned him to request that on the following morning, August 23, 1974, at ten o'clock, he be near the Moscow OVIR office.

"I'm sure," he said, "that it has to do with Silva! They're going to release Silva! I'm sure they'll release her." Then he grabbed me, lifted me up and kissed me. "Ida, Ida, you did so much for them! I believe it, they're going to release Silva!" He took a few quick steps in one direction, then turned quickly and walked back, clearly feeling cramped in the little room. His usually reserved face was now open and very lively, reflecting a storm of emotions. "Now they have to release the boys!"

I knocked on the bathroom door for Shimon. "Quick, come out; Yosif Davydovich is here; it seems as if they're releasing Silva!" He dashed out, still wiping his damp scalp. We talked almost the whole night. Shimon had been imprisoned with Yosif Zalmanson's oldest son and the father greedily absorbed every word about him.

We dozed a little in the morning. Shimon and I were impatient to go to OVIR but Yosif said firmly, "They told me to be there around ten o'clock and we will be there exactly at that time," which is what we did.

When Silva appeared he heaved a huge sigh, "There she is!" She was walking slowly but then stepped up her pace and suddenly ran toward her father. Yosif Davydovich grabbed her in an embrace and lifted her off the ground and she, like a little girl, wound her hands around his neck and buried her face in his chest. Yosif Davydovich wiped away just one tear. Silva did not cry at all. After her father had very carefully deposited her on the ground, she disengaged from his embrace, squatted on her haunches clutching her knees and began to laugh loudly and hysterically. I decided that she had gone crazy; I couldn't understand either the pose or the strange laughter.

"Is she all right?" I asked Yosif Davydovich.

"Yes, of course she's all right," he answered, with an enormous happy smile still lighting up his face.

When she calmed down somewhat and stopped laughing we got acquainted. "I thought you were a large woman and look what you're like!" she said, astonished.

In a little while they summoned her back into the OVIR office. She came out of the building quickly and told us, laughing radiantly, that they had suggested that she go immediately to the Dutch embassy where the consul had a visa and ticket ready for her; everything was paid for. That evening she was supposed to leave the Soviet Union.

"What is this—leaving the Soviet Union without seeing your husband and your brothers?" I said. "Silva, you mustn't do that. Demand a meeting with all of them. You haven't seen them for four years and you're leaving just like that? Demand a meeting."

Poor Silva went back alone into the OVIR building. We did not see with whom she talked but she came out sadly and said, "They wouldn't permit it."

"Did they tell you whether you're a free person or not?" I asked.

"Yes, they said I'm free!"

"Silva, if you insist now, they'll give in. They either sold you or exchanged you. Today *you*, not they, can dictate. Let them bring all three to Moscow. Silva, demand a meeting!" To make my words more convincing, I shook her by the cuff of her black prison jacket.

"Silva, when will you again have a chance to see your husband Eduard?"

"Where are my brothers?" she asked. "What should I do, Papa?"

"Demand a meeting with Eduard!" her father said.

She reentered the OVIR building, firmly resolved and returned to us radiantly in a few minutes. She had been told to come again the next day at the same time; there would be a meeting there at five o'clock.

We decided to go to the store and buy her some pretty clothing. It was August and Silva was wearing a striped prison dress peeping out from under her black padded jacket, black woolen pants, ragged winter half boots and an odd-colored scarf on her head. Many eyes followed her; she was a walking symbol of the Gulag out on the streets of Moscow.

We didn't buy a dress because we couldn't find the right size. I remembered a pretty dress which I had been saving for my arrival in Israel; it would fit Silva, as she was very thin. We went home to try it on and to rest a little.

Gradually the news about Silva's release spread through Moscow and my apartment filled up with people coming and going and talking constantly. We didn't notice that night had arrived and Silva was falling off her feet. Realizing her condition, I shooed everyone out of the flat and finally put her to bed.

In the middle of the night there was a ring at the door. I was sure that it wasn't the police. Two KGB cars had been standing under my apartment window; they had been following us ever since Silva appeared near OVIR. Without checking first, I opened the door and saw a friend of the Sakharovs.

"Elena Bonner and Andrei Sakharov ask Silva to call now," said the man.

"She's sleeping; it's a shame to wake her. This past day has been crazy and tomorrow will be the same. I can't wake her."

"Then you call yourself," he suggested.

I went downstairs to a pay phone and dialed the Sakharovs' number. Elena Bonner answered the phone nervously, "How is it that Silva is released and we don't know about it? Correspondents are tying up the phone and we don't know what to say. How did this happen?"

She was completely right, I did not know what to say.

"There is no justification; we are all insanely tired. You're right; Silva will call you early in the morning," I said.

"Call Silva, Ida, I beg you."

"She's sleeping and I can't wake her," I replied. "For her sleep is the most important thing now."

"Andrei," she called, "come talk to her, she refuses to wake Silva."

In a very calm voice Sakharov explained that we had acted incorrectly. "It's a shame that it happened this way," he said. "We forgive you but if anyone, the Sakharovs should have been the first to know."

The next day was again full of hustle and bustle—people and more people, preparing for the five o'clock meeting and drawing up plans for the future. Amid all the excitement I had prepared bouillon which was impossible to drink because I had completely forgotten to salt it. I was very upset when Silva's friends virtually kidnapped her from me. I had wanted to feed her and protect her from the sympathetic and curious crowd but they took her away from my house. In a few weeks Silva left for Israel.

In the immediate quiet I was able to return to the problem of exporting Aron and his paintings. The exhibition of dissident artists would decide the fate of his paintings but we needed some foreigners as witnesses to the fact that the artists and his paintings existed. Naum Meiman, a long-term refusenik and activist, helped arrange a meeting with two foreign embassy workers. Generally Aron did not sell his paintings because he could not bear to part with them. When he was distraught he could lose his passport, his jacket or his head, but never his package of drawings or paintings.

The next day my friends, Aron and I marched in a long file, dragging paintings by hand from the apartment near Izmailovsky Park where they had been stored for the night. When we reached the spot designated for the exhibition Aron took charge. I obediently followed his orders and continually kept him in my field of vision. At the announced time a rather large number of people gathered—both artists and spectators. Aron displayed three paintings: the largest crowd of spectators gathered around them and forced Aron to show everything that he had brought with him, and demanded explanations of his themes. Foreign correspondents approached and interviewed him. I stood near him and helped with the first interview but then he became bolder and didn't need to call me. Aron was in heaven with his success.

A constant problem that I encountered in my activity was the difficulty of obtaining reliable information from the prison zones. One night when I was not expecting anyone my doorbell rang. Something told me it was not the police—their ring was always insistent, even imperious and long, whereas this ring was delicate, cautious. I carefully looked to see a man standing outside the door.

A "criminal," flashed through my mind. Maybe he'd been sent? After all I was alone. But what if I was being sent news from the zone? If he was from there, he had no place to go at such a late hour. Any policeman would lock him up temporarily and investigate.

He rang again and slowly retreated down the hall, hands behind, measured steps, like a robot.

I opened the door.

"Are you Ida Nudel?"

"Yes."

"I bring you a greeting from the men in Zone 35."

"Come in."

He entered and surveyed everything cautiously. "Do you live alone."

"Yes."   .

"Good."

I also scrutinized him over carefully. His dull grayish face matched his clothing, with its disgusting, musty, prison odor. His face was tense and immobile like a mask from the shock of new impressions and circumstances.

"Excuse me," he said, "I have to go to the bathroom right away."

He soon returned and extended an open palm in which lay several little clumps. "Take them, they asked me to give them to you. Excuse me, there were four of them, but I lost one on the train. I couldn't hold them all in any longer, I was traveling for two days. You have to tear open the covering, the text is inside."

Those little pieces had a nightmarish smell that made me nauseous. I couldn't avoid taking them from the outstretched arm—these revolting, stinking valuable lumps were messages from a political camp.

"Good, thank you, I'll take care of it. In the meantime, take a shower and I'll get a bed ready for you."

"Thank you very much," he replied.

I quickly washed my hands, prepared some food, arranged the bed and decided to start reading. As soon as I unfolded the paper in which the lumps were wrapped, however, I was again engulfed by nausea. With difficulty I stifled the vomit which was already rising in my throat. I tried to control myself, but as soon as I touched the stinking lump, the queasiness returned.

He came out of the bathroom.

"Eat everything on the table; I'll try to read. I must warn you that my apartment is bugged."

"You don't say! You, too, live like you're in the zone. We didn't know that. We know so little about people who help us. I was waiting for you on the street for several hours while the grandmothers were taking their grandchildren for a walk. If you had passed by, I would have recognized you; I looked at your picture for a long time. But you're not at all like I had imagined. From the picture I thought you were a big woman, but the face is the same."

"You eat while I read," I said.

Returning to my desk I took the stinking messages in my hands. The sheets of very fine paper were covered with minute handwriting. I could not make it out without a magnifying glass. How did someone write it? I had to copy everything over by hand and destroy the original. I spent the whole night transcribing the fine, minuscule handwriting. But the last sentence of the third package struck me:

"Don't trust this man too much. He'll come to you once. Give him money. Goodbye."

October 1974

My Dears,

Oh, what a day it is! I received three of your letters right away.
Hooray! Hooray! We are rejoicing and laughing. Aron was given
his paintings. Now I can catch my breath after the excitement of the past
weeks.

Now it's time for me, too, to receive a visa although Lena warns
that I will receive it with the last prisoner. That probably means in
1985 if there won't be any new prisoners.

I am getting older and losing my professional qualifications. I am
not studying either English or Hebrew. What shall I do in Israel? The
years fly by and my health is deteriorating. Am I right?

> *I look forward to your letters.*
> *Love,*
> *Ida*

P.S. I reread one of Lena's letters and decided to add a few lines. I tell
a lot about myself in my letters to you. It's very annoying to give the
chekists so much material but there is no choice; either you will learn
about my life from me or you will have to sift rumors, and I don't like
the latter option. Please don't be angry at the tone of my letters, don't
carp at my words or punctuation, or at me. We mustn't torture each
other with this. When I arrive, I'll explain everything that you don't
understand.

> *In the meantime, all my love,*
> *Ida*

September 1975

My Dear Ones!

You will be happy to know that I am more and more occupied with my own matters. Yesterday I checked out two books in English from the library—Dickens's Oliver Twist *and Kipling's* The Brave Captain. *My problem is that I don't remember the meaning of new words although I spend a lot of time grinding away at it. Moreover, I don't understand conversational language, I only catch individual words. With patience it all will come, but at present I suffer from the fact that I cannot express myself at meetings with foreign friends. It's a terrible sensation to feel inarticulate. I don't like it the way I sit quietly in the corner and smile weakly like a dimwit. If I can just find enough time to cram, I'll start speaking.*

It seems like the two superpowers are flirting with each other; instead of elephants and diamonds they'll offer some person as a gift, but not me. I don't have a chance and I know it very well.

I do, however, have some good news to tell you. I am now the happy owner of American jeans and a jacket. A tourist gave me the jeans near the synagogue; it's a funny story how I acquired the jacket. We met a group of English tourists at Vladimir Slepak's apartment and I gave one of them a list of things which were needed to send to the camps. He then asked, "What about yourself? If you need anything, I'd be happy to send it."

"Please . . . I need a jacket," I said.

"What size?"

I told him that I didn't know. He then hugged me around the shoulders and said, "Now I know." A few weeks later another group of tourists arrived from England and delivered his gift to me. It was a perfect fit. Now I'm fully equipped with a foreign outfit.

On Saturday evening we celebrated Simchas Torah by the synagogue. There were not that many people—several thousand—but I was struck by something else: the average age was fifteen to twenty!

I would like to get a letter from Yakov. He doesn't have to be embarrassed that his written Russian is poor. I can read simple sentences in Hebrew, too. Has he really forgotten me completely?

My love to you, my saviors, and good luck and good health.

CHAPTER 14

"IDA, DID YOU READ TODAY'S ISSUE OF *IZVESTIA*?" ASKED MY neighbor, an older man who had served time under Stalin and, unlike the other neighbors, was willing to talk to me.

"No, I haven't read that paper for years."

"Come," he waved me into the hall and said quietly, "it has to do with you." He handed me the paper, "An Open Letter from Sanya Lipavsky," almost a full page in the issue of March 4, 1977.

Without a private phone at such a moment I felt totally isolated but I did not have the strength to go outside to the pay phone. I needed to sit all by myself and think it all over. I read the letter again. Lipavsky's penitent "confession" of how he and other Jewish activists were recruited by the CIA to spy on the Soviet Union was written like a novel, full of secret hiding spots, codes and out-of-town meetings. Lipavsky wrote that the Jewish refuseniks had betrayed their motherland and served the interests of worldwide Zionism. The Soviet state had given them everything—a homeland, education, an apartment, interesting work—but that wasn't enough. They sold their services and state secrets for American jeans and chewing gum.

That faceless Sanya who had first appeared at Azbel's apartment during our hunger strike. After that he would ingratiate himself with a family, earning their trust. When that family received a visa and emigrated, he quickly would befriend another, passing like a baton from family to family, never remaining in one place more than a few months. We had no idea what a viper we had harbored in our midst.

I had to face the facts: this most definitely meant arrest. Having fingered us years ago, the KGB had been saving us for this hour. What made the KGB spring its trap? How would the West react? Had something happened between the superpowers? We activists had been tested many times—and the West together with us— but this case was the most punishing.

While I was reading the article once more, the doorbell rang —a long, insistent ring.

"Who's there?"

"Open up, the police!"

Already? I stood silently by the door. The bell rang again.

"Open up, Ida Yakovlevna."

I opened the door. Pushing me aside, a crowd of men swept into the room. One of them presented me with a search warrant and at the same time the others started pacing around my apartment but it was hard for seven men to maneuver in such a small space.

I couldn't understand the text of the warrant; the only words that reached my consciousness were "KGB" and "investigative division." One man placed a chair near my balcony and, pointing to it, stood nearby. Another man who appeared to be the senior member of the team ordered me to sit still and not move. I had spotted him in the past at our demonstrations, I had been struck by his resemblance to Lenin, and now, when he was closer, the similarity was even more striking—the same short stature, malicious face, cruel eyes, quick sharp movements and flapping hands.

They rummaged through my closet, tossing papers and books and all my other belongings onto the floor. The most intelligent thing that I could do was to sit calmly and not talk to them. All my notes disappeared. Everything flew into a bag—letters to me from the zone and from abroad, books, journals, maps, postcards, pretty book covers with scenes of Israel, napkins—everything. They also took my typewriter. One of them said, "It's a good machine; we'll replace it."

One of them had found a wrapped package and stared at me as if he had found a bomb. Idiot, I thought to myself, unwrap it and you'll see my laundry. As if following my advice, he unwrapped it and didn't look at me again.

The one without a neck was checking a record but somehow he couldn't put the needle on the record properly. His hand trembled, the needle slipped and scratched the record.

"Are you also going to rip open the feather bed?" I asked, unable to contain myself any longer. I got up and wanted to put the needle on the record myself but my hand also trembled and the needle scratched the record again. Why was I helping them?

"Go ahead and break everything!" I said hollowly. He left the records. One put some books in his jacket pocket.

Suddenly one of them exclaimed, "Here it is, I found the fifth copy," and with a broad, happy smile he showed his valuable find to his boss. I also looked; I couldn't remember to whom this thin brochure belonged. Then I remembered that a long time ago Nina Bukovsky had given me this article by Esenin-Volpin on how to behave during an interrogation. Unfortunately, I had forgotten all about it.

"Sign here," said the one without a neck.

"No, sign yourself," I retorted.

I had only one thought in my head—would they tell me to collect my things or not. Not now, I prayed. You can arrest me tomorrow morning but not now.

The boss said, "Stop your anti-Soviet activity or we'll put a stop to it ourselves." After their departure I turned off the light and sat silently amid the upheaval of the search. The newspaper with the terrible accusation lay on the table. Although my name was not mentioned specifically, it did not change matters; I shared my friends' lot.

In the bathroom I tried to calm my tormented mind with a stream of warm water. I lay down in bed but, as if I were watching a movie, scenes from the day floated in front of my eyes. Russians are flying into a rage. Détente is a failure. Americans are not going to give them privileges in trade and in credit.

Gains in so-called "human rights" are over. A month ago Yuri Orlov—the initiator and head of the Moscow Helsinki watchdog group and Alexander Ginsburg—director of Solzenitsiv's fund for prisoners of conscience were arrested, and accused of anti-Soviet activity.

Now is the Jews' turn to pay the price. We are again facing the traditional accusation—spying.

In the morning I phoned Aleksander Lerner, one of the senior activists who had been accused in the *Izvestia* article. "Come over," he said, "the others will join us and we'll talk." When I arrived, the street outside the Lerners' house was full of men who had tailed us and KGB cars.

Our mood was heavy as we composed our statement. My voice had the high, excited pitch of a schoolgirl when I declared that I would refuse to participate in any investigation and if testimony would be published under my name they should know it was obtained under the influence of drugs. It was clear, however, that the KGB's main blow was reserved for Anatoly Sharansky. He was both the youngest among us and the most active; he was the most familiar with foreign correspondents, had elderly parents and his wife was far away in Israel. Trying to protect him, Vladimir Slepak told him, "Tolya, live with us."

We left, each taking his own tail, but it was awful to look at Tolya's entourage. Whereas the rest of us had four people tailing us, he had a dark group of figures behind him, in front of him, alongside of him, shoulder to shoulder, surrounding him. When he wanted to greet someone, he had to thrust his hand out through the human wall. They accompanied him like a pack of dogs waiting for the signal to attack.

Then on March 15 they circled him, grabbed him, pushed him into a car and took him away.

After Tolya's arrest there was an almost physically tangible quiet. I felt it personally—my guards were taken away. Jews hid in their homes and almost no one would show up at the synagogue. The brave ones, after standing for a few minutes, left silently. The charge frightened everyone and the stream of friends from various countries also seemed to have evaporated. It seemed like interrogations were being conducted all over the country. People were summoned from Moscow, Leningrad, Kiev and even from the Far East, but the first ones were those on the periphery of Tolya's life and some did not even know him at all.

Time is the greatest healer and gradually the fear receded. Friends began to visit us and to go to the synagogue on the Sabbath.

"No," I replied to a tourist's question, "we did not violate any laws or engage in espionage." He looked me carefully in the eye.

"Are you telling the truth?"

What a paradox! He believed Soviet propaganda more than he believed us.

For a few months near the end of 1977 there was no information about the fate of the political prisoners in the zone of so-called particularly dangerous criminals. Elena Bonner and Andrei Sakharov decided to try to obtain a meeting with Eduard Kuznetsov, who was serving a fifteen-year sentence in a strict regime camp in Mordovia for his part in the Leningrad hijacking attempt. Elena Bonner formally had the right to such a meeting because she was recorded as his relative in the official court transcript. The Sakharovs spend almost a week in the small hotel near the camp for visiting relatives but the KGB flatly denied them a meeting. In response Kuznetsov declared a hunger strike. Stuck in Mordovia, the Sakharovs were unable to make a breakthrough. Daily they phoned Elena's mother, Ruth Grigorievna, who passed on information to correspondents and others but time was passing without any results.

I decided to appeal to Albert Ivanov, the high official in the Central Committee of the CPSU with whom I had carried on many long and painful telephone debates over the years. We had talked so often on the phone that we had learned to distinguish each other's mood from our opening words.

"Something happened again; I hear metal in your voice," he said after my greeting.

"Yes, something did happen. I should like to request a personal meeting to discuss matters," I said.

"That's impossible," he declared.

"Are you afraid of me?" I asked slowly.

"It's the rules. They won't let you in to see me," he said.

"I have spent many hours in the waiting room of the Central Committee and I saw that some people have been invited into an inner office for a personal meeting."

"Only in very special cases," he replied. "They won't let you through."

"Do you think that I'll attack you?"

"No, I don't think so. Once when you were demonstrating in the waiting room of the Central Committee, they pointed you out to me."

"Then what are you worried about?"

"I've already told you and I repeat: there will be no personal meeting. What do you want from me, Ida Yakovlevna, I have an appointment in a few minutes."

I had to get to the point quickly. "Put yourself, Albert Ivanovich—for a moment—in the place of someone who is facing the death sentence and writes a book about himself. Can you do it?"

"I don't want to," he responded.

"Do you agree that one must be a very unusual individual to act that way on the verge of death."

"Yes, one must be strong," he agreed.

"Well, Eduard Kuznetsov, who recently declared a hunger strike in the zone for particularly dangerous prisoners, wrote a book while he was in the cell for condemned prisoners. Please phone the zone and order them to permit a meeting with Elena Bonner. She is mentioned in his personal file because she is his aunt and by law she has the right to see him."

"You ask the impossible from me."

"But you are the highest authority for the interior ministry," I persisted. I kept advancing one argument after the other in an attempt to convince Ivanov that his personal interference was indispensable. "Believe me, Albert Ivanovich, Kuznetsov's courage evoked great sympathy toward him in the world. His many friends are carefully following the hunger strike. What Soviet state interests will suffer if Kuznetsov is given a meeting? Doesn't the situation seem idiotically absurd?" I asked.

"The administration does not believe these visitors can have a positive influence on the convict," said Ivanov, meaning the Sakharovs.

"May *I* obtain a meeting?"

"No, you're not a relative!"

"Can his elderly mother receive a meeting?"

"Call me in three days."

Having finished speaking to Ivanov, I called Ruth Grigorievna and recounted my conversation with Ivanov. In the middle our phone connection was broken. I dialed the number again and again but the telephone did not work. I quickly called the telephone repair service and was given the district station.

After I had registered my complaint, the person on duty replied, "Why are you lying?" she asked me. "You spoke from that phone booth for half an hour without interruption."

"How do you know?" I asked.

"I know your voice," she answered.

"What does that mean—that you are eavesdropping on my conversations, is that it?"

"No one is listening in; I do repairs so I am connected to the network. You phoned from that number five times today and it worked."

"You even know how many times I phoned; perhaps you know my name and address?" The telephone clicked off; she had said too much. It had never occurred to me that pay phones were also bugged!

Ruth Grigorievna repeated my aborted conversation to the Sakharovs and they decided to return to Moscow. Three days later I spent an entire morning by the phone booth, trying to reach Ivanov. He picked up the receiver only after dinner.

"What news do you have about Eduard Kuznetsov?" I asked.

"First you tell me."

"I can say that there is confirmation that he received my letter. You told me that he is in a hospital, but the notification shows only the stamp of the zone, which means that your aides lied again. By law he should be sent to the hospital. What can you tell me about the possibility of a meeting? His hunger strike has been going on for a month. We talk about his situation every few days, but nothing changes."

"There can't be a meeting during a hunger strike. First he has to stop."

"Let's be logical. He declared a hunger strike only because they denied him a meeting. If I send a telegram with a request to end the hunger strike, can you arrange for my telegram to be delivered to Kuznetsov?"

"I want to know the text of the telegram," he said.

"Tell me when to call, and I'll read you the text."

"Call at three o'clock tomorrow."

The following day I read a text that had been prepared in coordination with the Sakharovs:

Millions of people are anxiously following your hunger strike. Public and political figures from many countries have turned to the Soviet authorities on your behalf. Continuation of the hunger strike is becoming meaningless. We are sending a ten-pound package of food; its delivery is coordinated with the deputy director of the administrative department of the Central Committee.

*With love,
Andrei Sakharov, Elena
Bonner, Ida Nudel*

"I don't like the text," said Albert Ivanovich.

"Saying less won't convince him to stop his hunger strike." We continued to argue but I insisted on our text. "Aren't you tired of my calls and commotion about the hunger strike? Where's your common sense, what do you need this for?"

"You know, you have a terrible nature. All right; send the telegram, I promise that it will be delivered," he said.

In a few days I phoned again.

"Well, what do you know about Kuznetsov?" he asked cheerfully.

"That's why I'm calling you—because I don't know anything," I answered.

"He stopped his hunger strike. I have his statement," he crowed quietly.

"Wonderful! When did he stop? Could you read me his statement?"

Ivanov read me the short text: "I am ending my declared hunger strike. Political prisoner Eduard Kuznetsov."

To myself I thought how smoothly he pronounced the words "political prisoner," but aloud I said, "So Kuznetsov fasted for thirty-nine or forty days. Now will they allow him a meeting?"

"Only with relatives," he replied coldly. I immediately phoned the Sakharovs.

"What are you happy about?" asked Elena Bonner in a disappointed tone. "We did not get a meeting with him."

"I am happy because he stopped his hunger strike."

What stimulated Ivanov to help us? Certainly not secret sympathies for dissidents or Jews.

*   *   *

Andrei Dmitrievich Sakharov's involvement with human rights issues also encompassed the Jewish movement. He took to heart all human tragedies. In March 1978 a group of Arab terrorists hijacked a bus on the coastal road between Haifa and Tel Aviv, killing twenty-eight people, including women and children. In an act of heartfelt, spontaneous identification, he once participated in one of our demonstrations.

On the morning after hearing the news on a foreign broadcast, I went to see him and Elena Bonner. Although I normally do not wear jewelry, as a sign of my sorrow and solidarity I wore an enormous Star of David on a chain around my neck.

"Why did you get dressed up?" asked Elena when she opened the door.

I explained what had happened in Israel and said, "I think we need to demonstrate; I can organize everything but I need your help. Would you take part in the demonstration?"

"Andrei," she said, calling into the other room, "in Israel terrorists killed twenty-eight women and children. It's awful! Ida thinks it's necessary to demonstrate."

Andrei Dmitrievich emerged from the other room, greeted me and said, "You're right, we must demonstrate, but to whom should we appeal?"

"To the Central Committee; they incite war and train terrorists in the Soviet Union," I replied.

"That's correct, but we need a different place." He took out his Moscow address book and we began to discuss possible alternatives; I even rushed by taxi to look at one of the places he proposed to see whether it was suitable. Finally we decided on Elena Georgievna's suggestion, opposite the International House of the Friendship of Nations, the site of receptions, conferences and workshops, where there was a sufficiently wide sidewalk and not very heavy traffic; symbolically it was also the most appropriate.

We agreed on the time and I left to organize people and correspondents. Boris Chernobylsky, Yakov Rakhlenko and Mikhail Kremen, a group of young refuseniks, agreed to participate in the demonstration on the next day and to inform people living near them. We decided that fifteen to twenty people was the right size for the sidewalk space. Viktor Elistratov, a refusenik who spoke English well, was to inform the correspondents.

Five minutes before the agreed-upon time I approached the designated spot. Like large crows the KGB agents had settled on the fence in a small square facing the House of Friendship.

Who informed them, I wondered, as the participants in the demonstration gradually approached. Viktor Elistratov appeared on the opposite side of the sidewalk with a few reporters. We stood in a close but small group opposite the House of Friendship. Without posters the passersby did not understand the purpose of our silent protest. Andrei Dmitrievich saved the situation by slowly and clearly explaining our action in a few short sentences. Others joined in his expressive rhythmic protest, which swelled to a choir of thirty voices repeating the same concise phrases.

Because it was a Sunday, we did not think we would be dispersed. With the big chiefs relaxing in their "people's" dachas outside the city, neither the junior KGB officers nor the high-ranking on-duty police officer would dare make such a decision. Nevertheless, the police kept moving in.

"Viktor," I asked, "did you talk with the correspondents in person?"

"You know, I wasn't able to; I had to phone them and explain things openly."

"Now I understand; it's too bad. You informed on yourself!"

The KGB men sitting on the fence were yelling loudly, arousing the police and the crowd but it was obvious that neither they nor the police had an order to disperse us.

Looking from one demonstrator to another, I noticed that all were tired from the tension. Even Andrei Dmitrievich had stopped. Leva Furman, one of our refusenik circle, was trembling slightly. I couldn't let his overwrought state infect the others.

"Leva, take yourself in hand, right away," I demanded, "or you'll ruin it for all of us."

"I can't do anything," he replied.

"Go away immediately," I demanded.

"I won't," he replied sharply.

Grabbing him quickly by the cuffs of his jacket and with all my strength I nailed him to the metal fence on the square.

"Beat him up, Ida," egged on the KGB men, "hit him!"

I shook him once more and Leva calmed down.

"It's time to go," announced Andrei Dmitrievich, and he was seconded by everyone.

A fat policeman with a row of large stars on his shoulder boards came up to us.

"Citizens, disperse, I am asking you to leave now," he said loudly. We obeyed and the police accompanied us to the doors of the subway station.

On the day after the demonstration Andrei Dmitrievich said to me, "Ida, I hope that Israel won't retaliate."

A few days later the Israeli air force bombed a Palestinian refugee camp and Soviet newspapers reported victims, and he told me, "I am very sorry that I participated in the demonstration. Israel carried out a retaliatory act."

Interrogations continued throughout the country in connection with the arrest of Anatoly Sharansky. He himself was concealed behind a thousand locks in Lefortovo Prison and we had not heard a word from him. The legally permissible span of time for completing the investigation had long passed and we feared to imagine what the KGB was concocting behind the impenetrable walls of the prison.

In the summer of 1978, although it was over a year after Sharansky's arrest, no one had been arrested in connection with his case. Nevertheless, we could not be sure that it would not happen the next day. We therefore decided that we could no longer remain silent. We had to speak for Sharansky and ourselves and decided to appeal to all Soviet institutions which deal with the emigration process. The women, however, felt that because of the difficult and unclear situation, the men, who were more vulnerable to arrest, should not take part in the protests.

Given my apparently hopeless situation, it seemed that only the most dramatic actions would have an effect. Selecting a group of women for demonstrations, I weighed the risks each was taking and felt that I was the only one seriously facing the possibility of conviction. I frankly discussed the possible consequences with each one and chose a group of six women—Faina Kogan, an older woman whose son was already in Israel; Natalya Khasin, Galina Nizhnikov, Elena Chernobylsky and Natalya Katz, refuseniks with young children; and myself.

The spot we chose for our demonstration, a grassy hill near the main gates of the Kremlin wall, was the very same place where a group of Jews had intended to demonstrate in the summer of 1973 when they had been detained.

May 23, 1978, was the day of our revenge and our triumph. Unnoticed by the flock of tails, we climbed to the top of the hill by attaching ourselves to a group of Soviet tourists. As soon as we had distanced ourselves enough from the tourists so that they could not turn around and crush us, we raised our posters. In front of the astonished eyes of passersby, a small group of women, sharply delineated against the background of the red brick wall and the green hill, raised posters in Russian and Hebrew that said "Visas to Israel!" Our move was so unexpected that it took even the chekists some moments before they started to mobilize their forces.

We stood for what to us seemed an eternity; five minutes passed. Finally a car drove up and the chekists poured out, followed by two police cars. They surrounded us in a tight ring and began to drag us nonresisting from the hill. Our demonstration was a sign that we were determined and organized and there were no informers amongst us. I am sure that all six women will remember that day as one of the most glorious of their lives.

We refused to speak to the KGB investigators and repeated, "Visas to Israel!" Not having obtained any testimony, the KGB handed us over to the police investigators. It was obvious that no one knew what to do with us and in the evening they let us go home.

When I was released in 1977, she met me and was very happy that I was free. We drank a little wine and then she prepared tea. I was very surprised that she prepared tea the way prisoners do. She took a cup, put the tea leaves in it, poured in the boiling water, covered it on top with a saucer and waited for the tea to steep. I was so delighted and surprised that she knew all this because tea is prepared that way only in camp. Tea is one of the prisoner's greatest pleasures.

I asked, "Where do you know this from?"

She answered, "Oh! There have been so many 'criminals' here already that it's impossible to count them."

She then took me to the synagogue and introduced me to many people. I stayed with her for a while, sleeping in the kitchen. I always felt at home and could do what I wanted. Her apartment was very cozy —a couch, two arm chairs, table, a radio and a lot of books. Everything was always in its place.

She was a good cook; everything was so tasty, especially the cauliflower, perhaps just because Ida prepared it, because I never used to like it before.

She invited me to spend ten days at a tent camp organized by refuseniks on vacation. We gathered together a pile of things and Ida left with a knapsack in a cheerful mood. We took a motorboat down the river, with the spray splashing in our face. It was so pleasant to be traveling along the river, to be free after those years of imprisonment, to be among people who thought as I did.

When we arrived at this tent city the first thing I noticed was a little girl who ran up to Ida and began hugging her and saying, "I've been waiting for you so long; I was bored without you."

In the evening I felt sad and sat in my tent instead of joining them when they were singing near a campfire. Ida would sit there on the bank of the river and they would sing, talk and listen to the Voice of Israel. She was very sociable. There were a lot of children by the campfire and they all knew and loved her.

Ida is the only person I respect because she is unselfish. She lives for the sake of her goal and I always liked people like that.

During the day, when we went to the village for food, they would call out to her and say, "Girlie!" She looked so young then and really looked after herself—she was an elegant woman.

When I left for Israel, we were almost late for the plane and she got a taxi to take us to the airport. I asked, "How can I help you?"

She said, "You can't help me at all. Everything is being done, but in my case it's not helping at all. The only thing you can do to help is to write me." I must have sent her about four letters but then I received a monetary reimbursement because my registered letters did not reach her and our link was broken.

Mark Slogin

CHAPTER 15

ON JUNE 1, 1978, THE INTERNATIONAL DAY FOR THE PROTEC-
tion of children's right to a peaceful and happy life, a group of
Jewish women and children held demonstrations in five Moscow
districts in defense of their and their children's personal right to
be free and happy. Participating in a demonstration while facing a
hostile crowd and police force can be traumatic for a young psyche,
but years of living as a refusenik facing constant stress and uncertainty were certainly no healthier. In fact, the difficult situation
turned the children of refuseniks into little old people. A child's
mind does not want to accept an illogical situation and the little
one would ask his parents, "Why are they leaving and we aren't?
Perhaps you are behaving badly, Daddy?" It was very difficult to
answer such questions.

In planning the demonstration the women decided not to part
with their children and not to go out to the street where conflict
was inevitable, but instead to stay at home and demonstrate from
there. We figured that the police would not know how to react to
the unexpected situation.

According to our plan, five to six women would stay in each
apartment with their children behind closed doors. They would
put posters on their windows or balconies with our usual appeals
—"KGB, Give Us Visas to Israel" or "Let Us and Our Children
Go to Our Homeland." The demonstrations were scheduled to
take place in six locations in Moscow, one after the other, at in-
tervals of forty-five minutes in order to give foreign correspondents

an opportunity to arrive. I decided that with my reputation as a troublemaker, I would remain alone. The first one was set for noon at the apartment of Natalya Rozenshtein, a religious activist and refusenik; my turn was to come at six in the evening.

Obviously not everything worked out according to our plan. One woman changed her mind on the morning of the demonstration and several women and children moved to the Rozenshteins' apartment. Some had arrived the previous evening. They camped out in sleeping bags and on blankets spread across the floor.

I took care of my own preparations, assembling a roll of wallpaper, a small brush and ink. I decided to reinforce my placards with some skis which were standing on the balcony.

The evening before the demonstrations the police circled the building. There were police cars on four sides, attracting the attention of passersby, as did the police unit which began patrolling around the building in the morning. Long before the start of the demonstration the chekists installed television cameras in the building under construction to the side of my house; in addition they brought in a large number of people in plainclothes; I could see very young faces. The day dragged on endlessly: the police kept up their motorized and foot patrols, the curious gathered in groups, and I observed it all from my fourth-floor balcony. I tried to distract myself by reading a book but I could not concentrate.

I took a long time choosing the text to write on my piece of wallpaper and finally picked the most strongly worded one: "KGB—Give Me a Visa to Israel!" I barricaded myself in my apartment by moving all the furniture into the little hall. I did not know what else to do to make the time pass more quickly.

In the meantime, the chekists were making their own preparations. A bulldozer was placed directly under my balcony and its motor started racing from early morning. Four plainclothesmen appeared on the neighbor's balcony. Realizing that their job would be to tear down my poster, I decided to defend myself and prepared a bucket of water and a mug. To keep them from jumping onto my balcony, I gathered all the wooden pieces in the house, mainly boards from boxes, drove nails into them, and spread them on the floor of the balcony, with the nails protruding upward. I left myself a narrow path free of nails in which to maneuver and I was ready long before the time set for the demonstration.

After lunchtime, carloads of important people began arriving;

majors and colonels walked past the police up to the building itself.
I looked from the balcony at the growing crowd of passersby, police
and chekists, and at moments it seemed like it was all a dream.
Stand, I thought to myself, until tomorrow; I'll laugh at them and
at myself. But then these healthy thoughts were replaced by fears:
the KGB will decide I was simply scared off and then it will be
harder for me to act, they will begin to break me in the hope of
winning a repentant soul; each one will no doubt think he can
receive another star on his uniform, an extra vacation in a sanato-
rium with his entire family, a raise in pay and many other real and
imagined privileges. There is no more destructive force on earth
than shattered illusions. I would follow the plan after all; otherwise
what would I say to the other women—that I had decided to fool
the KGB and foil their expectations? Who would understand my
humor in the present state of tension we all were in?

At three minutes before six the chekists shouted on the neighboring balcony: "In three minutes they'll arrest you, Ida." At one
minute before six I held up my first poster, which was stretched
between the skis—"KGB—Give Me a Visa to Israel!" The chekists
on the neighboring balcony began lashing at my poster with flexible
metal rods. After one of these blows the poster was gone, flying
off into two pieces. I wrote the text again, but this time I didn't
have room to write any more than "A Visa to Israel." I attached it
to the skis, moved the bucket of water to the balcony door, ex-
hibited my poster and began desperately to douse them with water
from the mug. The KGB men choked in surprise. "Look at what
she's doing," they called down to their boss, "she's throwing water
on us."

I looked and saw that now there were three, not four of them.
Nevertheless, they got hold of their rods and ripped my poster
again. While I was preparing another one, their numbers decreased
to two. Excited and frenzied from my triumph, instead of making
a poster, I simply splashed water on them until no one was left on
the balcony.

Their life, however, was easier than mine; they had more
resources than I did—they had all the neighbors and apartments
at their disposal. They entered the apartment directly above me
on the fifth floor, tied strong cord to a long stick, and on the end
they attached a heavy wrench. Swinging the heavy burden, they
clearly were aiming at the glass window. Gathering speed, the

wrench moved closer and closer to the glass. Under my balcony the crowd held their breath in expectation of the blow.

I stood on the balcony and silently watched the scene—the blazing eyes of the majors and colonels standing below, the noise of the crowd gathered not far away—and listened to the now familiar cries—"Hitler, Hitler, didn't finish his job! Where is Hitler? There's no Hitler for the Jews!" The wrench kept swinging in a wider and wider arc, with each swing approaching closer until the sound of broken glass finally rang out and a triumphant cry burst from the throats of the crowd. It was the exact same howl as the crowd screaming at a stadium when their team would win a point. I thought to myself, You're dealing with evil, with sick children. What am I doing here? It's either a visa or prison.

While I was standing on the balcony, I suddenly heard someone nearby call, "Ida!" and I turned my head. From the window of the neighboring apartment on the same floor emerged a man's head, then shoulders, a hand, and a mug in the hand.

"Ida," he cried. "Go away, I'm going to douse you now!"

I silently looked the chekist in the eye and he splashed the mug of water straight in my face. I continued to stare at him and the smile forming on his lips froze. He spit, put the mug on the windowsill and disappeared into the apartment.

With the arrival of darkness the chekists departed in their cars, taking their cameras and KGB trainees. I remained alone in the barricaded apartment and lay down on the couch to calm my pounding heart. What had I achieved? They hadn't arrested me, but they could do so at any moment now. On the other hand, I was satisfied: I had won, I had resisted them in public. Moreover, I was not alone. Over a period of six hours, in other Moscow districts, groups of women and children one after the other had locked themselves in apartments and hung placards in the windows declaring: "Give Us Visas to Israel!" The chekists gasped at such impudence and were confused by the unprecedented happenings.

I went to sleep without taking off my clothing but no one came to arrest me during the night. I woke up early and went outside to the courtyard to discover there was no police guard. Instead, the air was full of the pleasant scents of spring and the song of birds. At such an early hour everyone was asleep and no one disturbed the peaceful natural scene. Perhaps yesterday's crazy day had not occurred? But when I returned to my apartment with the broken windows and furniture in disarray, I had no doubts that it had indeed been all too real.

The next day, I was still in shock over the previous day's events, but Zhenya Shvartsman, another member of our small circle of refuseniks, dropped by and suggested that I take part in a press conference that day. I agreed and accompanied her on the long subway ride from one end of Moscow to the other.

After telling the correspondents my part of the story, I left but I had barely gotten out of the subway station when three policemen surrounded me and ordered me to follow them. Taken aback, I started to obey, but soon regained my composure. "What's going on and where are we headed?" I asked, slowing down.

"You'll find out when you're supposed to," replied one who walked behind, pushing me in the back.

"Get your hands off, I won't go anywhere; why did you grab me in the middle of the square?" I demanded. The passersby began looking at us, some stopped to listen, and a crowd gathered.

"Why did you grab me, because I'm a Jew?"

One policeman twisted my arms behind my back and dragged me. I began screaming from the pain, the surprise and the humiliation. "Beasts," I yelled, "monsters, you torture people and trade us like potatoes!" They released my arms but positioned them in such a way that I could not move them. One of them clamped both his hands tightly around my upper arm and began to twist the skin in opposite directions. It felt like my skin was tearing apart into strips.

Having led me toward a waiting bus, the policeman pushed me aboard with a heavy blow on the back. I flew forward until I grabbed the arm of a seat. More and more people were pushed into the bus. Some of the unfamiliar ones quietly complained. "You look like a Jew, that's why they grabbed you," someone explained to a woman who was the most nervous of all.

The anxious woman looked around with a grim look and said, "All peoples are equal in our country."

"Then sit with us like an equal," Yakov Rakhlenko, who had also been detained, told her.

When the bus was full, they brought us to some place that looked like a clubhouse, where I was separated from the rest and ordered into a car. KGB men sat on both sides of me while a third jumped into the front seat next to the driver. The car started and I wondered: is this really an arrest?

The four KGB men in the black car brought me to my home, where a few others were waiting. I was ordered out of the car and at once KGB men appeared from all directions. In a tangle we entered the elevator, where it was so crowded that we stood pressed up against each other like sardines. In the same tangle we spilled out of the elevator and they let me go ahead. A piece of paper was hanging on my apartment door and a chekist and I reached for it simultaneously. On the paper the words "Zionist swine" accompanied a sketch of three pigs.

I stood indecisively in front of the door, not sure whether to open it or not. "Do you have the key?" asked one. I didn't answer. "If you have it, open up or we'll open it ourselves. There's going to be a search." My brain started racing—what papers do I have that I don't want to give to them? There were letters from my family in Israel, letters from the camps, my complaints and the replies of the camp administration—all had been received through the Soviet mail and read by my censor. What could be illegal about that? I opened the door and, shoving me aside, they ran in.

I was ordered to sit on a chair and not stir; a chekist stood next to me. The house was an indescribable mess. The furniture was overturned, broken glass lay around, and the wind blew through the apartment from the empty pane in the kitchen window. The chekists turned everything upside down and gathered up all my papers, letters, postcards from Israel, stamps, books in English— even those published in the Soviet Union—and Hebrew books. After they had taken my typewriter in the last search, someone had given me a used one; now they took that, too. Suddenly the window panes clinked and stones began flying in. Finding themselves in the line of fire, the chekists became frightened—pretending that it was not their colleagues doing the shouting, they shouted—"Look what Zionists do!" In my apartment the glass tinkled as stones flew in. One of them hastily went outside and the barrage stopped.

I was told that I had to sign a document promising not to leave town. Then they presented me with a charge of malicious hooliganism. According to the criminal code, a crime under this article can be punished by up to five years' imprisonment.

Could I really endure five years of imprisonment, I wondered?

I was forty-seven years old but the past seven years had been so stressful that they were the equivalent of twenty normal ones. I had to admit to myself that I had lost and would not get a visa.

I told them I would not sign: "You were the ones who acted like hooligans, amused yourselves to your heart's content, took pictures and trained your students from the KGB school. I didn't commit a crime and I won't sign." They called in the old Jew who was the chairman of the cooperative.

"Darling," he said, "perhaps you'll sign that you won't leave town."

"Don't meddle in my affairs," I answered sharply.

They soon left, leaving me alone in the ransacked, over-turned apartment. I had to sit down for a while to collect my thoughts. I wanted nothing more than to climb into a bath, wash away all the agitation and lie in a clean bed where I would not see or hear a thing. But I could not. I had to get up, open the door, go downstairs to a pay phone and tell my story. I sat, delaying that moment.

As soon as I left the house, the tails leaped out of two cars and followed me, stopping next to the phone booth and listening to the conversation.

In the morning as soon as I left the house the doors of the two cars opened, sturdy men got out and arranged themselves around me. In this absurd configuration we moved everywhere— on the street, to the subway, in the store. Previously, if there was only one tail following me, I sometimes managed to get away from him, especially in the subway. It's hard to get away from two, but I didn't even consider escaping from a brigade of them.

I spent the entire next day trying to restore order to the apartment after the chekists' pogrom. I, or rather we, since the chekists followed me everywhere, went through the courtyards where I found a large piece of cardboard. I got a second piece from my elderly neighbor, my secret sympathizer, with whom in the years before I applied to emigrate I had listened to broadcasts of the Voice of Israel. His hands shook when he opened the door to let me into his apartment and they trembled as he embraced me, pressing me to his chest. "Oh, if I were only at least ten years younger," he said, wiping away the tears. "Bandits, real bandits, they went on a rampage, like in the terrible years. What do they want from you, darling, what do they want?"

* * *

I traced a bright yellow Star of David on two pieces of plywood and filled the empty window opening with them. After a day of cares, sorrowful thoughts and painstaking analysis of events, I quietly sat alone in the apartment, licking my spiritual wounds.

Suddenly someone knocked on the door. At that point, I didn't care whether it was the police or friends and I opened it. A dark-haired, very tan young woman stood in front of me. She spoke in English, saying that she had just arrived from Israel. We sat in the kitchen, drank tea and conversed quietly. I told her a lot about myself and others and she understood. She took a chain off her neck, removed a small metal object from it, and then extended it to me on her open palm.

"Take it, I'm giving it to you. You need it more than I do now. It was given to me by a very wonderful but fatally ill woman who gave it to me not long before her death. She wore this tiny chai [meaning life in Hebrew] for thirty years. I have worn it for several years and think it helps me, but now you need it more. Take it, I give it to you with all my heart. It will protect you."

I felt uneasy about taking such a cherished object from her. I refused, but she insisted. I found a compromise, "I'll return it to you when I get to Israel. Do you agree?" I extended my open palm to her and the tiny metallic object, still warm from her palm, slipped into mine.

I received a notice that my trial for malicious hooliganism would take place on June 20. Undoubtedly I would receive a prison term. Although I had realized when I chose the group of women to participate in the demonstrations that I was the most likely to be arrested, deep down I had hoped that the KGB would give me a visa to Israel. Didn't they have enough trouble with Sharansky? I didn't know that relations with America—always a factor in their treatment of refuseniks—were bad at the time.

The women activists designated June 9 for the most difficult demonstration; it was to be the last in our planned series of four. We intended to go directly to KGB headquarters. At the same time, my trial date was approaching fast and I thought I ought to have concentrated on my own problem; yet I was the one who had organized and planned the whole campaign of demonstrations and I could not leave my friends as they faced the most difficult ordeal.

Before we women had begun the series of demonstrations, we had agreed to tell no one of our plans, except for our husbands, because of the danger that the KGB, warned in advance of a demonstration, would organize a "protesting" crowd. Soviet people are the most self-disciplined because we have been taught ever since childhood that initiative is punishable. When we went to a demonstration which had not been announced in advance, I had almost no doubt that there would be no clashes with the crowd if the demonstrators themselves remained restrained and were not drawn into an argument.

On June 7, two days before our last demonstration, Galya Kremen, a refusenik whose husband had been put in prison for fifteen days for his own home demonstration, sighed that she was so tired of demonstrations and the terrible tension that she had been unable to keep silent any longer. She had told Viktor Furman, who had told us he was a refusenik, about the planned demonstration.

"Galya," I groaned, "we agreed not to tell anyone!" And worst of all, she found just the person to tell—an informer for the KGB!

Galya said that she had never believed he worked for the KGB nor did her husband, but that morning she herself had been convinced that he was a scoundrel. "We left the house and were supposed to go to my husband in prison. Viktor said, 'You wait here, I have to make an urgent call.' I stood nearby and heard his conversation. He did not give his name but said, 'Number so-and-so is speaking; very urgent information.' And he briefly repeated everything that I had told him."

We decided not to cancel the last demonstration on June 9. When I arrived at the designated spot three minutes late, the place was already full of men and women. They surrounded us even before we unfolded our posters with the words in Russian and Hebrew: "Let Us Go to Israel." In two or three locations hysterical female voices began to shout the traditional appeals to Hitler. The crowd quickly joined in.

When the police did not interfere, I realized that they wanted to intimidate us by stirring up the crowd. One hysterically screaming woman latched on to Galina Nizhnikov, one of the refuseniks, and began to shake her by the collar. I caught sight of Galina's stunned eyes. We had agreed in advance of the first demonstration that we must not enter into conversations with the crowd and never yield to provocations. Galina, her mouth clamped shut, looked into the face of her attacker. At the same time, eleven-year-old Sasha Kremen, whose father had been arrested a week before, ran around in a circle, his father's portrait on his chest with the inscription, "Free my Daddy." Small and nimble, he eluded the chekists.

I could not understand the KGB's motives in not preventing this demonstration near the holy of holies—the main headquarters of the KGB. When the crowd had become sufficiently large and began yelling, "Let them go, don't let them disgrace us, let them go to their Israel," the KGB decided to make their move. As if they had been awaiting the order from around the corner, police cars immediately appeared and we were surrounded by police who began shoving us into cars, hitting some of the women heavily on the back. The police cars turned on their sirens and, ignoring a red light, zoomed off with their valuable cargo of nine Jewish women and two Jewish children.

We were taken to a police station and detained for several hours. While the police were drawing up a report, a brigade of chekists arrived and called out the women one by one to their office upstairs. The returning women recounted the essence of the KGB's conversations—if one could call it that, for unfortunately, they contained only threats of reprisals and no serious talk. The women were distressed and complained to me, "We suffered so much in vain; nothing came of it."

"Girls, it would be naive to think that you'll get visas right away. If the KGB handed out visas after each demonstration, the chekists wouldn't have time to sleep; everybody would be running to demonstrate. You'll see, some of us will leave!"

I was one of the last to be called. "Our talk with you is yet to come," said a plainclothesman to me, referring to my trial. At that point deputy district police chief Zagladin entered the office. "Take her to her apartment," the chekist ordered.

I took stock of what I had to do in the days remaining before the June 20 trial. I had to check over my clothing and mend and wash the most necessary items. I had to write to Lena, Leva and

My mother and father, my sister Lena (on the right) and me,
with my maternal grandfather, 1935.

With friends in the mountains, 1962.

In 1977 before my exile.

The village in Siberia where I lived for four years.

Jane Fonda and Sovietologist Marshall Grossman visited me in April 1984 in Kishinev, Soviet Moldavia. (CREDIT: STEPHEN M. RIVERS)

The world remembers: these women were part of "I WIN," or Israeli Women for Ida Nudel, who demonstrated on my behalf in 1979. (CREDIT: GREGORY ROZANSKI)

In New York City, many people voiced their support of Soviet Jews, 1985.
(CREDIT: RIVKA FINDER)

In 1986, the years of exile have taken their toll.

Meeting in 1987 with some of the people who became my spokesmen after I was arrested. Left to right: Hannah Rabinovitz, Lena, Peter Krauss, myself, and Michal Erlichman. (CREDIT: GREGORY ROZANSKI)

My sister Lena (center) with Lova and Raiza Polatnik in Vienna on a hunger strike on my behalf ,1986. (CREDIT: ELENA FRIDMAN)

At last: Lena and me, Ben-Gurion Airport in Israel on October 15, 1987.
We had not seen each other since 1972. (CREDIT: MIKI KRATSMAN)

Pizer and me, home, in Israel, in the spring of 1988. (CREDIT: JUDIE PARTNER)

Yakov and to the fellows in the zone. I had to think about how I should conduct myself at the trial, rest and not talk to people in order to store up some mental energy. I did not, however, succeed in keeping quiet because people came in and out all day and even at night.

In the remaining days Elena Chernobylsky sewed a special sturdy bag for me that was convenient for prison conditions. I had to take things for the heat and the cold yet keep my pack from getting too heavy. My heaviest possession was my English-Russian dictionary, which I hoped would enable me to pass the tedious days in prison. At the last moment I put in an additional pair of glasses.

The last weeks had been so physically and emotionally tense that I did not even have the strength to dream. The chekists did not leave me alone, accompanying me at all times with the brain-shattering sound of their slamming car doors. I even found it difficult to be with friends. I hoped very much that I would not fall apart under the pressure and let out a stream of unnecessary words or start to scream or break down into tears.

Convincing myself that I had to do for myself what I had done for others, I wrote dozens of statements to various Soviet bodies, which Yakov Rakhlenko distributed.

Statement on the Eve of My Trial

For seven years I have been trying to obtain permission to emigrate from the U.S.S.R.; for seven years I have been waiting for a visa.

During these years of waiting, I became known to a wide circle of people because I actively tried to oppose the violence of the regime.

I helped many people whose situation was worse than mine—prisoners, particularly those who by their self-sacrifice in 1970 gave me the opportunity to attain my national and human dignity.

I am deeply grateful to these people. They were the first who raised their heads and said to the Soviet authorities, "Give us visas!" They gave me the confidence that sooner or later I shall be with my people in Israel.

Tomorrow I shall be tried because, as the official charge reads, I "prepared and hung posters with slander about the state institutions, did not react to remarks by citizens and the police, acted provocatively and like a hooligan splashed water on citizens."

For these terrible crimes they are preparing a judicial reprisal, but even before the trial the KGB organized psychological pressure on me. For twenty days—workdays and holidays—I have been followed by four KGB men and two cars. They never leave me and walk directly behind and alongside me.

I declare: Yes, this is a difficult ordeal, this is an enormous psychological burden and it becomes more difficult with every day.

Yes, rejoice, you who torment me. I feel tenser.

But what does it give you, representatives of a great power? Does the knowledge of my suffering bring you joy?

Rejoice, it is difficult for me, but it is also easy.

I feel the support of many friends—both those by my side, and those who are far away—and to all distant and close friends I am deeply and sincerely grateful.

Ida Nudel
Moscow, June 19, 1978

I also met with officials of the justice ministry and the district communist party and pointed out the investigation's complete disregard for the law. When I stated that "this is a reprisal against a political opponent," their faces turned white and their eyes dark.

Thinking they could break me, the chekists wanted to make a show of my trial, but I decided not to participate in the performance. I therefore refused a lawyer because by taking one, I would indirectly legitimize their game. Nevertheless, without my knowledge, the "humane" Soviet court appointed my defense. On the day before the trial, a policeman brought a notice summoning me to court "in connection with a complaint." Assuming that it had to do with a complaint that I had sent to the chief judge two days earlier, I went to him. He looked at me in astonishment, "I did not summon you."

A figure loomed behind my back saying, "Ida Yakovlevna, I summoned you, come to this room." I followed, harboring the faint hope that he would reply to my complaint. The few other people in the room he brought me to disappeared instantly, as if they had evaporated into thin air. "This is your lawyer," said the robust man who had brought me there, introducing me to another man. So that was it! They had deceived me into a meeting with a court-appointed lawyer. They could not do even this honestly.

I refused to discuss anything with the lawyer, saying, "I did not commit any crime; this is the chekists' revenge for my open position in defense of the right of Jews to emigrate. I didn't commit a crime and I will not take part in the trial. I have nothing against you personally, but you represent the regime and I refuse to co-operate with you."

He started asking questions but I repeated very loudly and hotly, "I refuse to speak with you." He said that he was insulted by my sharp tone and refusal. "No matter how unpleasant it is for me, I can't act any other way," I told him. How I wished that some supernatural force would intervene and the reprisal would be averted.

I had asked Viktor Elistratov, who had become more active in speaking with foreigners after Sharansky's arrest, to convey to our friends in America that I was appealing to Sister Ann Gillen for help. I had known for several years about the activity of this remarkable American woman, who was active in a Christian group that worked on behalf of Soviet Jewry.

Late in the evening before the trial there was a ring at the door and I opened it. I did not recognize the two women standing there but from their clothing it was easy to identify them as foreigners. Viktor stood behind the women and introduced them. I was so surprised that I didn't know what to say or do— one of the women was Sister Ann and we embraced. As in a fairy tale, I had barely managed to express a wish and it had been granted.

Sister Ann told me that she had had a premonition that she would need to go to the Soviet Union and had applied for a visa two weeks before she had been phoned about me. She had just received the visa when the call came.

When we accompanied the guests outside, it was completely dark. I took my flashlight. As soon as we stepped outside, the doors of the two cars standing in the courtyard opened and four men jumped out, slamming the doors with a resounding crash.

"Don't be afraid," I warned the women, "they're only after me. They won't touch you."

"How can you live this way?" asked Sister Ann, her face pale. "It's a nightmare."

"You're right," I agreed. "It is very difficult." We parted near the subway stop and I returned under the surveillance of the chekists. Sister Ann was returning to freedom as soon as she crossed the border, but in the meantime, even she felt like a prisoner.

Back in my apartment, I set the alarm clock for three A.M. in order to think over my final words.

June 1978

Don't cry my dears,
I think it is harder for you than for me because I am living the reality, even though it is a very difficult one, and you are forced to imagine what is happening to me.
I emancipated my soul and I am at complete peace with my conscience.
One has to pay for everything in this world; that is the law.
Don't cry; without prison I will not gain freedom.

All my love,
Ida

C H A P T E R 16

ON THE MORNING OF THE TRIAL FRIENDS CAME TO ACCOMPANY me and we left the house in a small group. A crowd of chekists immediately surrounded us and their cars followed on the fifteen-minute walk to the court building.

When we approached, we saw that the police had cordoned off the building and were not letting anyone in, including the refuseniks, dissidents and foreign correspondents who gradually arrived. I refused to go into the courtroom without my friends, explaining to a policeman that the article under which I was charged allows for an open hearing.

He left and shortly afterward a police colonel accompanied by several policemen arrived. I repeated my demand for an open judicial examination as required by law and they left silently. The courthouse doors then opened, and we entered, hoping against all odds that our demands were being met, but fearing a trap. Two policeman walked ahead, showing us the way. They lured us into a dead end; people pressed against us from behind. My friends surrounded me and the policemen crowded around us. At this point the police colonel again suggested that I go into the courtroom.

Tension in the crowd grew. In a few minutes the court secretary arrived and read aloud a decision that I would be forcibly brought into the courtroom. The policemen rushed at me and tore me out of my friends' arms. They shoved the crowd to the side and dragged me toward the courtroom, pushed me inside and slammed the door behind me. One guard edged me through another smaller door into a partitioned area as policemen appeared to flank me.

Strange as it seems, I was completely calm. I took out my prepared statement and looked out into the small room overflowing with people; there was not one familiar face, not one friendly glance.

The court secretary announced, "Stand up; the court is in session." For a moment I hesitated, but decided to follow the rules of the game and I stood up. "Sit down," the secretary declared and the hearing began.

I requested that the judges invite witnesses who had seen what had happened near my house. Having conferred, the court refused. I petitioned to allow the presence of my friends, or the two proxies to whom I had given power of attorney to handle my affairs after the trial, but that was also rejected. I then declared that I did not trust the court because even before the start of the judicial examination it had acted in a clearly tendentious manner, discriminating against me. Having conferred, the court rejected my challenge of the composition of the court.

Expecting very little from the court-appointed lawyer, I was astonished when he also petitioned the court to allow my proxies into the room. Having conferred, the court rejected the lawyer's petition. Then I submitted a petition to hand over the material of the investigation for a supplementary examination and presented a list of witnesses I requested be questioned. The court refused the petition. Even the lawyer supported my petition to hand the material over for further investigation. Having conferred, the court rejected the lawyer's appeal.

On the table in front of the judges and assessors lay the material evidence of my crimes: a bottle of ink, a brush, a rolled-up piece of paper. The witnesses continually got confused in their testimony and the judges patiently guided them. I refused to take part in the judicial examination, reserving the right to deliver my final words.

During the recess, I went to the open window and shouted to my friends who were waiting below that the demonstration of May 23 at the Kremlin gates was excluded from the material of the case. The chekists immediately shoved me away from the window and the police were ordered to watch me.

Having been surprised by the lawyer's initial words on my behalf, I was even more shocked when he made the following unusual speech in my defense: "Having familiarized myself with the material of the case and the testimony of witnesses, and having heard the speech of the state prosecutor, I have come to the conclusion that my client, Nudel, Ida Yakovlevna, is innocent and I petition for a sentence of acquittal. The action committed by Nudel not only does not fall under Article 206, part 2, but also does not fall under any other article of the Criminal Code of the RSFSR. As a lawyer I consider that the investigation has not proven the guilt of Nudel, Ida Yakovlevna, under Article 206, part 2. The witnesses continually modified their testimony during their appearance in court. This circumstance affords the court a basis to hand the case over for a supplementary investigation. Nudel, Ida Yakovlevna, petitions the court to summon witnesses who by their testimony could help the court in determining the truth as she considers it. And I support this petition. Furthermore, this provides a basis for the court to hand the case over to further investigation.

"Nudel does not get along very well with our society but this is not a basis for holding her criminally responsible. There is a group of people in the investigation who have a negative reaction to the behavior of Nudel, Ida Yakovlevna, but can one reach the conclusion that the official reaction to Nudel's means of expressing her desire to emigrate is a basis for charging her with a criminal act? I ask the court for a sentence of acquittal."

All hell broke loose. The "public" in the courtroom began to whistle and scream, and the judge called for order.

The state prosecutor suggested a punishment of four years' exile instead of five years of prison camp, alluding to a good recommendation from my place of work, my age and the humaneness of the Soviet system.

The lawyer, an older man who otherwise undoubtedly knew how to control his emotions, exclaimed sincerely, "Four years! For what?"

In the course of the trial I had decided to ignore the judicial examination altogether and to express my protest by remaining silent instead of delivering my final words, but at the last moment in gratitude to the lawyer for his sincere remark, I decided to turn to him alone in my final speech. It was not easy and I was glad that I had prepared it in advance. When I began to read it, my voice trembled and I was afraid that I would burst out crying at any moment. But I controlled myself and my voice grew stronger as I heaped my scorn on them:

On June 1 of this year I committed an act of desperation; I asserted the right to a public expression of protest. Although I am formally charged with a demonstration on the balcony of the home in which I am living, that is not what you are trying me for. You are trying me for the seven preceding years, the most glorious ones of my life. Many years from now, if I again have to deliver final words, I am absolutely certain that then, too, I shall repeat: these seven years of my life for which I now sit on the defendant's bench have been the most difficult and the most splendid years of my life. During these seven years I learned to walk with my head proudly held high as a human being and as a Jew. These years were full of daily struggles for myself and for others. And each time that I succeeded in keeping another victim alive, my heart was filled with an extraordinary feeling which is like no other. Even if my remaining years are dull and monotonous, this time will warm my heart and provide the knowledge that I have not lived in vain. None of you, my judges, can think up a punishment to take revenge for the triumph and victory of these seven years.

How the "public" and witnesses in that overflowing courtroom shouted—"They didn't give her enough!" "The court gave too little, review it!" "Why did they give her exile!" "Too little, too little, too little!"

As I was taken away from the courtroom under guard, I was terribly dissatisfied with myself. I should have said to them: "Not I, but you, are standing on trial now and everything that you will do to me today will become known to millions tomorrow. Yes, what I shall have to endure will be very difficult and frightening but my confidence that you will have to pay a price for my suffering gives me the strength to bear what you have prepared for me. I know that every day and hour thousands of people—Jews and non-Jews—will demand an accounting from you about where I am and what is happening to me. I am happy in this knowledge, no matter how difficult my fate. And I also want to say to you, my tormentors and judges, that the more you torture my people, the more clearly the world will see your true face—the face of barbarians. You can take away the health and life of those who dared declare this to you, but your end is already approaching. You are afraid to give free rein to your cruel will in full view of the civilized world because now you are dependent on it. You use my people as a commodity and in order to raise the value, you abuse them in full view of the world, demanding: either sell us goods at cheap prices or we shall torment them. Possibly the world will concede, and a stream of food products and contemporary technology will be forthcoming. Will this save my brethren from slavery or your people from starvation?"

The trial ended and I joined a new social caste, that of criminal offender. One of the policemen ordered me to take my bag with my belongings; as he led me out of the courtroom and into another room I saw my lawyer and several women. Turning to the lawyer I said, "I felt that there was only one human being in the courtroom and that was you. I delivered my final words so that you would understand what happened."

The lawyer asked whether I was willing to make an appeal.

"What for? You saw yourself that this was a reprisal. The KGB was settling scores with me and nothing will change its decision."

The lawyer left, and the women standing nearby ordered me to undress.

"Why should I undress? Are you going to take me naked?"

"You were told to undress; there will be a personal search." I knew what that meant, but at that moment, in that large room, still excited from the agitation of the trial and my speech, I felt that I could not bear another ordeal.

"Woman, why are you standing still? You are delaying us, you were ordered to undress; otherwise we will do it by force." These words reminded me of previous occasions when I had been stripped and I did not want a repetition of that. They took one thing after another out of my hands, carefully checking and feeling each object.

"Can you tell me what you are looking for in my underpants? What could there possibly be there?"

"Stop talking or we'll punish you," ordered a policeman standing behind a screen. "We've heard enough from you."

I was then taken outside to a car. There were a lot of people in the yard of the court building and when they saw me, they began to shout words of greeting. I lifted my arm so I could be seen among the crowd of policemen.

At the Krasnopresnenskaya transit prison I was again checked, ordered to undress and once more they poked through my things. My fingerprints were retaken and I was photographed looking straight ahead and in profile. Sitting alone in some cell for what seemed like ages, I thought, You can't measure time in prison. I wondered whether it was day or the dark of night. Perhaps it was already the next morning and my second day of life as a Soviet criminal offender was dawning. But what difference did it make whether it was day or night outside the prison walls? I would not participate in that life. I wanted only one thing right then more than anything else in the world—to lie down and sleep, but there was no place to rest and even sitting was uncomfortable. The bench was narrower than the human buttocks and I was almost sitting but, in fact, my weight fell forward onto my feet, which became numb, and the board cut into my flesh. I sat, stood up, and again sat down. Walking in the room was not easy because it was very small—one step in length and two in width. I had to circle around all the time and this was worse than sitting and standing, sitting and standing.

Finally the key clanged, the door opened, and in front of me I saw several women, the likes of which I had never seen in my life. Where had they picked up these strange creatures? What city back streets had they been hiding in? They looked at me with equal amazement. What kind of bird flew in here, I read in their eyes—in American jeans and an American jacket—an unbelievable picture for a prison scene. With a female guard in front and another one in back, our procession moved on, both guards continually clanging their keys as they led us up and down, as if they wanted us to lose our orientation. At this point I was indifferent; I just wanted it all to end.

We were given a mattress, pillow, blanket, metal bowl, mug and something resembling a spoon. I already had a bag with my personal things, which weighed over thirteen pounds because of the thick English-Russian dictionary. I put everything together and tried to lift it, but it was clear that I could not carry all this baggage at once; the mattress alone weighed at least twenty-two pounds and measured about three feet by six feet. I divided my burden into two parts and first went a short distance with one part and returned for the second, but in the meantime, the prisoners had already been led off somewhere. Orienting myself by the sound of people in motion, I slowly and gradually carried my load from place to place. They appeared to have made some turn because it became silent, but I continued to drag my load, one half at a time, slowly moving along. Suddenly I heard the staccato tapping of feet and in my unhappy mind I imagined that someone had run away, and they were going to shoot me on the spot; it never occurred to me that the police were running through the prison in search of me! They finally discovered me and cursed my slowness.

I sat down on my pile of belongings and announced that I could not drag them, I was staying put, and they could do whatever they wanted with me. Perhaps they believed me or were afraid that the rest of the group would scatter; in any case each guard took something from my pile, leaving me the large and heavy mattress. As if it were alive, the mattress tried to slip out of my arms, which simply were not long enough to keep hold of it. Every few steps it would slide down again, forcing me to stop and roll it up. Keeping their eyes glued to me, the guards first barked and cursed, hoping that I would not fall back, but seeing that it did not help any, they began to walk more slowly.

Finally, they led me into a cell, the door closed and the lock clanged. Although my eyes were clouded from exhaustion and emotion, I remembered how I had decided to behave during my first moments in the cell. I knew that criminals have a highly developed sense of their own dignity; they can forgive some things but not arrogance. Following the scenario that I had already played in my imagination, I said loudly and calmly, "Hello, girls." To my great relief I saw that there were only two young women in the room and my fear vanished. I could not lift my heavy burden onto the free upper bunk so I left the mattress on the floor, put the pillow and my bag of things under my head, covered myself with the blanket, and disappeared into blessed sleep. In a little while I was awakened by a familiar, despised melody—the anthem of the Soviet Union.

I spent a week in this small cell, slowly soothing my jangled nerves; the silence helped to cure me. I was then transferred to a larger cell which was meant to hold twenty people, but I was the thirty-ninth to enter. Directly opposite the door, high up near the ceiling, was a small window; the bars across it were not that close together and it was possible to stick a hand through. Under the window was a table for twenty people that was fastened to the floor, as were the wooden benches on both sides of the table. Women were usually kept no more than two weeks in this cell while waiting for transit.

Unluckily for me it was terribly hot in Moscow during the time I was in that cell and quite impossible to breathe in the suffocating cell. Large groups of women were continually being brought into the cell, where they washed their clothing in the sink and hung it up to dry wherever they could. The street temperature was over ninety-five degrees Fahrenheit but it was even hotter in the perpetually unventilated prison cell, and the forty sweaty women stayed half naked. The combined odor of steaming bodies, damp laundry, defecation, prison food and dirt was a terribly nauseating mix. An additional punishment was the painful bites of the innumerable bedbugs.

At night the cell would quiet down, the guards would be less zealous in keeping order and might even doze off, and the inhabitants of the prison would begin their night life, an existence full of anguished love, meetings and partings, conflicts and reconciliations, confessions of love and hatred, but all on paper.

Prison cells are placed one above the other, male on one level and female on another, and the windows are conveniently aligned. The initiative came from the cell on the upper floor; while one person kept an eye on the door's peephole, the second tried to lower a tiny letter by string weighted with a stone in a small bag. Someone watching at the lower window fished in the catch. At first the letter was addressed simply to whoever wanted to reply. When the answer was ready the string was tugged and the return missive climbed upward where it was seized by some impatient hands. Sometimes events developed so quickly and dramatically that the whole cell became involved in the game; everyone sharing the excitement of the participants in the romance. Sometimes this commotion lasted until morning. Even if these affairs were fictitious and imaginary, the participants' energy and emotions found an outlet which helped them to resist the harsh inhuman conditions imposed upon them.

Occasionally the guards also wanted to amuse themselves and if they were patrolling when the string dropped down into the cell, the door would open instantly and the guilty ones would be caught in the act. The most terrible retribution was not the punishment cell; instead the guards would bring the poor woman to the men's cell. With her head shaved bare because the doctors would have found lice in her hair, a not so youthful woman who had described herself as young and beautiful would appear in all her squalor before the gaze of her "partner." The terrible, merciless laughter of criminals and guards would ring out, followed by hooting and crude comments. The humiliated, crushed woman would no longer participate in such games and would most often spend her time lying indifferently on her bunk.

My relations with the criminal women proceeded smoothly; I wrote their complaints, which enabled me to stand for hours under the window where it was a little easier to breathe because a small quantity of air occasionally passed through the bars.

During the twelve days I spent in this cell, I saw a large number of human types that I had never encountered before and I heard fantastic stories, both real and imagined. Each time the guard began to clang her keys before opening the door, everyone would become silent. The tense, expectant faces turned toward the door expressed only one feeling: hope. The face of the murderess who was waiting for her final sentence or that of the thief who had sold a dead dog instead of lamb meat at the market expressed one single dream— perhaps this means my release? In this respect I was just like my cell mates; no matter how much I tried to convince myself that the chekists had decided to take revenge and would not release me, every time the key turned in the lock and the guard opened the door, my fantasy would take me far from the prison cell and I would pray, "God, release me from here now." The door would open and some names would be called out but they were not mine.

As the days dragged on, I stopped dreaming of release and dreamed only that they would take me quickly out of the prison where it was impossible to breathe and where even the night brought no relief to the inhabitants. One evening as I was lying on the floor, the keys jangled and the whole cell tensed up with the usual hopes; the door opened and the guard announced: "Nudel, without her things."

Me, but without my things? "Ida, don't worry, it's probably to go to a lawyer or a meeting with family," my cell mates whispered. I got up and quickly left the room, wearing just what I had on, a light dress over a bare body. The guard led me through long corridors, constantly playing the prison melody with her keys, taking me in circles that descended lower and lower. Finally she handed me over to a male guard, who led me into a room with heavy tables separated by a thick plastic partition. There were three telephones on the tables and an equal number of chairs next to them. Another chair, probably for the guard, stood near the door. Through the thick plastic wall I could see three chairs and three telephones and a door in the other half of the room.

I had barely managed to look around as the door opened and through the thick pane I saw my refusenik friends, Isai Goldshtein and Yakov Rakhlenko, enter the room. It was wonderful to see their familiar and dear faces. Conversing over the telephone, they urged me to make an appeal.

"Are you kidding? Who should I ask—the KGB, as if to say, beat me, but not till the blood flows! I did nothing criminal; I didn't even violate the law. They're the ones who arranged the jolly extravaganza beneath the windows of my home with broken glass and threats. I should ask their pardon? No, I won't do it, I don't need a lawyer. I learned to walk with my head proudly held high and I have to pay for it."

During the day there was a constant din in the room. The women spoke mostly in slang and a few days after I had been put in the cell I noticed strange things happening. First of all I began to stutter. Then I reached a state where I could not focus on anything but slang. Horrified by this unexpected situation, I dug into my English-Russian dictionary and would sit or stand by the window for hours, cramming in words, but I could not memorize one of them during those crazy days.

They gave us nothing to write with but I still had a pen refill taken from home. I saved the small square pieces of paper that they gave us each morning for the toilet, sometimes taking two or three at a time, and collecting any that remained. The prisoners' tales were very interesting and some women were brilliant storytellers, portraying incidents so vividly and with such humor that the whole cell laughed. The most striking were the tales of women who had murdered their husbands. They told about the unbelievably sadistic indignities to which the men had subjected them, the complete indifference of society and the police, and the sweet relief they felt after the murder, which was usually committed with an ax while the husband was sleeping off a drinking spree. Afterward, the children usually defended the mother and only asked why she had not done it earlier. These women were happy prisoners because each day brought them closer to complete freedom. There was also a large group of teenage criminals; they were nasty and I did not talk to them.

I began to record the stories, not only because they were interesting but also because it was an occupation which somehow linked me to the normal world. I began to classify my notes according to the nature of the crimes and had begun to discern a definite pattern but these notes were confiscated during a search while I was in the exercise yard.

Under prison conditions a person's senses grow dull, reactions slow down, thoughts diminish and focus only on the very closest matters: family and oneself. The longer this continues, the narrower the range of thoughts becomes. I began to notice that, in general, I was not thinking about anything in particular and was becoming indifferent to the sound of the keys opening the door and was no longer looking through the English-Russian dictionary, my sole link with the civilized world.

One rule which I tried to adhere to strictly was not to miss the exercise period. Once I discovered that during the exercise period someone had eaten some of my food supplies. It was easy to identify the thief—the woman would arrange to sleep next to me all the time—but the question was what to do about it. Had I accused someone of stealing my food but could not prove it, it would be as if I were accusing the whole cell. I had already seen several wild quarrels among these women—never before had I even heard such words as they spat at each other during these scenes— and I was loathe to get involved in them. I decided that I would survive even if they ate all my food. Although I needed the energy the food gave me, I was not willing to declare war on the cell. I continued to go out for the exercise period and each time I returned, I found my food bag lighter and lighter.

When finally one day the cell door opened noisily and the guard said, "Nudel, with your things," almost the entire cell rushed to help me collect my belongings. "Ida, don't ever land here again!" they shouted.

The guard hurried me along. "Get dressed or I'll send you to the punishment cell!" She literally dragged me out of the cell by the arm.

"Who are you?" she asked.

"A political prisoner," I replied.

"We don't have any politicals here," she retorted sharply.

Ida,

I am writing to you because I have, through contact with your sister and her family, come to feel something special for you. First, you amaze me. I read and reread the transcript of your phone call to Ilana. I must say that I fully understand and appreciate the particular stand that you have adopted. I admire it, but shudder and shrink from it. I have silently tried to think whether in similar circumstances, God forbid, I or anyone I know, would have the inner fiber and courage, the power of soul, to do what you are doing. The answer is that I would not and could not. Where did you obtain your inner strength? What nourishes it? To my wife I said, she is made of iron, but we know that is not so. We know that it is the power of soul wrought from iron conviction, fed from years spent giving life and comfort to others. However intangible these things are, they form indeed the strongest fiber in the world. We know very little about the human soul. Only when we come into contact with someone such as yourself, do we really begin to perceive a glimmer of its ultimate reaches. As long as there are examples such as yourself, human kind may indeed still have possibilities even in our horrendous world.

I study Talmud regularly. Yesterday I came across a passage that opened vistas for me. It explained so much, and especially within the context of Ida Nudel. The passage is long, the important pieces for the moment are the final two sentences. The Sages, who were the only real probers of the power of the human soul, said, "Just as God gives strength to the wicked to bear their punishment, so He gives strength to the righteous to bear their reward." Within the context that this appears in the Talmud, I think they mean to say quite simply, but quite devastatingly deeply, that the human being is a kind of infinite creation. The depths and heights that are his are unfathomable, and these depend only upon the manner in which he chooses to live his life. If he chooses goodness, he has infinite capacity, within his limited frame, for goodness. If he chooses the reverse, he has infinite capacity for its consequences. If he chooses suffering, he has infinite capacity for that also. The human being is unaware of this, usually. It is only that the depths of his capacity are brought out, shown to him and to others, by circumstances.

God grant you the strength and courage to continue the glorious path that has been thrust upon you, for as long as it takes until we can welcome you joyously here, in Israel, amongst us.

Sincerely yours,
A. H. Rabinowitz*

---

*Avraham Hirsch Rabinowitz was the first rabbi of the Israeli Air Force. He died on March 26, 1987.

CHAPTER 17

SHORTLY AFTER I WAS TAKEN TO A TRANSIT CELL, A PRISON
officer arrived and read me the decision of the supreme court of
the Russian Republic, which upheld the verdict of the district court.
I was now being sent to a place of exile and would have to face an
etape, the long and difficult transit journey.

Every doomed or condemned person is sustained by one wish:
to be saved by a miracle. I had not asked my tormentors for con-
descension or mercy and had not appealed to them; therefore my
pain did not come from deceived hopes or crushed illusions. My
heart constricted and became reconciled.

At the last moment before I was taken out of the prison the
KGB decided to show their magnanimity and gave me a ten-pound
package of food which my friends Grigory and Isai Goldshtein,
Yakov Rakhlenko and Elena Sirotenko had put together. I can still
remember the wonderful taste of the cake, the sight of the incom-
parably beautiful cucumbers and tomatoes, the smell of the sausage.

Twenty prisoners were assembled in one large cell; I kept my
distance because I was the only woman and understandably apprehensive. The head of the convoy arrived with our papers and
began to familiarize himself with the prisoners. He called out a
name, the prisoner stepped in front of the crowd and gave his name
and patronymic, the article under which he had been convicted
and the term of punishment. When my turn came, he looked with
astonishment, even disbelief, at this middle-aged, gray-haired

woman in a sporty American jacket and Levi-Strauss jeans. "Convict Nudel, come to me," he ordered. I approached. "Your appearance . . . how did you land here? Why were you given exile instead of camp?"

"I am a political prisoner; put me separately."

"I'm taking more people than I can, there's no room."

During an etape, when you are transported from place to place, you are given only a few pieces of rotten salty sprats and a portion of bread. For the first three-day stretch of the journey I was given a loaf of bread and a small paper parcel of the fish. I took the bread but left the package untouched. Someone asked whether I was going to take it; when I said no, the package disappeared.

We were taken from the prison, surrounded by guards with dogs, and loaded into cars that brought us to the train station. The guards were nervous, and continually stirred up the dogs, who were straining at the leash. I was ordered to walk near the head of the convoy, but when I could not keep up the pace and started to fall behind, a guard urged me, "Stay near me, it's dangerous."As I struggled along, I wished I didn't have to carry the food package I had so gratefully welcomed in the morning.

At the back entrance to the train station, they stopped the group of prisoners, ordering men to their knees and counted off again. The dogs were going crazy, straining and barking. The guards kept warning me, "Stay closer, don't go near the men." The head of the convoy and I were standing opposite the men on their knees. I looked at the dull, colorless faces of old men and young boys.

"Take the woman first," the officer commanded. When I saw the high step of the train car, I wondered how to get on it. I decided to throw my heavy bag first, but I was able to lift it only as far as the first step. The guard was already pushing from behind and the dog was straining from the side. I wish you would all go to hell, you and your chekists, you torture me so, I thought.

"Take her bag; this boarding will never end," ordered the boss. I don't know where I got the strength or skill—perhaps simply from fear of the jaws of the German shepherd, but I managed to scramble into the car quickly and safely. I was the first to board the car. After the noise and tension of the last hour, the silence was deafening. The car was divided into several cells; instead of a door, there was a sliding metal grate which locked on the outside.

The head of the convoy held the key. Gradually, the car filled up with prisoners and the train started moving. There was no more stamping of boots, and I entered a new, unfamiliar phase of my life. From having read and heard a lot about the life of prisoners, I knew that the etape was one of the worst stages in a prisoner's life and I was prepared for it as I lay down on the bare wooden bunk.

Even though it was summer, it was cold inside. The wagon rocked rhythmically, lulling me. The day had been so draining both emotionally and physically that I drifted into sleep. From time to time I woke up from a sharp jolt; in my semiconscious state my brain indifferently registered the loud commands of the guards, the clacking of the metallic heel taps on their boots and the sharp sounds of the locking and unlocking of the metal grates. Only when the metallic sounds echoed right above my head did I open my eyes. The guards brought an enormous woman into the cell; she must have weighed over two hundred and twenty pounds. When she had settled in a bit, I asked her in what city had she been put aboard the car.

"I'm from the special psychiatric hospital in Kazan. I killed two people."

Goose pimples crawled down my back, and I felt terrified and disgusted at having to lie next to her. Although I had food in my bag, I decided not to give her any.

As the train continued its slow journey eastward, it stopped in several towns. At each place others were brought on or taken off. At one stop a whole group of women were put together in one cell. The cells quieted down until prisoners heard the sound of the keys and all eyes quickly turned to see who was being led past the grating. When the two guards accompanied these women along the corridor in front of the open grating of the men's cell, it was an event in which all participated, including the guards. The women acted in indescribably vulgar ways. They hurled disgusting, vindictive words at the men, which drove even those primitive creatures into a fury. I had the suspicion that this was a joint game, whether conscious or not; the exchange served as a kind of emotional nourishment. In these mutual curses and unthinkable accusations people who had never seen each other before poured out their personal pain in a frenzy.

These scenes were a nightmare for me and I found my unwilling presence loathsome. The threats of the guards never helped until passions calmed down on their own. On my way from Moscow to Siberia I rode in five different prison cars and each time the conflict between the men and women—always initiated by the women—was repeated with the same remarkable intensity.

Somewhere along the way the guard brought one more woman into the cell. She had a pleasant face, spoke agitatedly, and from time to time she began to cry and asked the guard to release her.

I shared some of the food from my pack with her and we began to talk. I was attracted by her open, broad face and sincere telling of her life story. Impulsively I trusted her and decided to relate a recurring dream to her.

"Can you interpret dreams?" I asked. She nodded yes, and I told her about it.

In it I saw myself walking along a dark wall, which at that moment seemed infinitely high and long.

I knew I had to get over to the other side, but how could I do it? Suddenly I noticed that in one spot the wall was significantly lighter and had some kind of broad and deep modular structures built into it that were open only to the outside and were piled one on top of the other. They were enormous—about my height—and I could not imagine how I would scale them. Somehow I nevertheless managed to climb onto the first one and noticed a large vessel covered with a white cloth.

Behind me a voice proclaimed, "Careful, don't spill it, it's full!"

I then saw myself on the next structure and it, too, contained a vessel with a white cover and there, too, I heard the warning, "Don't spill it!"

The same sequence of events repeated itself a third time. When I raised my head to see what loomed above, I saw that very little of the wall remained—one more ascent and the shining blue sky would be over my head.

I observed myself as if from a distance, I raised my right foot and put it on the edge of the wall; then, holding on to the edge, I slowly moved my left foot toward the top. I had almost put my foot on the wall when some strong hand grabbed me from behind and with this sensation I woke up. I was alone in the room and the bright sun was shining in my eyes. Ever since, the white covered vessels and the sound of an unfamiliar voice saying, "Don't spill it, it's full," flashed through my mind.

She told me, "I believe your dream is about the future. I don't know exactly what it is about but I can tell you that you still must face many difficulties, that is, vessels filled with your tears. The fact that the vessels were covered in white means that your wish will come true. And when that moment arrives, it will be beyond your wildest imaginings. You saw a cheerful clear sky above your head; I don't know who you are but yours is a very special dream."

"Tell me, what is the symbolism of the four structures which I climbed?"

"I don't know, my dear, but your dream will come true, believe me. Probably the time is not yet ripe."

At almost every large city on our way to Siberia the police with the help of German shepherds unloaded the prisoners into the cars known as Black Marias and brought us to the city prison. We remained in the prison for several days until a new convoy arrived. Then we would be led back to the prison car with the new group. This procedure repeated itself monotonously until we reached our destination.

In Sverdlovsk we were joined by a whole flock of teenagers. Although they had the external characteristics of human beings, whether as a result of upbringing or some other reason, they totally lacked the ethical and moral norms of civilization. That group, who apparently declared war on me, had originally been assigned to a prison camp, but the administration had been completely unable to control them. They had set fire to buildings with sleeping prisoners inside, started fights, destroyed equipment and books and protested whenever they could. The youths had then been dispatched to a mental hospital which had performed the task of "taming" their rebellious energy with insulin shocks and drugs before sending them back to the zone. Although far from passive, they were thus somewhat slowed down at the time that fate brought us together in a large cell in the Sverdlovsk prison.

Trying to amuse themselves, the young women stripped naked and began to jump from bunk to bunk, screeching and entwining and untwining in a tangle. Howling, they would rush at a victim. Bunched together in one spot, the other women looked on, but no one defended the attacked person. The law was harsh—each one fended for herself. The experienced women drove them away with profanity but I could not curse and was completely defenseless. They could not understand my language, and I resorted to defending myself with my hands and feet. Ironically, the prison guards saved me from these "playful kids," as they called them. Running into the room armed with clubs they began to grab them by the hair, hands and feet and drag the slippery creatures into the hall. There, using all their might, they beat them savagely, deriving enjoyment from the fierce cries and howls. Having thus "pacified" them, they tossed them back into the cell.

Toward evening I was transferred to a solitary cell for over a day, where I was able to recover a little from my overwhelming experiences, but on a train again I was soon stuck with these youths. They knew that I had food in my bag and they, of course, were hungry. I decided to defend myself rather than hand over my food to them. When the fight erupted in the train car, however, it was clear that these young ones had planned everything in advance. That hunk of a woman, the murderess who had been put into my prison car at Kazan, barricaded the metal grating for them with her body, and the horde descended from the upper bunk and piled on me. One held my right hand, a second my left hand and a third sat on my foot. "Hand over the food of your own free will," demanded the leader.

"I won't, I want to eat it myself," I replied, guarding the bag behind my back.

Then she began to poke me underneath my glasses with her fingers.

"You're afraid, you're afraid," she hissed.

"Go away or I'll call the guard," I shouted.

"No you won't," replied the youngster confidently.

Then the murderess couldn't contain herself and struck me on the face with her sturdy fist, aiming directly at my glasses. I kicked her with my free foot as hard as I could. Then she punched me again in the face. I screamed, "Guard!" and I heard the sound of boots. The woman clung to the grating, covering the cell with her enormous body, while the delinquents seized my bag of food from behind my back and quickly scrambled to the upper bunk.

"Get away from the grating immediately!" ordered the guard.

The head of the convoy ran to the cell and demanded, "What kind of fight is going on here?"

"She's a Jew! She's a kike! She has sausage!" came howls from the women's cell. The convoy head quickly unlocked the iron grating and dragged me by the arm out of the cell; with the same hand he led me to the platform and left me there alone. I couldn't see anything because my glasses had been shattered. "Stay here," he said. "I'll have to switch everything around in order to separate you." Little splinters of glass from my eyeglasses were strewn over my face and chest; I very cautiously wiped them off. My God, I thought, what would have happened if even the smallest splinter had fallen into my eyes?

At night the train would stop and we were ordered to get ready to leave. "Women first," commanded the head of the convoy. Two guards went up to the women's cell and stood on both sides of the grating waiting for the chief, who was the only one with the key. The whole cell watched through the grating as they called two women and the guards led them to the exit; the chief locked the door, a new convoy took that pair, and to the cry of "Send some more," the cell gradually emptied as the women were transferred to the Black Marias. Each time they led out a new group of women, the men in the neighboring cells began to yell, "Show her to us, is that the one who screamed so loudly? Chief, be a sport, show me, I liked her," someone began to clown. Locked in iron cages and debased to the lowest human level, some nevertheless maintained the ability to joke. I couldn't see the humor in my situation but I didn't make a tragedy out of it either; I knew that everything would come to an end.

A few days later I found myself occupying a large metal cage in the hold of a steamship. The floor of the cage was made of wood and even had a little elevation at one end which I used as a head rest. Three men were already there, in other cages, but talking between the cells was strictly forbidden. These cages were locked with two locks each and guarded by two armed soldiers; in addition, the officer in charge of the convoy often went down to the hold. The steamship sailed slowly, moving constantly north against the current. In August it was not very cold in the hold and I wore my jacket and jeans. From time to time the ship docked and I could hear the stamping of feet. In the daytime I could see a sliver of the river and sometimes even the shore through a tiny porthole, but the hold was so low down that I saw mainly water.

Although I wondered how long the journey would last and what would await me at my new destination, I had learned the prisoners' rule—whatever will be will be, and if they tell you "with your things" it means you're going on the road.

June 1979

Ida,

I have seen in wars men and boys, whom I had thought weaklings and lacking in dimension, rise to heights of self-sacrifice, heroism and dignity. Trial and suffering are indeed hard and even cruel. But they teach man more about himself than any other teacher. Through them man becomes more man. He becomes a real man. A full man. A man amongst so-called men. I write in the male gender, but Ida dear, you know that it is you of whom I am speaking.

The true hero is not he who seeks heroism by prowess, but he who, as you, shows prowess when forced to the brink. It is he who says, I will not give in.

Ida, do you pray? Can you pray? I do not know the answer to these questions, you will have to tell me in person when you come. But bear with me a little while, and I will tell you what a great teacher in Israel, the late Chief Rabbi of Eretz Yisrael, Rabbi Kook, said. The soul, that intangible, unknowable part of God that is within us and pervades our being, always prays. It seeks the way to its source, to God. He called this the unceasing prayer of the soul. This, for the human being, is unconscious prayer. Conscious prayer is the effort to delve down within oneself, into one's being and join in with the prayer of the soul. Such effort is cleansing and uplifting. It succeeds in both retaining the reality of being, and transcending it. It transports. No walls can contain it, no exile suppress it. It says, contemplate and I will be with you though you walk in the valley of death. There is no light that shines so brightly as that kindled in utter blackness. That light means hope. It shines within the breast of each one of us, Ida. We have but to recognize it. God does not demand words. He seeks the broken, downtrodden soul that seeks him. We, Ida, are doing whatever is

*possible for you. You can do little, but so much. Turn your thoughts to
the God of Israel, He will hear your prayer. Ask Him for courage,
stamina and strength to wait and to remain that same, wonderful Ida,
till freedom comes.*

*Sincerly yours,
A. H. Rabinowitz*

CHAPTER 18

THE STEAMBOAT FINALLY REACHED ITS DESTINATION AND one by one we were signed over to the police, loaded into a Black Maria and taken to the local police station.

An enormous surprise awaited me on the night I was deposited on shore. I was greeted at the police station by Viktor Elistratov. Making the long journey from Moscow to Siberia in order to welcome me was an invaluable gift.

Fortunately, despite the distance, the phone connection between Siberia and Moscow was on a relatively high technological level and thus during my exile I was able to talk long-distance to my Moscow friends regularly. Telling them about my life became a source of much needed support, but ultimately I had to live on my own in this tiny settlement where everyone knew absolutely everything about everyone else. I had to start life anew in a hostile environment, and I had to live every moment of the one thousand four hundred days of my sentence under the constant gaze of hate-filled eyes.

I was taken to the village of Krivosheino, a small settlement of about two thousand people on the River Ob, one of the largest Siberian waterways. The land had been wrested from the swamps by exiles, who had been sent there since the tsarist times; indeed, I wondered who would voluntarily have settled in such a harsh climate. The villagers used to lament jokingly that they had nine months of winter and three of summer. In winter the temperature hovered between five and forty below zero, occasionally dropping as low as seventy-five degrees below zero on the Fahrenheit scale, making it difficult even to breathe. A thick constant fog covered the ground, making it impossible to see even a short distance. In summer the temperature sometimes climbed to ninety-five or a hundred and five and the mosquitoes made life unbearable, crawling into your nose, mouth and ears. In the brief fall and spring it rained constantly. The sky was gray, oppressive and gloomy and the people were always behaving the same way; they never smiled walked with their heads down, staring at their feet. Outside the village stretched the taiga—the dense, pathless forest—in summer a kingdom of mushrooms, berries, birds and flowers.

My appearance in such a godforsaken place caused a certain sensation. On the very day after my arrival, no matter where I went, everybody knew that a political exile had come to the village. Whenever I opened the door to the office of some local petty official, he would instantly exclaim, "Oh, that's you," with a mixture of astonishment and disappointment. My appearance, after all, did not inspire respect—short in height, wearing glasses and dressed in pants and a Levi's jacket, I seemed like an adolescent. This impression was intensified by my rapid, light stride, open gestures, lively facial expressions, passionate speech and openness in conversation, which seemed at odds with the formidable term "a political."

"Go find work for yourself," a police officer told me. "You have fifteen days to find a job and housing." I trod the worn, clay roads of the village in the rainy autumn weather. After each step I had to balance on one foot in order to drag the other shoe out of the thick mud, but sometimes I lost my balance and my foot fell out of the shoe and plunged directly into the mud. I tried to walk along the tracks left by trucks whenever possible, but this usually did not save me. In some places along the road boards had been strewn, resembling a sidewalk, but they were full of gaps. I went from house to house, knocking at each one. If they opened the door, I asked whether they took boarders but the answer was invariably negative. Completely soaked after having wandered around the village for half a day, I returned to the little house for travelers where the police had sent me on the first night.

Fifteen days flew by and I had no success in my searches. Realizing, however, that the police were responsible for my housing and employment, I wrote them the following statement: "I have made the rounds of all the organizations in the village and none were willing to offer me work. For reasons of health, I am unfit for heavy physical labor."

In a few days they sent me to a small settlement over three miles from the village known as the PMK, the mobile land reclamation colony. The colony consisted of several houses, a small store, an office for the land reclamation project, a boiler house and a small one-story wooden barrack, with sinks at the end of the hall and drafty, crude toilet facilities in a separate shed. I was sent to work as a draftsman in the office of the land reclamation project and I was assigned a room in the barrack with two beds and a little space for a small table between them. The woman in charge of the dormitory gave me a key and bed linen, and warned me not to bring men into my room; she promised to come to the room to check. "There's no need for you to come to my room. I am capable of maintaining order on my own," I told her, insulted by her warning.

"I am the one in charge here and I'm allowed to," was the reply.

I discovered that the mattress and pillow were stained with dried blood and requested, "Please replace them, they're all bloody."

"We don't have any other. They all have blood. No one's going to buy anything especially for you."

I managed to make do with the mattress by putting a blanket on top of it and wrapping it in sheets, but the pillow was another story. No matter how much I tried to convince myself that no one had been murdered on it, I couldn't bring myself to touch it. I tossed it aside, rolled up my jacket and slept that way until Evgeni Tsirlin, the person whom I had designated as my legal proxy to care for my affairs in Moscow, arrived in the fall bringing me a new pillow, along with a radio, books, including a Hebrew-Russian dictionary and some of my clothing.

The other inhabitants of the dormitory—all men—were former criminals who worked all week draining swamps. They returned on Friday, dirty, hungry and wild. I saw my neighbors in the evening after they had washed off the dirt, shaved, and filled their stomachs with the cafeteria food. They were bored from the lack of anything to do.

"What kind of little birdie flew in here?" someone asked when

I entered the barrack. "Who are you?" he asked as a hand grabbed me by the arm.

"Please, remove your hands!"

"Who are you, the new engineer?"

I silently opened the door to my room.

"I told you to stop it!" I insisted. Someone's foot appeared in the room, preventing me from closing the door. Although quite a few men were in the hall, none interfered.

"Oh ho, there are two beds here; who are you that they gave you a separate room? I'm going to live here, too. You'll have one bed and I'll take the other," he declared, grasping my hand.

"Stop it right now. Take your hands off me and leave me alone," I yelled.

"Who are you? I'm going to live here." Pushing me inside, he followed me into the room.

"I'm a political exile. Get out of this room this minute," I demanded. He couldn't digest the word "political," but he let go of my arm and finally left. I turned the key in the lock and leaned my face against the door. Only after the man had left did I realize how frightened I was.

I was sitting on my bed, wondering how I would survive when someone kicked the door. I didn't say anything. "Don't you hear? Open!" I was silent. "Open or I'll break the door!"

"Break it and you'll get charged with hooliganism," I answered.

I spent the night locked up in my room but I could not sit there forever, so the next day, when it seemed to have quieted down, I ventured outside. Smoking and talking, the men were standing near the entrance to the barrack. My heart dropped to my heels as I approached them.

Again someone grabbed my arm.

"Talk without your hands," I stated strongly—but I was shivering inside.

"Who are you to give orders here?"

I pulled my hand away and left without saying anything and didn't return until it was almost evening. While I was opening the door to my room, some man came up and asked if he could go into my room.

"Why?"

"Just to see how you settled in."

"You have no business in my room."

"You don't have to pretend," he said, "you're no engineer."

The KGB had really pushed me into a corner and what good did it do even if I locked the door twice? The door was only plywood and any of the men now standing behind it could kick it down in one blow. I sat in my room like a mouse, afraid even to go to the primitive toilet outside the barrack, and wished it were evening so they would run off to their "princesses," as they called their local female companions. I reminded myself that I was lucky that they had exiled me and not sent me to a prison zone or psychiatric hospital. But still, how could I get these criminals to leave me alone?

On Monday morning I went to the police station and informed them I refused to live in a male dormitory.

"We don't have anything else."

"I'll kill the first one who breaks into my room," I declared, and I handed him a protest, a copy of which had been registered with the on-duty police officer. Although as a result of my action the director of the land reclamation project gave me a reprimand for leaving work, he did assure me that no one would touch me and I could live in peace. That indeed was the case.

Time passed quickly and fall arrived in full force. It got dark early and rained either from morning to evening or from evening to morning. There was nothing to do and no place to go to in the colony other than to the small store which sold milk, grain, bread, soap, matches and odds and ends. On "festive" occasions, such as the first of May or the anniversary of the October Revolution, they even had duck, and we residents would line up, waiting excitedly to see whether we might get one.

My next encounter with the police chief came when I decided it was time to start writing again to the fellows in the zone and to report to them about myself. I was summoned to him, and he informed me, "You are not permitted to correspond with other prisoners."

"I'm an exile, not a prisoner. I live under the same conditions as you do in this village! Perhaps you are a prisoner, too?" I asked him.

"Get out of my office," he roared. What else could he say to me?

I began to receive many letters from Israel, England, France, the United States, Germany and other countries where friends were eager to help. At first the postal workers were visibly nervous about handling these letters but I taught them how to fill out the necessary forms.

Correspondents who sent letters by registered mail could pay an extra fee for a pink card that was attached to their letter. This pink card had to be signed by the recipient and was then returned to the sender; if the form was not filled out and returned, the local post office had to pay a fine for nondelivery. I took advantage of these pink cards by writing protests in English about the fabricated charge against me, and along with the card, my words reached the senders. This worked for several weeks until I made the mistake of writing the text of my protest in Russian on a card which was attached to my sister's letter, and the post office immediately stopped giving me the cards. Without them my personal contact with many people was lost and I turned into a distant apparition. If I could not remind people of my existence during the four years of isolation, the world would forget that I was alive, I thought.

As a protest against the KGB action I decided to refuse to receive my international mail. I wrote on registered forms: "Please turn to the Soviet embassy in your country in order to receive information about me. I am refusing my mail as an act of protest." It was difficult to convince Lena that I was right because my refusal disrupted the sole opportunity for contact, creating new problems for her. Via friends I communicated the following open letter:

My Dear Loved Ones!
I know how difficult it is for you, how you are tormented by fear for me, and how you wait for even the slightest news. During these last few months after my trial I have thought a lot about my new situation and how I should respond to it.
My tormentors could have sent me to a camp where they could have starved or tortured me with cold and humiliated me daily and hourly with the most refined methods, but they knew that the knowledge of my suffering would not give you any peace and therefore you would not give any peace to their high-level representatives in various countries. Exile is something else; you know that I am surrounded by warmth and the constant concern of friends, that I have enough to eat and am

*warmly dressed and my letters stream out and everything
seems to be calm and fine . . . . No, I am not willing to play their
game, don't expect news from me; there won't be any. I am
becoming silent now, when it has not yet become routine that
somewhere in Siberia yet another victim is suffering.*

*I become silent, confident that you will not be silent. Don't turn
to me, but to my tormentors for information about me and then
my suffering will have meaning and their victory over me will be
uneasy and their revenge bitter. I know that in refusing to write
letters I distress my relatives and friends even more deeply, but
what can I do? How else can I resist the violence done to me;
otherwise I will only help my murderers.*

Please understand and accept my position.

> *With love,*
> *Ida*
> *September 24, 1978*
> *Krivosheino, Tomsk region.*

I also sent an open letter to the *Jerusalem Post*, which they
printed:

My dear friends, I understand that many of you felt bewildered
and insulted when my letters were returned unopened. How else
could I express my protests; what else could I deprive myself of?
Water? Food? Housing? Life?

No, I want my dream to come true. I want to live with my
people and, if I can, be useful to them.

The chekists did not like this but of course they did not like
anything I initiated, since my position also put pressure on their
missions abroad. To persuade me to change my mind they began
to send all my mail to the village, not just the registered items,
but even simple postcards and letters. Although the mountain of
correspondence grew daily, I only looked at the enormous packets
of letters and postcards from a distance. Sometimes the postmistress
asked me to translate the name of a country from which my mail
had arrived and I would hurriedly skim the text:

"Ida, be brave!"

"Ida, hold on until we succeed in liberating you!"

"Ida, don't despair, we love you!"

They represented so much support and warmth and protection! My desire simply to touch them became irresistible. "Let me help you register them in your entry journal," I suggested once to the head of the post office.

"I beg you to take it all away; I have a huge amount of work as it is and half the personnel in the post office are working on your mail alone," she said.

"I can't," I explained to her. "I have no other way of protesting against the false charge and conviction. I can't accept it in silence."

Although I believed in the correctness of my decision, I was sometimes forced to act inconsistently. Occasionally I sent long letters with a description of everything that was happening to me to general delivery in Moscow, in the name of Evgeni Tsirlin. But these letters were delivered to his personal mailbox. The chekists thus demonstrated that I could not have such a thing as a secret correspondence. Intolerable pressure was put on me to renounce my statement, not only by the KGB but also by my friends, but I persisted stubbornly. I refused to accept my mail for a year but eventually I gave in; I discovered that my family and friends in the West had not accepted my decision and it became senseless for me to continue.

In autumn, when darkness fell early and the dawn arrived so late, it was frightening to leave the colony but I desperately wanted to be alone—away from those voices and idiotic songs and constant cursing, if only for a few minutes. On my long-awaited day off from work I decided to walk into the taiga, but not stray too far from the road—just enough to be alone among the trees and birds. Nothing helped, however; neither books nor the taiga relieved my unbearable feelings. Externally it seemed as if I were free. I walked around the village and no one stopped me; I went to the store, the post office or the taiga without anyone following me. Yet there seemed to be two simultaneous incompatible states of my consciousness—free and not free. Probably the people around me also feel miserable, I reasoned; why else do they all get drunk? Even though they are primitive, they have feelings like I do.

I bought a bottle of cognac which knocked me off my feet, but soothed and calmed me a little. I now understand what people were looking for at the bottom of a bottle, but I felt I had to find some other way of keeping my equilibrium.

"Zhenya," I wrote to my friend Evgeni Tsirlin, "please bring me a puppy, an auburn female collie."

Ever since our youth, my sister and I had dreamed about owning a dog, but our complicated life had never permitted it. We knew exactly what kind we wanted—it had to be an auburn female collie. When I was locked in Siberia in a hostile environment and deprived of companionship with people of a similar cultural level, I decided that I could not stand it without a dog. The chekists, who listened to all my phone conversations, warned me through the police that they would not let me keep a dog. I decided to again test whether they were already sick of the commotion concerning my fate. If they accepted my decision silently, it meant that pressure from the West was sufficiently strong; if they got into a conflict with me, it meant that my affairs were in very bad shape. Their reactions would help me analyze what I could and could not do, where the limits existed in this boundary-less zone.

At last Evgeni arrived with two hundred pounds of food and a wonderful, cheerful auburn puppy, just like I had asked for. The local people were thrilled with the puppy; neither the adults nor the children had ever seen a collie in real life. In their own way people there loved animals and a little dog could be found near every home. The police remained silent.

My glorious puppy needed an appropriate name, but not a Russian one. I had wanted her because I was alone and needed protection from my enemies. In my Russian-Hebrew dictionary I found the verb "pizer"—to scatter or disperse; and thus the dog acquired her name, Pizer.

November 1978

My Dears,

To give you a better idea of how I am living I must tell you that my small little room serves simultaneously as my fortress and bedroom, my kitchen and dressing room, bath and hall.

Sometimes I weep about the senselessness of my existence. There are moments when I think that I made an enormous mistake in not having my own family. There are other moments when I don't have the strength to bear the crushing physical burden and I think that if only I had a man by my side, then everything would be much easier.

It seems I am becoming fatalistic. The thought that everyone's fate is predetermined comes to mind more and more frequently. Nevertheless, most often I believe that my suffering is not in vain.

My love to all of you,
Ida

ONE NIGHT I WAS AWAKENED BY A TERRIBLE NOISE AND THE yelping of my puppy. An indescribable fight was raging in the hall. I heard the heavy stamping of male feet, screaming and cursing. Someone was beating someone else's head against the wall. The whole barrack shook and my dog trembled. I felt cramped in my tiny cell-like room. Someone screamed, "I'll kill you, I'll kill you! Where's my knife!" Someone else was already wheezing, and I heard the blows of heavy male bodies against the shaky walls. My God, I thought fearfully, what will happen if they suddenly remember me now? I'm all alone, there's no one, no telephone . . . I took the dog into my bed and she stopped yelping and trembling. Turning on the light to dispel my fear, I sat on the edge of the bed, dressed in coat and hat, ready for any turn of events, pressing the puppy to me and passionately praying that they would not remember me. Finally the police came, took away those who had been stabbed as well as some others, and quiet reigned.

In the morning I appeared at the police station. "Solve my housing problem, I can't live like this. What will happen if they remember me in the heat of a fight? Move me immediately into normal conditions or I'll run away."

"Go to work, we'll decide, and for leaving work without permission you'll get a reprimand."

Although the men's fights subsided for a while, my life was endangered in another way. One day I could not understand what was happening to me. My throat and stomach were burning. I drank and drank but couldn't extinguish the fire. I barely managed to make it to the end of the workday, but sick or not, I had to take my puppy for a walk. Locked in the room, she either quietly whimpered or stormily protested, scratching the door with her paws.

Every bone in my body hurt; every hair on my body stood on end; and I was shivering with a light chill. I did not understand, however, why my throat was so terribly dry that water would not quench my thirst and why I had such chills while my temperature was normal. Having walked the dog with great difficulty, I returned to my room and lay down in bed but it did not warm me. Even piling on all my warm clothing did not stop the chills and at times I dozed or fell unconscious.

Very late at night, when the dormitory was quiet, it suddenly struck me—I had probably been poisoned. I had observed men doing it to the rats in the dormitory only a few weeks earlier—and now someone had done it to me!

In late fall the dormitory had been invaded by enormous three-colored rats the size of cats. They acted like they owned the place, strolling around in groups or alone. I was deathly afraid of them and was paralyzed when a band of these creatures came toward me in the hall. No knocking, stamping or shrieking would deter them. Gathering around the wash basin in the morning, the men would relay to each other how the rats ran across them during the night. Imagining them running across me at night, I panicked; I was unable to sleep because as soon as I closed my eyes, I felt them. In horror I would jump out of bed and shake all my things but there wouldn't be anything there. I turned off the light but the awful feeling of these vile creatures running across me would come back to me. It became impossible for me to turn off the light. I was going crazy, hallucinating; there were no rats in my room. If there had been, the dog would have sensed it and looked for them. I tried to convince myself but logic did not work. My inflamed brain could concentrate only on one thing—I heard them rustling under the floor of my room and running back and forth on the road; I heard the squeak of their young. This continued for several days. Kafka, Kafka, where are you? I moaned. Your unlimited fantasy could rival my reality. I could not read nor write nor even think. No matter where I went—to the taiga, the office, on the road or near the private houses—I was haunted by hordes of rats.

I left work and went to the chief doctor of the small clinic in the village. He listened but said that he did not deal with rats and I had to go the the public health station. "Yes," they told me there, "you're at the right place, but you have to sign a contract with us, pay and then they will come and get rid of the rats." I took a blank for the contract but the chief bookkeeper of the land reclamation project said that there was no money for battling the rats. "The dormitory has existed for many years and no one ever complained. There's no money for such nonsense. Get used to living with these creatures!"

I then went on to the director of the project and said, "You settled me in a zoo. Rats are running around everywhere day and night. I arranged everything and here is a form for extermination but your bookkeeper refuses to pay the fee."

"Fine, he'll do it," he agreed. "No one should live in a zoo."

Thus the war began against those rats. Their fur on end and their bodies shuddering, they staggered around the dormitory shaking from illness. The corpses piled up all around. Finally, as if mourning their brethren, the ones who survived left the dormitory at night, quietly whining. In the morning the men told me, "We've been living this way for years; the rats ran on our beds day and night and no one cared. No one treats us like people. It's only because of you that they exterminated the rats."

I recalled all this when I was lying in bed, shivering with uncontrollable chills: someone had put poison in my drinking glass. I reconstructed a picture of the previous day in its entirety, minute by minute, and realized how the crime had been committed although I could not prove it definitively. I had to call Zhenya in Moscow, but it was three miles to the telegraph office and I did not have the strength to go that far. If I woke someone up and asked him to summon a doctor, they would probably do a blood analysis, and if they found any poison, they would definitely hide me away in a psychiatric hospital. From there I would never be able to prove that I had in fact been poisoned and had not tried to kill myself and changed my mind at the last moment. No, I could not turn to a doctor. I had to drink and drink; that was all I could do to help myself.

Suddenly remembering that there was a guard and telephone in the boiler house, I somehow made it, staggering the three hundred feet to the building, but the telephone operator refused to let me use the phone because I had not paid for an intercity call in advance. I spent the rest of the night waking and falling into oblivion. Probably understanding that I was fighting a battle against death, my dear and cheerful puppy lay ever so quietly, stretching her lean body along my bed without causing any problems or distracting me from my struggle for life. By the morning I felt a little better and the agonizing chills had gone. Although I realized that I would live, nevertheless I wrote a final testament—"In case I die, bury me in Jerusalem"—and brought a copy to the police station. In addition, I asked an exile from the Caucasus, who chauffered between cities, to post a letter for me to the address of Evgeni Tsirlin in Moscow. By having him mail the letter from a different location, I hoped to keep it away from the chekists' eyes. Via the office manager I was summoned to appear immediately at the police station. I knew that I could not prove anything to the police, for they would take it as the delirium of an ill mind. No logical explanations would convince them.

"How am I supposed to understand your testament, Ida Yakovlevna? Is this a warning that you are planning to commit suicide?"

"Oh no," I said, "I won't give the KGB a gift like that; don't expect it."

"Then what's the matter? Is someone threatening your life?"

I couldn't go on and all at once the tears came flowing down my cheeks. I got up and called back, "I'm sorry, but I can't," and I hurriedly left. At the door I bumped into two little boys who sometimes played with my dog but I continued on my way.

What a senseless, humiliating existence—a war with rats on four and on two feet. Life was rushing by and I had to listen to the drunken shouts and curses of my neighbors in the barrack and to hear the insulting remarks of the primitive colleagues at work. I couldn't bear it any longer! The office will survive without me, I decided, and I turned toward the taiga. It was close to noon on a day without any rain. The forest had been washed by the fall showers and the trees were beginning to shed their leaves. The dead leaves rustled monotonously and soothingly under my feet. I went even deeper into the taiga, knowing that the woods would comfort and calm me, renewing my strength and patience to follow my difficult route just so long as I did not lose my direction.

When I finally returned to the colony at the end of the working day, I was told, "The police were looking for you, phone them immediately."

"Ida Yakovlevna, where were you for so long?" the policeman asked.

"I'm not obligated to give you an accounting within the borders of the village," I replied.

"We were afraid that you had gone away. The police chief is personally responsible for you."

The two little boys I had run into at the police station were waiting for me near the dormitory. They told me that the police had summoned them to an interrogation. "Ida Yakovlenva, we saw that you were crying. Did they hit you?"

"Oh, no, boys, they didn't touch me." I was moved to tears by their sincere concern.

In the evening a woman who had once invited me to wash in the bathhouse knocked. "Yakovlevna, you were crying in the police station, did they hit you? The boys ran over and said that they probably beat you."

Until then I had not known that some people in the colony had indeed accepted me as one of its citizens.

Nature, however, celebrated my first winter in Siberia with unusual severity. Temperatures reached sixty degrees below zero on the Fahrenheit scale—a rarity even for native Siberians. Such winters used to be more frequent about forty years ago, but in recent decades the climate has warmed up somewhat. I took the harshness of the winter as a personal message. You, Ida Nudel, ought to know that that's what Siberia is like. In the barrack it was freezing cold. When the temperature outside was at minus forty, it was from forty-five to fifty degrees inside the building and on the days when it was minus sixty outside, it was only forty to forty-five degrees inside while the wind blew in through all the cracks. On those cold nights the dog seemed to be searching for something, restlessly moving from place to place, dragging her bedding with her. Finally, I realized that she was looking for a warmer spot and commanded, "Up," pointing to my bed. She obeyed like lightning and fell asleep. I was envious of her luxurious fur. I was so cold that even when I lay down fully dressed, under my coat and all my blankets, I was able to sleep only for brief moments when sheer exhaustion conquered the cold.

Life itself froze at that time. It was almost impossible to breathe outside when the temperature reached sixty below; children did not go to school and the adults did not work. People stoked their stoves incessantly; even the poorest of them did not save wood on such days. The most important thing was to retain the heat, which meant survival. If you were conserving wood and letting your hut freeze, it would be almost impossible to warm it again in such severe weather. The air was completely still and the little homes, snowed in up to their windows, seemed to be sketched on a white canvas.

The air was full of frosty powder in the form of the most minute, prickly crystals, making it impenetrable. The trees, which were completely covered by this fine powder, seemed like white giants through the snowy fog. It was impossible to distinguish objects at a distance of more than forty feet. And what a smell! It was an indescribable mixture of smoke from burning firewood, saturated with pure snow and the delicate aroma of vital, resinous trees. Immobile and heavy, the air pressed this smell to the earth.

The dog still had to take care of her needs, even if it was sixty below and she was freezing. She would run up to me, stick out her freezing paws and I would rub them, then we would race each other back to the dormitory. I would be wrapped from head to toe in every article of my scant wardrobe, with a small opening just for my eyes, but even that didn't help, and my face, especially the nose and cheeks, would sting for a long time.

The severe cold created an atmosphere of mystery and if my body had been able to stand it, I would not have returned home. My mood became joyful and excited by the enchanting surroundings; even to this day I can remember that astounding sensation of being in touch with the surreal reality.

When winter's savage celebration had continued for over a week, people became tired of remaining locked inside and the children would begin to dash outdoors. When the temperature reached forty below, it seemed as if it were already warm outside.

The cold weather was hardest on those who lived in the barrack. The heating pipes cracked and the water pipes froze; everyone had to melt snow in order to get water, and the temperature inside fell to almost zero. While I was being transported in the prison car from Moscow to Siberia, my imagination had sketched pictures of the future, but never such as I actually encountered.

Living in isolation, with no companionship, I had planned to keep busy by writing, reading and studying languages, but in fact I had very little time for such activities; all my time and physical and mental energy were devoted to the most primitive problems of feeding, warming and defending myself—in other words, sheer survival.

My only companion and comfort was my dog, whose eyes radiated warmth and care. She understood everything I said to her and every shift of my moods. As I lay under all the blankets, I sometimes pictured the life of those who had preferred not to risk their well-being and comfort and asked myself the agonizing question: who was right—they or I?

Evgeni Tsirlin arrived again with two enormous knapsacks bursting with food, books, letters, gifts and greetings from many people, including my sister, Lena. When he unpacked this wonderful treasure, my nerves gave out and I broke down crying. Until then, I had always prided myself on being an independent being who did not take orders from anyone and resolved her own problems, but in looking at what Tsirlin had brought, I suddenly realized that my independence had actually disappeared. It is difficult to describe my conflicting feelings. On the one hand, I knew full well that I could not meet all my needs and I welcomed the wonderful things and the warm feelings they represented. On the other hand, I wanted to be sure that I was doing what I could on my own, remaining as independent as possible in the new situation. But I was so excited by the treasures in the knapsacks and so delighted to see Tsirlin that I talked without stopping. Fortunately Evgeni was the silent type or else I would not have succeeded in spilling out everything that I had kept inside during those months of forced silence.

Evgeni had mentioned in passing that he would like to practice using the new Japanese movie camera that he had brought with him. At first I had not paid much attention to this, but the next day at work, thinking about our conversation of the previous day, I remembered what he had said about the camera. If he wanted to practice, what could be better than photographing the village and making a film about my everyday life? Let the world see how political exiles live in the Soviet Union; after all, my living conditions were no different from those of many others who had entered into a "dialogue" with the penal system of a developed socialist society.

"Zhenya, I have a marvelous idea," I told him when I returned from work. "Let's make a film; we have three days until you leave Monday morning. Even if this room is bugged, they won't be able to find you. When they realize that you've left and decide what to do, you'll be in Tomsk. You can get on the train in any direction and let them find you in the vast expanses of Siberia."

Zhenya had no objections and we began to work. I wrote the text, listed the scenes and worked on my monologues and Zhenya translated them into English. On Saturday, while there were still people in the dormitory, we filmed inside the room without anyone suspecting us. We left the more difficult task of outdoor filming for Sunday, when the men usually ran off to their women friends.

Our outdoor filming did not take more than ten minutes, but during that time Zhenya's cheeks almost froze and we had to drink some wine to warm up. I felt confident that no one had seen us because the windows in the huts were all frosted up. No one other than Tsirlin and I was brave enough to walk around outside, but we had a good reason for taking the risk.

We decided that once Zhenya was on the road he would send a telegram with a pre-arranged message. I received the message from the Siberian town of Omsk in two days and felt more relaxed; he had gotten away with the film. The next stage, getting it abroad, was also dangerous, because it could either get lost or fall into KGB hands. We were lucky, however, and in a month and a half I found out that the film had reached London safely and had been shown for the first time in a large church; afterward, copies were shown in various places.

As a result of the film I began to receive an enormous amount of letters, arriving first by the dozens, then by the hundreds, then by the thousands; I drowned in them. My correspondents would begin their letters with the words, "Ida, your suffering is not in vain!" They were responding to my filmed appeal to the viewer: "If our suffering does not arouse each of you to come to our help, then all this is in vain."

"Ida, we love you," wrote a boy from America, hesitantly tracing the Russian letters, and I was touched to the point of tears. "Ida, we think of you often and protest against the behavior of

Soviet authorities. Don't lose hope, we are with you," related messages signed with dozens of signatures from Italy. "May God protect you and lead you to Israel. Believe and pray," wrote someone from Germany. I believed and I hoped, and at the same time I didn't believe and I asked myself—isn't my life as sacred as the lives of those whom I defended? It is, I told myself. But it was the only way I could live in peace with myself.

The colony's only telephone was by the guard in the boiler house. In the summer months when the boiler house was closed, we had no phone link with the outside world. The workers had a simple explanation—we were not people and not worth listening to. I did not consider myself in such a category and decided to tell the authorities what I thought about a situation in which almost two hundred people lived completely cut off from the police, doctors and fire department. The director of the land reclamation project listened calmly to my arguments and promised to think it over. He then switched to personal matters, relating that the KGB was spreading the story among the villagers that I had lived in Israel, asked to return to the Soviet Union and then had reconsidered and begun to organize demonstrations. According to this story, they had exiled me because I had insulted the Soviet regime.

The director was interested in it all and began to ask me about Andrei Dmitrievich Sakharov and the democratic movement, which he knew about only from reports at party conferences. He perceived all dissidents as spies and enemies. Belonging to the younger generation of leaders who had sprung from the ranks of the Komsomol, the communist youth organization, he considered himself abused by the communist party because it had not allowed him to rise higher and instead had sent party leaders from the regional center to run the village. With almost no prospects of escaping the situation, he hated the back-breaking village life. A man had to grow almost all his food by himself because it was much cheaper, and there was a very limited number of items for sale. The nearest city was almost one hundred twenty-five miles away; in spring and fall the roads were all out and there was no bridge across the River Ob. After work people had to feed the pigs, poultry and cattle, clean up after them, drag water from the well for themselves and the animals. People wore themselves out, using the short Siberian summer to grow vegetables and potatoes for their own consumption, pitch hay for the animals and gather wood for the stove. In the fall people set out for the taiga and gathered nuts and mushrooms for the winter, when there was hunting as an addition to the daily routine and diet. Then in the movie theater the Siberians saw how gloriously people live in the city, doing nothing and buying everything in the store. By the end of the day a person would fall off his feet and rebel by drinking himself into a drunken stupor— party and nonparty members and the simplest workman alike.

The land reclamation director agreed to grant my request and a telephone was installed in the barrack. Although none of the men ever expected a call, nevertheless they rejoiced because the telephone was a sort of symbol that they, too, were people. Treating my calls from friends as a sensation, they would begin to call excitedly, "Moscow, Moscow, hurry, Ida!" and several men would rush to report the news to me at once. No matter how primitive they were, they also suffered severely from emotional starvation. Everything that fell outside of the framework of the ordinary would excite them like children. Something was always happening with me, and they began to sympathize with me in their way. Whereas before they had crudely attacked me, considering me an easy prey, now they acted "politely." One of them knocked once on my door asking, "Ida, may I come in, I would like to borrow some salt from you." How could I refuse him, I thought, even though I worried that it was not a matter of salt at all. He came in, sat on the chair and I started to hand him the salt shaker. Then with one quick movement he grabbed me by the shoulders and pushed me down onto the bed. I started to holler and with the dog barking he muttered, "Excuse me," and left at once.

Such incidents happened again and again. After a while I refused to open the door to them and neither pleas for salt nor matches helped. I hated the men's drunken singing and vicious drunken brawls. The songs they sang were the same in prison and at liberty.

One night in the spring of 1979 I heard men shouting in the hall, "Ida, quick, the phone." I picked up the receiver and heard an unfamiliar voice say, "Ida, this is Vulf Zalmanson. We're free, they freed us today, the four of us are here. You'll speak with everyone now. We're free! Now it's your turn." The receiver passed from one to the other. Anatoly Altman, Aryeh Chanoch, and

Hillel Butman were all excited and each tried to cheer me up in his own way. I was so floored by surprise and joy at the release of the Leningrand hijacking group I couldn't say anything. I was happy for them and myself and I was proud of my victory. I had invested a considerable amount of effort in the struggle for their liberation. I had written them hundreds of letters, trying to keep up their spirits; with my own hands I had dragged hundreds of pounds of food for packages; I had written numerous complaints to Soviet official organizations, and had spent interminable hours hanging around Gulag offices, the Presidium of the Supreme Soviet, offices of procurators and lawyers and the waiting room of the Central Committee of the CPSU. I had exhausted myself with agonizing sparring matches over the phone with Albert Ivanov, the representative of the Central Committee. How many sleepless nights had I spent planning my moves to attract world attention to their plight and on how many occasions had I risked my own freedom by describing their situation to foreign correspondents, politicians and public figures in full sight of the KGB? It did not matter whether others knew or not; I knew that I personally had played a role in their release.

Now they were free and I was occupying the discomforting space they had just vacated. I sat alone in the tiny room of a male barrack in a remote, deserted Siberian village, a single, middle-aged, educated woman who had suddenly and unexpectedly fallen in with the dregs of society, and I sought the inner strength to withstand it all. As if detached from myself, I pictured myself sitting on the edge of the metal bed with its mattress and pillow stained by the blood of murdered men, my feet encased in enormous felt boots and a warm scarf around my shoulders. It was spring but it was still cold in the drafty barrack, particularly after sitting and writing for hours on end. Yes, I did feel sorry for myself, but I had gone through this many times.

The first time had been at the end of 1972 when a large group of about forty refusenik families had been summoned to the Moscow OVIR but probably five times that amount actually showed up. It was announced that those who had been summoned would receive exit visas. It was impossible to breathe or move in the waiting room crowded with the happy ones who would receive visas and the unhappy ones who stubbornly refused to leave the office although they knew it was not their lucky day.

I had also been in that room at that moment and had shivered from the tension and excitement. I had asked myself what I was doing there; I had not been summoned. Why was I making my heart sink when the official pronounced a name? Was something wrong with me—this was pure masochism. Go home, I said to myself, go about your business and when you don't have any, read a book. At home, having shaken off the hypnotic effect of the crowd, I pledged to myself that my next visit to OVIR would be only for a visa.

While sitting on the edge of my bed engrossed in these memories, I suddenly looked up and saw an enormous fiery ring on the wall. At first I enjoyed the sight—the flaming circle with its sparkling gleam was a physical expression of the feelings churning inside me. What striking symbolism, flashed through my mind! These men who broke through the wall of silence of Soviet Jewry; passed through the fiery circle of the prison camps to attain their freedom.

Suddenly I realized the danger of what was happening on the wall. I jumped up and stretched my hand out to the ring. I had simply no recollection of plugging the electric immersion coil into the outlet while forgetting to put the other end into the teapot.

The next day I received a telegram from the freed Zalmansons telling me of their release. It had lain in the censor's office for thirty-two hours.

April 1979

Shalom Dear Ida,

Excuse me for writing so informally, but I can't help it. I feel as if I know you because you are dear to every Jew who loves his people.

Ida, I'm not sure that refusing to receive your mail is a correct or expedient form of protest. You, more than any other refusenik, enjoy the attention of Jewish and international society. In particular, various women's organizations and several outstanding women have taken up your cause.

We are very worried about your health. I'm sure that it will improve when you come to Israel. But even now, when you are living in such difficult circumstances in a distant alien country, the knowledge that you are not alone and are beloved by your people must give you sustenance and the strength to wait and struggle.

I shall be happy to send you material about our country. As someone who came from the USSR myself, I understand very well how much you need this.

Of course, write me if you need any help. I shall be happy to do anything I can for you.

Best wishes until we meet
Yours, Talmon Pachevsky*

---

*Talmon immigrated to Israel from the USSR in 1973 and settled in Beersheva with his family. He did everything he could to help Soviet Jews immigrate to Israel. He died in 1986.

CHAPTER 20

EVERY SATURDAY I USED TO WALK THREE MILES ON THE DIRT road from the colony to the village post office. As I stumbled through the mud, trying to stick to the tire tracks left by heavy trucks, no one ever stopped to give me a lift; indeed, it seemed as if the drivers intentionally speeded up as they passed me by, splattering me with clumps of dirt and mud.

At the post office I would receive hundreds of letters weekly. I was worried I would seem ungrateful but how could I answer thousands of letters and what could I say—that everything was fine and there was nothing to worry about? I found the answer in a form which I had adopted even before my exile—the open letter in which I addressed all my concerned correspondents.

Curious villagers would come to look at the thick bundles of letters tied together with string, and the children would note each foreign stamp with shining eyes. Naturally, the KGB took measures to avoid this and as soon as I entered the post office, the building would empty as if by the wave of a magic wand. I then collected a large number of the foreign stamps, put them into several envelopes and offered them to the children at school. They accepted my gift with gratitude and great curiosity and immediately proceeded to look over the stamps and ask me what countries they were from. I suggested they bring an atlas and I would show them. I promised to bring them more stamps and invited them to visit me. Our friendly talk was interrupted when the teacher ran out and dispersed them.

The next day I was summoned to the police station and the chief threatened me with a new term for anti-Soviet agitation among children. "You are forbidden to distribute foreign stamps to the children, to meet with them or talk with them."

"Do you really think that innocent foreign stamps can make your children anti-Soviet?"

Although his answer was the usual threats, the police chief did not summon me again after this conversation. Some of the local inhabitants, however, began to greet me, in a halfhearted, not very friendly way, but nevertheless they accepted me as an existing fact.

My dog was the one who really broke down the KGB-inspired hostility, as well as the fear of me. It was an indescribable pleasure for me and others to watch Pizer's elegant motions as she ran or jumped, and to see how she played with other dogs and children. I taught her to play with a ball and brought her to the schoolyard. The children surrounded her in a noisy throng but were not her equals in the game and no one could get the ball from her. She was remarkably clever; she understood how to play with a soccer ball, and became a marvelous goalie, playing offense and defense simultaneously. The children, who had never seen such a dog before, were delighted. In the morning as I went to work, I would meet the smiling, grateful glances of their mothers.

I succeeded in moving out of the dormitory in the summer of 1979 thanks to the help of Yakov Rakhlenko, Evgeni Tsirlin and Boris Chernobylsky. They arrived at the village to earn some money over the summer and I asked them to look for a hut for sale. They succeeded admirably and with my savings and money collected from friends—Semyen Gluzman, in particular, sent me a considerable amount—I bought (with the permission of the police and despite Soviet legislation) a small log peasant hut consisting of a large bright room with a stove in the middle. It also had an enclosed front porch, a covered courtyard for wood or livestock and a large plot of land which I eagerly decided to cultivate. The most difficult thing was dragging water from the well, and in the frustrating moments when I slipped and slid carrying the water buckets, I wondered whether there really was any meaning to my life. But when I would pick up my packs of mail, my doubts would ease and I felt my tears were not in vain.

At first I continued to walk back to the colony for my work at the office, but it was too difficult to bear their repeated scornful remarks. They would say, "You're a criminal and ought to be performing heavy labor; it's insulting for us to breathe the same air as you." My petty revenge was to tell them about the Moscow society in which I had lived. Eventually I found a job in the village as a night watchman for the trucks of the road repair department.

It was already getting dark one winter day in 1980 when someone knocked on my door. I had a million things to do before my night guard duty and receiving unexpected guests was not part of my plans. I therefore was not too pleased to see a woman standing at my door.

"May I come in?" she asked.

I had never seen her in the village and the thought crossed my mind that she was from the KGB. While I was thinking, she entered the room.

"You came in without my permission. Who are you and what do you want from me?"

"I would like to speak to you," she said.

"I don't have any time; in a few hours I have to go to work, the stove isn't stoked and I have to sleep a little."

"It won't take long, just a few minutes; I'll just ask a few questions."

"Are you from the KGB?" I asked.

"No, I'm not from the KGB; I'm a journalist."

"They have already slandered me enough in the Soviet press and I have no desire to talk with a journalist. You'll distort all my words." She entered the room and sat at the table. "Please leave, you entered without permission," I insisted.

"I won't bother you, I'll help you stoke the stove, I know how," she persisted.

"Get out of my house, I don't want to speak to you," I repeated.

"I traveled so far; just answer two questions and I'll go. Why did you decide to leave the Soviet Union?"

She was annoying me with her arrogant stubbornness. "Your anti-Semitism sticks in my throat."

"There is no anti-Semitism in the country. I have many Jewish friends and none of them want to leave."

"They don't tell you the truth because they're afraid of you.

I'm finished with questions; get out of the house or I will be forced to leave myself."

If I would leave, however, she would rummage through my papers and letters, steal something and then use it as evidence, saying I had given it to her. How could I get her out of the house?

"Go; I can't prepare for my night guard duty."

"One more question," she said. "In an Israeli paper it was written that they treat you badly here. I spoke to people in the party district committee and the police and they told me that you were given work and housing and no one bothers you."

At that moment I surrendered. I told her about the tragic fate of my people, the millions burned in the crematoria, the tragedy of my own family where five children from the age of two weeks to eleven years and four adults had been killed in a portable gas chamber on the road from Simferopol to the dump and that their ashes still burned in my heart. I told about the suffering of the 1950's, when the stage had been set for genocide by accusations of espionage and treason. I recalled the meeting at my institute, where my classmates had said to my face, "Hitler didn't finish the job; all the Jews ought to have been annihilated," how my friends' betrayal opened my eyes to see and realize who I was and how those around me perceived me. I said that perhaps she shared this view and therefore I expected a base article. I also told her about my life in the male dormitory and how unbearable it was to live among perpetually drunk, rough men who demanded that I sleep with them and how much anguish it caused me. As a woman of intellect she understood my suffering and tears welled in her eyes. And when I confessed about how I had suffered from poisoning, her body trembled in horror as she imagined herself in my place.

I gave her tea to drink and then took her to the hotel because it was dark outside and she could have gotten lost easily in the unfamiliar location. She said she would not write anything.

Despite her promise, the journalist wrote a vicious, untrue article about me, which appeared in the Tomsk regional paper. In it she asked, "Why have her foreign protectors elevated her?" And she answered for herself, "It's to their advantage to have the martyr's halo shine over her forehead in order to falsify the Jewish question in the Soviet Union." They created the Jewish problem through "provocation and lies," she contended. "The film which her hirelings sent abroad told about Nudel's 'unbearable' living conditions but the scenes were falsely contrived. Vestiges of shame prevent her from saying to those around her what she conveys for use abroad. Her guardians from Tel Aviv do not toss away money for nothing. Ida has to pay with the shreds of her conscience and dirty fabrications. The writers from Tel Aviv will not succeed in defaming the great rights and freedom of the Soviet citizen nor demean his spiritual potential."

Of course I could not publish a reply in the Soviet Union but my answering letter was published in the Jewish press around the world. I wrote, "It wasn't difficult to 'cultivate' a martyr, even one with an international reputation—you just had to beat him often and painfully enough so that his cries were carried to all ends of the earth and you had a ready-made martyr available as the reward in exchange for goods, instruments, lower tariffs, most-favored nation status or as a way of wreaking revenge for intractability." As an example I pointed out that a week after the Soviet regime failed to receive the most-favored nation status from the U.S. government, the KGB began arresting activists in both the dissident and Jewish movements and intensified the harshness of prisoners' conditions in political camps, a clear sign of disappointment and desire for revenge.

As for the claim that "vestiges of shame" prevented me from saying the same thing to my neighbors that I sent abroad, I stated, "No, they are wrong, I am not ashamed of one word of mine. And those daring people in the village who ask me questions receive a frank story about my past, present and projected future. I'm not sure they always understand me but I do know that they don't doubt the sincerity of my words."

Although the days after the publication of the article were hard for me, I went around with my head proudly held high. The inhabitants of the village crowded around the stores, which displayed copies of the issue with the article. The people on the street I was living on demanded that I be expelled from the village because they were afraid I would poison their wells, ruin their livestock or generally bring bad luck to the village. As local patriots they were deeply insulted that such a criminal had been put in their midst.

On one of those crazy days, when I was walking through a glade that divided the village into two parts, a group of men caught up with me somewhere in the middle so that I had to walk in front of them for some time. When I heard the voices approaching and glanced back over my shoulder, my heart fluttered at the thought of crossing the woods with them. The distance between us soon diminished and my mind kept on weighing the possibilities—I could let them pass and be freed of a danger from behind, but if I stopped to let them go ahead, they would know I did not trust them and was expecting the worst. If I was expecting the worst it meant I acknowledged my guilt. How tired I was of living under such tension, like an animal in a trap! I kept ordering myself forward but it was hard to obey my own commands. At the same time I tried to assess whether their voices were hostile or not. It seemed to me I was doing the right thing, walking in my usual brisk manner, but would they throw stones at me or not? They neither approached nor fell behind. As I realized later, after turning into the gates of my house, they also were weighing the situation.

The next day I went to the police chief to ask for assurances that measures would be taken for my safety, but he did not give me any. "Don't go out of the house, don't go alone," was his only advice.

I decided to do what I used to do when one of my "clients" got into trouble—publicize the matter. I ordered a phone conversation with Moscow and spoke to my friend Lev Blitshtein, my new proxy because Tsirlin had left for Israel, and we coordinated our actions. I prepared a packet of telegrams which I mailed to him, insuring it for two hundred rubles to guarantee its delivery. Blitshtein then sent them on to the West. Our swift action caught the chekists by surprise.

As soon as information about my situation reached the West, more and more people began to get involved and express their concern. Whereas Lena's requests for a phone conversation with me were usually thwarted by their telling her, "The respondent did not show up at the post office for the call," this time her request got through to me.

"Tell me, how is the local population acting after the article?" Lena asked.

"I went to the police chief," I told her, "and demanded that he take preventive measures and declare that no one has the right to apply a lynch law to me. We spoke for a very long time and he let me understand that he also viewed the situation quite seriously and he realized that he would have to answer for me personally.

"He did not say so directly, but I understood that he would do as I requested. I want the police to do only one thing now— to explain to the villagers that no one has the right to interfere."

"All your friends know what happened and they have confidence in you. We receive so many letters that they don't all fit into our mailbox," Lena told me.

"Tell my friends that I am grateful to all of them."

"The most important thing now is for you to look after yourself. You have already served half of your term; do you have a legal basis to ask for your release?"

"Never in my life will I do this. They lied to me and insulted me. What should I ask them for?"

"Okay. Do you need anything?"

"Don't even think about it; my friends bring things to me. They are very considerate and caring and I have food and warm clothing and wood."

"Be strong, Ida. We're all with you."

Perhaps it was a crazy idea but the next day I decided to walk through the village. Let them get accustomed to the idea that I live here and nothing has changed. As I walked, I was accompanied by hate-filled stares and whispers. The weather was simply marvelous—not too cold with a bright sun. Life is so beautiful but so strange! Man, that miracle of nature, is so weak and so strong. His life on earth is so short and these years of life go by so insanely. Every day there's a war and someone kills somebody else, and even without all that, life is but a moment. What does the Soviet regime want from me and what do they want in exchange for me? A bag of potatoes? And for this they are tormenting me and my sister, my family, my people?

"Ida," I suddenly heard someone driving a wagon call, "get in, I'll take you."

Engrossed in my painful thoughts, I did not understand who this man was and what he really wanted. I was so tensed up in expectation of a blow or a scandal that at first I was unable to comprehend a sudden friendly word.

"Ida," he yelled out so the whole street could hear, "don't you hear me, get in, I'll take you." I had been living in that village for two years and no one had ever given me a lift, even on the muddiest days; perhaps it was a provocation. I silently approached the horse-drawn wagon.

"Sit down, Yakovlevna, I'll take you. After all, we're neighbors." To tell the truth it was the first time I had seen him; if we were neighbors, then we were not close ones.

"You're not afraid to talk with me?" I asked him directly.

"What should I be afraid of, what can they take away from me? I'm a simple stoker, working twenty-five years, a union member, I pay my dues on time, what else do I have?" He helped me climb into the wagon, which was used to transport coal. "Don't be afraid, Yakovlevna," he told me. "Be what may, I don't believe all this prattle. Of course the women are afraid, but I don't fear you."

"Thank you for the kind word," I said. "Stop the horse, we're already here."

Although I refrained from going into the taiga during the first week after the newspaper article, it was unnerving just to sit home so I decided to walk along the streets on the edge of the village. I ran into an older man who was slightly tipsy but spoke clearly, "Yakovlevna, I want to tell you something."

"Go ahead."

"Why do you act that way? After all, you're an intelligent woman, you graduated from an institute."

"What don't you like about my behavior?"

"Did you read what they wrote about you in the paper?"

"Yes, and it's a lie. You, too, know that what's written there about the village and the dormitory is not true. Who doesn't know that there are brawls and murders there?"

"You're right, I can't argue with you, but why do they write about you?"

"Tell me, were you in the war?"

"Yes, I was."

"Did you take part in an attack?"

"Yes."

"Did you see the people who were getting fired upon?"

"Yes, Yakovlevna, I saw them."

"Well, that's what's happening to me. It's a war for the dignity of my people. You know that I'm a Jew, don't you?"

"Give me your hand, please, Yakovlevna."

He gave me his hand and shook mine, then he silently went away.

I did not want to accept the isolation and silence of my life in Siberia or the possibility that henceforth I would be occupied only with the struggle for my physical survival. Although I could keep myself busy on my own, I missed contact with people.

In those years Pizer was my chief companion. I often invited the children to walk with us in the taiga but none of them went along with me more than once. The adults did not trust me and the KGB spread all kinds of rumors, threatening the residents with punishments for associating with or helping me. They always depicted me as a paid agent of a hostile power, who could soon expect the just retribution from society. I tried to act naturally as if I were not an exile, a political or an enemy. I did just what the local women did—I carried water from the well, stoked the oven, washed my clothing in the sink and dried it for weeks in the yard since the humidity was usually high.

It was a real spectacle for the local residents to see me carry water from the well. Most people transported water in large lead tanks on carts which in winter were mounted on runners and the rest of the time on wheels, but I didn't have the strength to move such a cart. The whole village was quietly amused when I learned to carry water on a yoke. I filled two buckets of water, suspecting that I could not lift such a weight although local women carried three buckets at one time, two on the yoke and another in the hand. I couldn't even lift the two buckets off the ground, never mind get them on my shoulders. People silently watched my battle with the buckets. I poured out a lot of water from each and lifted them onto my shoulders.

"Why are you so bent over?" asked some man. "Straighten up your back."

I obediently followed his suggestion, but the yoke slid off my shoulder. "I straightened up too early, I'll have to get used to it," I said.

"You'll get used to it; no one will bring you water." I already knew that even for money no one would help me. In the end I got used to dragging the water by hand in one half-filled bucket, stopping every few steps in order to calm my irregular heartbeat. This, too, became part of my sentence.

Learning the art of stoking the stove was almost as painful. The danger lay in the carbon monoxide, which is released when the fuel, either coal or wood, burns. If the chimney flue is closed too late, the heat escapes into the air and an enormous amount of valuable warmth inside the stove is lost. On the other hand, if the chimney flue is closed too early, before the last coal has burned out and while combustion is still taking place, then dying from carbon monoxide poisoning is a definite risk, and even experienced Siberian families sometimes perish, whether from greed or inattention or drunkenness. I simply did not know how to stoke the stove and, overcoming my embarrassment, I knocked on the door of a house and asked the woman what to do.

"You never stoked a stove?" she asked in astonishment.

"No, but I have a head on my shoulders, I'll learn," I assured her.

"You'll study and you'll learn, but make sure you don't choke yourself to death while you're learning."

I did poison myself many times. Once I woke up in the middle of the night from an awful headache and nausea. I didn't understand what was happening but I was aware of only one thing—that I had to get quickly to the bucket so as not to soil the bed. I don't remember how I made it to the door, I found myself on the floor alongside the half-open door. There were many such ordeals which were not written in my court sentence. The sentence is merely a formula; the essence of the punishment is revealed at the spot where it is carried out.

There were three ways of leaving the boundaries of the village—by bus along the well-traveled road leading to the north or south; by steamship or hydrofoil up and down the Ob; or through the endless expanse of forest and swamps of the taiga in any direction the eye could see. I personally was prohibited from going to the bus station or to the landing dock.

The river, which was several miles away, tempted me; I was bored with the taiga. Like an old horse I walked on familiar paths, fearing to venture into the thick depths. The river became somewhat of an obsession—I wanted to look at something new, at the ships passing by, and at free people swimming according to their heart's desire. Unable to resist any longer, one Sunday I went toward the river, the dog running along with me, enjoying the new places. I did not make it, however, because I was overtaken by a truck from which a policeman jumped out, blocked my way and said, "Where are you going? You are not allowed to approach the river. Turn back."

But I was more fortunate than many other exiles because as soon as the transition between seasons ended and a reliable way was cleared—whether on the frozen river in the winter or the river freed of ice in the spring—guests came to visit me. They stimulated not only me but also the people of the village, who were always glad to see new faces. They usually came a few at a time—bearded Jews, shaven Jews, but very rarely women because the road was difficult and the KGB reaction unpredictable. Each visitor brought food and books. The police tried to supervise everything but I refused to report who was coming and why.

After I acquired my hut, I decided to grow my own vegetables. I felt that by working in the kitchen garden like everyone else around me, I would gain the sympathy of my neighbors. I needed this badly not only in order to survive under those harsh conditions but also because I was the first dissident and first Jew exiled to this place and their attitude toward me would determine their attitude toward the dissident movement as a whole and the Jewish movement in particular. My first summer playing the role of a farmer was very hot with the temperature climbing to ninety-five degrees Fahrenheit almost half the month. My poor plants drooped and dried out. I tried again to learn how to carry water on the yoke but remained unsuccessful and had to continue carrying what I could by hand.

Despite the heat and problems with getting water, the land paid me back generously for my labor. The harvest was so enormous that I did not know what to do with the surplus vegetables. Although I offered them to the local hospital to feed the sick, the nurse in charge refused to take them from me. I then decided to send them to Andrei Sakharov, who was then living alone in Gorky, where he had been deported. I found out at the local post office that my package would arrive there in eight days. I carefully wrapped the vegetables and sent them off and twenty days later I received a telegram of thanks from Sakharov. I was so happy that Andrei Dmitrievich had enjoyed the fruits of my labor and that my greetings and sympathy had broken through his isolation.

In early spring, when the women began to buy day-old chicks, I decided that I would also try my hand at raising them. "Please help me pick the chicks," I asked a woman who looked kinder than the others.

"What do you need them for? You'll kill them; after all, you're from the city."

"I never raised them, but I'll read how it's done," I replied. "Please pick me twenty."

"It's a waste of your money and a pity on the chicks."

I insisted and she helped me pick twenty yellow cheeping little balls; she put them in a box and gave them to me with a laugh. "Bring them to me when you have second thoughts."

"Okay," I retorted, "but I won't, I'm stubborn."

From then on my guests and I became slaves to this farm of chickens, a dog and a vegetable garden into which I put my whole heart and the desperation of my stormy soul. I didn't have a moment's peace to read books and barely wrote letters. Returning at eight in the morning, tired and hungry from my nightly guard duty, I entered the chilly unheated hut, and unable to overcome the agonizing need for sleep, I would fall on the bed with my clothing on, ignoring the furious cheeping of my chicks.

The squeaking, hungry chicks had an ally in Pizer, who attacked me in support of their demands. "Go to hell," I cried to them, "I'm a human being, I also feel bad. I want to sleep." I would throw a dark rag on their box so that the chicks would think it was already night, walk my dog to the yard, fill up the stove with wood, light it and put myself in the hands of fate—whatever will be, will be; if there's no fire, that's my luck. I did not have the energy to wait another two to three hours until the stove was heated.

Sometimes I fell asleep sitting on the floor near the stove, which was the most dangerous thing to do. In two hours I would wake up wondering whether my hut was burning. Sniffing the air and realizing that I had been lucky, I would begin my working day. Usually by that time the stove had burned out and a large part of the warmth had flown out the chimney. I would throw on a little more wood and begin to stoke it again. Next in line were the chicks, giving them food and water and washing them. They often got sick but there was no place to get medicine and I had to fight their illnesses the way mothers treat their sick children when the doctor is not around. I gave each chick vitamins from a medicine dropper, cleaned each one and talked to them. Even so, I could not save them all and eight out of the twenty died, but so did some of the chicks the local women had raised.

For a month and a half my heart, soul and time were tied up with those chicks. Some women offered to relieve me of my torments, but I insisted, "No, I'll raise them myself, you'll see." They laughed, but did so kindly. The simple people got used to my being different from them and became more kindly disposed, although this does not at all mean that they invited me to their homes or gossiped with me in the street in full view of everyone else. No one dropped in on my house for a visit although several times people asked me for medicine for a headache; but this practice was quickly stopped as people were constantly reminded that I could never be trusted. Nevertheless, whether waiting my turn in line at the store, or near the water pump, or in the bathhouse, I exchanged a few words with the women who looked at me without any hatred.

As the chicks grew bigger and stronger, it became increasingly difficult to keep them in the box. One night I left the box open when I went out to my job and in the morning I could not understand what had happened: everything was topsy-turvy, including the bed on which I found them. My harried dog was running around the room, chasing the chicks, who dashed about, clearly not intimidated by her. I was rewarded in the evening, however, when the chicks settled down to sleep; what pleasant tales they cheeped to me. It was surprisingly interesting to listen to developments in the chicken box—each one wanted a cozy corner and the struggle for it was remarkably reminiscent of the human situation. While a chick was searching for a spot, he did not hesitate to walk over the heads and feet of his brethren, evoking their outraged protests. The whole fraternity changed places several times, reacting unanimously and stormily to the fidgeter. Finally the racket began to quiet down a little, a single but loud and insistent sound came forth, and instantly all were quiet, although that did not mean all were satisfied or even warm.

Then the chicks began to tell their tales or maybe their dreams, first one in a thin, timid voice as if fearful of hearing the bossy "shush" and then another. They argued, interrupting each other, and new ones kept joining in until the critical moment was reached when all were screeching, pushing and moving and the incident ended with an imperative demand for silence. Sometimes I would sit for a long time near the box, listening and imagining what they were arguing about. At such moments I did not at all regret the labor and time I had invested in them. When the chickens got bigger, I taught Pizer to protect them from hawks and to keep them from wandering out onto the street or into someone else's yard. My marvelous, intelligent dog performed the role of mother hen with great diligence. She let the chicks jump all over her and climb onto her head. The only thing she did not permit was pecking at her eyes; if a chick got brazen and reached her eyes, she would jump up, forcefully shake off all the brood and leave in a huff for another place. She did not, however, like solitude and would return, lie down near the chicks and the whole story would be repeated.

The village children enjoyed watching near the fence as the dog looked after the chicks. Sometimes adults would also stop and laugh, praising the dog. When one chick broke a claw, Pizer took on the role of therapist and seized the chick in her mouth and licked the painful wound. The chick with the broken claw developed into a plump hen, who hobbled diligently after the others.

The first frost occurred at the end of August and the last in mid June. Of course there were no paved thoroughfares in the village and only the road for the trucks was cleared. Each resident had to clean out his own path from his house. Most often people would melt down the path, foot by foot in the deep snow.

In the beginning of the winter I was given a warm but bulky sheepskin coat for my night watchman's job. When I walked through the village on my way to work wrapped in this enormous coat, I could not help but laugh when I imagined how I looked. It covered me from head to toe and from the side it might seem as if the coat was moving by itself.

When I went out to guard I held the dog's leash in one hand and a heavy bag with a radio in the other. Pizer was not yet trained to go without the leash; her unrestrained youth drove her constantly forward, but her natural curiosity forced her to stop and discover everything on the way. If she made an abrupt movement, I would lose my balance and fall into a snow drift, holding firmly on to the leash. If I could not step across the snow drifts, I would sit on it, throw my feet across, and slide quietly down to the other side, quickly wiping off a tear so that it would not freeze on my cheeks.

Sometimes I did not manage to conquer the drift or the dog's leap was so abrupt that I buried myself up to my nose in snow. I felt painfully bitter about the humiliating situation I had landed in. No one, however, ever laughed at me, even when I myself sometimes joked at my own frustration. People got used to me and even began to sympathize. I often heard words like: "Yakovlevna, I look at you and I'm astonished. How they beat you and insult you. You seem to be bowed over, but then you straighten up again. And you're a woman and alone, with no one to advise you, no one to help!"

As soon as the KGB noticed that people were talking to me on the street, they immediately took measures, spreading the most absurd threats and rumors. Once at the police station they asked a man they had seen talking to me, "Why does she always go into the woods with the dog at the exact same time? What do you suppose?" What could he say; he shrugged his shoulders.

"She goes out to contact the Americans. She has a transmitter and in the taiga she transmits coded information. Do you want your name mentioned tomorrow on the Voice of America? And do you know what lies she spreads?" This man did not approach me again.

Once I received an enormous package of letters and the young ones crowded around. Seeing their eyes shining with excitement, I said, "If you want stamps, come to my house and I'll give them to you." Two days later they came in a big crowd, pushing each other and laughing out of embarrassment. Having played with the dog, they began looking at everything in my house, and with their very limited village background, there was much that was fascinating. I decided to amuse them and quietly turned on the tape recorder. Then I played it back and the boys burst into cries of rapture, recognizing each other's voices. Growing bolder, they asked me to show them the transmitter which I used to make contact with America and they were very disappointed when I said it was all invented and I didn't have one.

August 1980

My Dear Friends!

The mail has brought your letters here to distant Siberia. Words of support and approval, hope and faith in the victory of justice. It is difficult to express the feelings I experience when I read your letters— astonishment that people understand me and share my convictions, as well as pain from your compassionate suffering, and a multitude of other feelings for which I have no name.

When a person lands in a situation like mine, when life itself depends on the degree of others' participation in his fate, when the spirit is crushed by the difficulties along the way and doubts creep into the soul, letters of support provide a vitalizing strength.

When a person lands in a situation like mine and suddenly senses hundreds and thousands of outstretched hands, which he never shook or even knew about earlier, then he feels most vividly the links between people separated by space and language but united by the recognition of human dignity and the desire to defend it.

The Soviet regime acted basely with me and it's not clear whether it will release me from its cruel claws. This does not mean, however, that we must be silent and reconciled to the situation. No, I ask you in the name of those who are locked behind the iron bars of prisons and those who cannot raise their voices from fear, I beg you not to be silent!

Political prisoner Ida Nudel

CHAPTER 21

It was frightening guarding trucks and cars alone all night in the yard of the road repair department. I had neither a pistol nor rifle; in fact, there wasn't even a latch on the door of the hut in which I warmed up from the cold. A policeman told me that one was not allowed because then I could lock myself in the room and never go out to guard.

"If someone wanted to steal a truck, the first thing he'll do is try to get rid of me. I would not have a chance to inform you by phone—the door is open and I'm unarmed."

"No one will steal the trucks," he replied.

"Then why am I suffering here every night?" was my foolish question.

"You have to work."

I had no choice; I worked. During the brief summer it was not so dreary. The nights were warm and starry and it was an indescribable pleasure to watch the dawn of a new day. Some tiny, drowsy little bird with a thin voice would begin to rouse nature from slumber. She was probably also a rebel by nature, awake when everyone else was still sleeping. At the same time the sun would pierce the sky with its distant glow. Although the forest concealed the sunrise from me, I saw the stunningly beautiful weaving of hues and colors, fantastic landscapes and remarkable animals; it was as if I were removed to a fairy-tale world beyond the bounds of my real-life surroundings. I stood in the midst of a yard, surrounded by heaps of junk metal, and stared at the heavens, while my dog ran around, warning me of approaching cats or people. Her bark would return me to reality, to the knowledge that I was another day closer to the end of my exile, but also that in a few hours I would return exhausted to my hut and once again begin the round of domestic chores.

Sometimes I left Pizer alone in the hut when I was working. I would return home, open the gate, check with a flashlight, run the distance between the gate and the door, hastily open the heavy, secure lock and rapidly lock myself inside the hut. My dog would lift her upper lip, baring her snow-white teeth in a smile. She would stretch after her sweet sleep and then, as if remembering she was supposed to greet me, press up to my knees, or if I had been gone a long time, throw herself on my chest. Then she would tell me a secret and sometimes I even understood. I learned to read her behavior. If in my absence she had climbed up on my bed and slept in my place, she would hang her tail and lower her head. She knew that she had behaved badly, but couldn't stop herself.

"Pizer, I'm angry at you; you're a bad dog."

She would look back intently into my eyes. Sometimes I thought that had I gotten a more aggressive dog, I would have felt less anxious, but then I decided that such an animal would only have caused more problems than this intelligent beauty, the favorite of the whole village.

Whenever a noisy gang of children ran by, she always wanted to go and run with them but the fence was in her way. In one second with a fluid and graceful leap she would fly into the air and land somewhere in the middle of the street. In another second she would realize that she had landed outside her territory without permission and she would stand dejectedly near the gate, awaiting punishment. I practically never punished her, although once she got me very angry and I tied her leash to the foot of the table and kept her there several hours repeating, "You're being punished, you're being punished." I relied on her native intellect and I was right. She hated the word "punished" and I only occasionally used this threat.

One summer when she was in heat and made eyes at every passing male dog, I said to her, "Listen, my beauty, my life is hard enough as it is; having to take care of your pups will be the last straw."

"I'm not even thinking about it," she seemed to say, but to

herself she obviously declared, "Why should I sacrifice myself? I want it!" and she ran away from me when she needed to. The women sympathized and laughed when I told them about my conversation with her. But terribly afraid that she had left me forever, I burst out crying at the thought that I remained completely alone. I wandered for four hours in the taiga near the village, shouting and calling for my naughty wanderer. Then some boys ran over and led me to where she was cavorting in the company of a crowd of lovers. I was so happy to see her again that I did not even scold her. When she saw me, she felt terribly guilty and was afraid to come near me.

"Go home!" I ordered in a harsh voice.

"What about them?" she seemed to ask, turning her handsome head toward the pack of dogs.

"They will remain here. Go home now," I repeated. "Right away or I'll punish you."

Hearing the word "punish," she wiggled her ears rapidly in discomfort.

"Straight home, do you hear me, Pizer?"

She had heard me all right, and tired from love's pleasures, she obeyed. She even seemed pleased that I had found her but I couldn't bring such a filthy dog, who stunk from hanging out with the stray dogs, into my room.

"Sit in the yard, you bad dog. I told you not to leave me and look what you did," I reprimanded her. I fetched some water, heated it and washed her outside, trembling for fear she would catch a cold. Taking her in, I wrapped her tightly in various rags so she couldn't move around, let alone escape, covered her with my coat and a blanket and she fell asleep, clean, sated and happy.

Sixty-three days later she bestowed on me eight healthy puppies. They were not full-bred collies but they were handsome, little creatures the size of a man's palm. When Pizer's milk did not flow for three full days, I decided to raise them no matter what and fed them out of a medicine dropper.

I was so isolated from everyone else that only by accident did I find out that during one night in August a family of four people had been murdered in the village. Frightened by the news and its possible implications for my work as a night watchman, I went to a few homes and found out that the victims were members of one family. They had been shot, the bodies mutilated by an ax and piled into a cellar. The murderer had then set fire to the house and when the firemen, police and villagers had arrived, the grisly picture had been gradually revealed. The murderer had holed himself up in the cellar of his girlfriend's home.

I stood guard that night, trembling from fear. What will happen if he decides to flee the village and comes to steal a car, I wondered nervously. I had no desire to sacrifice my life in order to save any socialist property. Consumed by these thoughts and fears for two frantic nights, I decided to quit the job. I went to the police chief and declared that I could not work any longer because I was terrified. "Give me a gun and teach me how to shoot or dismiss me. I am afraid, being alone at night, unarmed, without even a latch on the door."

"We can't give you a gun, exiles are not permitted to have a weapon," he replied.

"Then dismiss me, I can't work that way."

"Okay," he relented a little, "work just another week."

"In a week he could shoot us all," I said.

"No, he won't leave the cellar. He knows that they're waiting for him."

When I began searching for a new job, I realized how much people were still intimidated by me. No one would give me work, and neither the police nor the party nor the procurator's office, which was supposed to look after my rights, could break down their resistance. The procurator declared that he would give me a document declaring that I was not working for a valid reason, but such a document did not guarantee protection from a charge of parasitism or a new criminal prosecution so I felt uneasy. Finally the police arranged work for me sewing heavy padded jackets on a machine. Later on, when that proved too exhausting, they found me a job as a sweeper in a hairdressing salon, where I worked almost until the completion of my exile at the end of March.

One cold night in November I was sitting and writing in a far corner, hidden from the door by the stove, when a strange man entered my hut. I don't know how he got in; I turned intuitively when he came in, but perhaps he had already been watching me. Pizer stood next to him, wagging her tail guiltily, as if saying, "Please don't get angry at me, I liked this man." I had grown accustomed to trusting her instinct about people, and therefore her willingness to stand next to this complete stranger lowered my guard.

"I've already made friends with your pet," he said without a trace of embarrassment. "I have a dog, too, a marvelous Saint Bernard, and I miss him a lot."

"Who are you and why did you come in without permission; what do you want from me?" I asked him sharply.

"I'm on a business trip to Tomsk and heard a lot about you from various people and decided to stop by and talk to you."

"How did you drop by when the roads aren't open now?"

"I flew in a postal plane."

He's probably lying, I thought. "Are you from the KGB?" I asked.

"What are you talking about? I'm a literary critic and an art critic; perhaps you heard of my name—Magidson?"

"No, I never did."

"A lot of my friends emigrated, but I don't want to. I've talked it over with them but no one could give me a rational and logical explanation for their behavior. I don't plan to write anything, but since I was near you on my trip, I wanted to talk with you on this topic."

"I'm sure you're from the KGB and I have nothing to do with them. I am not plotting anything against the Soviet regime; I just don't want to live with them."

"Let's talk about it."

"I have other things to do, go away."

"I won't keep you long, but I traveled so far. I'm really frozen, please give me tea; in the hotel where I'm staying there's not even boiling water."

I weighed the possibilities—who else but a chekist could fly on a postal plane and dare to visit such a godforsaken hole, register in a hotel and visit a political prisoner, knowing that the police and KGB will learn of it?

"Go away."

The house was relatively warm, there was an odor of pine wood from the stove and the teapot was boiling noisily.

"Please give me tea," he asked again. "Boil up half a box; I drink it very strong."

"Did you serve time?"

"No, where did you get that idea from?"

"Usually criminals drink it that way."

"No, I never served time, but I like strong tea."

I boiled up the tea, thinking only a chekist could be so brazen, and he drank the whole pot. He then started walking around the room, pacing and turning because it was too cramped for his long legs in the tiny hut. When he turned his back to me, some picture momentarily flashed through my mind; I couldn't place it, but it seemed to me that I had seen this back before.

"How long are you going to stick around in front of my eyes? Go away. I treated you decently. Leave my house!"

"I just want to ask a few questions."

"Leave; I already told you, I have nothing to do with the KGB."

"I told you already, I'm not from the KGB."

"Are you a Jew?" I asked.

"Yes."

"Do you have children?"

"Two sons."

"How old are they?"

"Eleven and eight."

"For the sake of your children, I'm willing to answer your questions so that if one of them says, 'Give me permission to leave for Israel,' you'll understand what is happening and won't hide him in an insane asylum."

"Why do you want to emigrate?"

"I want to have my own motherland, not someone else's."

"But you had everything here—an apartment, education, friends."

"When you say there's no anti-Semitism here, you are lying," I asserted. "And everyone around you knows it." He kept pacing back and forth, limping on his left foot.

I was very tired that evening after another long day. I had carried out all my domestic chores, stopped by the post office to pick up my correspondence and had appeared at the police station to sign a special document ensuring that I had not run away and remained at the place where I was registered. I had planned on getting to bed earlier that night and now this impudent man had stealthily broken into my home, was taking up all my time and energy and was forcing me to deliver a lecture on the Jewish people.

I did not think he would change his convictions in any way and I could see that he was a cynical pragmatist when he let slip that he hoped to receive a residence permit for Moscow. I had seen people like that who were ready to sell their own mother for the sake of this privilege. I spoke in the hope that his sons, if they would grow to become more honest than their father, would not encounter the same difficulties as others whose parents opposed their desire to emigrate.

I spoke until nightfall. The village was enveloped in a heavy darkness, illuminated only by the sliver of the moon and the light from the tiny windows of the small houses. A cloud of smoke from the burning stoves hung over every roof. The little houses were wrapped up to the windows in drifts of crystal-pure snow, draped in white silence and tranquility. Even the village dogs were now silent.

"Enough; do what you want with your sons, I'm tired." I showed him the road to the hotel as he embraced my dog and left.

In a few days the police chief summoned me and said I should stop dreaming about emigration or returning to Moscow. The authorities would never permit either of the two. "Time will pass and people will forget you. We can't let people like you out," he said.

"Time will tell," I replied defiantly, but my heart was weeping when I returned home to my miserable, freezing hut, full of anguish at the thought that I would have to live alone forever in such miserable places, and would never see my sister and family or get to Israel. Pizer read my thoughts and stared at me with her black eyes. I did not have the strength to withstand her inquisitive look.

"Go take a walk, Pizer. Go see what's going on outside." She obeyed reluctantly, clearly not wanting to leave me alone in such a sad mood. I was too weak at the moment not to burst out crying, but Pizer could not stand my weeping and she jumped on me with a bark, trying to lick the tears streaming down my cheeks. I wiped them away and felt some relief from my pain. Time *would* tell who was right and I was definitely not going to give in.

In the busy period after my talk with the Jewish chekist, out of the blue I would sometimes picture that man's back and slightly limping gait which I had seen before but couldn't remember where. Suddenly, during a conversation with a village woman about some

totally banal topics, in a flashback I visualized where I had seen
the man who had burst into my Siberian hut. It had been in December 1974, four years after the Leningrad hijacking trial. On the
anniversary of our friends' conviction, about thirty of us had gathered on the steps of the Lenin Public Library with our faces turned
toward the Presidium of the Supreme Soviet in a silent protest,
standing in a tight circle without placards, surrounded by chekists.
A car drove up and several men got out, clearly acting as if they
were in charge. Many of us noted a tall, red-haired man who limped
slightly, moving from one group of chekists to another.

"Look, there's a Jew among them," someone said.

He was so close that he must have heard the exclamation. The
other chekists reacted by flowing around him protectively while
keeping him in the center of their group. The man was clearly out
of sorts and tried to keep his back to us all the time, but we
stubbornly tried to stare him in the face. Adjusting our position in
response to his maneuvers, we gradually shifted around in the small
place. Caught in a rather ridiculous situation, the chekists rolled
off in their black Volga sedans and the police began to disperse
us.

"Yes, that's him, that's the man, now I remember it all
clearly," I said to the woman.

"What are you talking about Yakovlevna, I don't understand
you."

"Excuse me, I suddenly remembered a man who visited from
Moscow this winter and recalled where I had seen him before."
Why hadn't I remembered who he was when he was in my house?
Then he wouldn't have had to play the innocent fool in front of
me. There was no point, however, in crying over spilt milk.

The Siberian hut led into a covered yard convenient for storing
wood and food for the livestock in the case of extended snowfalls.
One time the snow fell steadily for an entire week, burying my
hut well above the windows. By the end of the week I was unable
to leave my house. The drift was so high that it hid me from sight.

At the time I was ill and not working and I knew that no one
would notice that there was no path from my house nor would
anyone inquire whether I was still alive. The gate of the closed
yard opened inward, which allowed me to begin my snow shoveling.
I spent several hours daily removing snow and moving it to another

place farther away from the gate. I actually was scraping the snow because the shovel by itself was just too heavy for me, and when it was piled with snow I could not lift it more than three times. I racked my brains for a long time for an easier method until I finally came up with one that would help me. I began to chisel slices of snow with a large kitchen knife. It was not hard to do, as the knife easily cut the tightly compressed mass. I carried it in my hands or poured it into a bucket if it suddenly melted. After several days of this exhausting task, I succeeded in digging out a narrow tunnel through which I could move outside. This tunnel was another victory over my isolation and physical weakness.

Finally the sun began not only to blind us from the reflected white cover of the taiga, but also to warm us. What a remarkable time of year! All living nature was full of excited expectation. My tormentor, the snow, melted and disappeared from the roof. It seemed as if only yesterday the columns of snow were howling and whirling in the streets but already we could change our winter felt boots for rubber shoes.

For some reason Pizer kept sniffing all day at the roof of the hatch which led to the cellar under the house. Have the rats come here too, I wondered. I did not have time to see what was happening there as spring brought other tasks, but the dog was uneasy and would sometimes sit down next to me and stare hypnotically into my eyes.

"What do you want from me, Pizer? You see how hard it is for me to deal with this household. Go take a walk and don't look at me." I sent her out to the yard. But when she began to run around the hatch and bark, I decided that it was foolish to avoid it any longer. I opened the hatch and was horrified—the water had risen so high it was almost under the floor. It was another disaster I had to face but I was impressed at how clever my dog was. She had sensed something wrong and had tried to explain it to me in her own way. I scooped out water for hours with the bucket and took it far way from the house.

Thus I lived for almost four years, from hardship to hardship. I had not managed to catch my breath from one problem when something new happened. My life in the village, however, introduced me to the world of animals and plants which I loved. It saved me from the anguish and introspection that were so usual in such circumstances and from unjustified hopes and illusions. With no time for mental excursions to Moscow or to friends, I accepted my new rural life, though it was difficult both physically and emotionally, and survived its challenges, still confident of the rightness of my demands.

Even though I had less than half a year left before the end of my exile, I still waited impatiently for mail. As soon as I saw my sister's handwriting on an envelope, I would open up the letter right there at the post office and quickly scan it. Of course, I looked at it again at home, trying to read between the lines, and would pore over it once more word by word while replying to each and every question. In one of Lena's letters she informed me that a woman's organization, Wizo, had initiated a campaign for my nomination for the 1982 Nobel Peace Prize for my human rights work.

Once in one of my many letters from abroad I found a Jewish Star of David and the Christian image of Saint Mary tied together, and I carried the two symbols with me, my heart full of gratitude to the sender.

In January 1982, a few months before the end of my exile, I decided that it was time to sell my hut. If they released me, they would do it on time. My term actually ended earlier than four years after the sentence because the time I spent in convoy on the trip to Siberia counted as double time. I had checked the exact date many times at the police station and they, in turn, made inquiries with a higher authority in Tomsk, where the date was confirmed.

I hung announcements at every corner in the village and even published a notice in the local printed sheet about the upcoming sale, but no one came. I wondered what I would do with the property if I received my passport and became free. People were looking for housing—I saw that all those who hung up notices at the same time as I had already sold their property long ago—but still no one came to me. I asked everyone I met at the well or those I passed on the way to the post office and even began to speak to the policemen in hopes of understanding why my home was not sold. Finally, an old woman opened my eyes, telling me that someone had spread the rumor around the village that the house and the kitchen garden were mined. It was so absurd that at first I burst out laughing. It was another reminder of what a deep backwoods hole I was living in, among people who were so ignorant that they were prepared to believe the most infantile foolishness. I felt uncertain about my release and uneasy about the KGB threats conveyed by the police chief that they would never let me out of the Soviet Union or allow me to be registered to live in Moscow again. Even Pizer's fate was uncertain; I was worried that I would have to give her to someone. All in all, my heart was full of fears and heavy forebodings.

Each day brought me closer to the end of my term; time never passed so quickly. It was March and only two weeks were left. I looked forward to leaving Siberia, the village and all that I had endured there, the good and the bad. I wanted to rip out of my mind and heart the pain and tears of those one thousand four hundred days and nights—the real and imagined fears—and then I would be ready for a new life.

The police chief informed me that I would be given the document of my release and my passport on the morning of my liberation. He also said that he personally would see to it that the necessary people would show up and all the papers would be ready on time.

"I suspect that you are awaiting my release with great impatience," I commented.

"Why? Didn't we learn to live with each other over these years?" he asked.

"Nevertheless, you'll heave a sigh of relief after I get on the bus, and I have no doubt that one of your men will be there to check with his own eyes that I have left this charming spot."

"You're right again," he said. "I would confirm it myself with pleasure, but I am not permitted to stand at the bus station during working hours."

In the final days some refusenik friends such as Mark Nashpitz and Naum Kosiansky had arrived to help me and the time had flown by in conversations concerning plans and projects. I finally sold my hut and my friend Naum, who lived in the Siberian town of Novosibirsk, took care of the final arrangements after my departure.

The day before I left I had everything packed and had distributed to the neighbors whatever I was not taking with me. I made the rounds of all those I had managed to develop some relations with over the years.

As I was walking on the road from the village, some older

women caught up with me. "Ida," they called out. "We know you're leaving the village tomorrow." They began to bless me and make the sign of the cross over me. One after the other wished me an "easy and quick road home." "Home," one of them emphasized, "not Moscow," and I understood that she meant Israel. They left me standing stunned in the middle of the road. I had not expected such a farewell and I had not even suspected that underneath the cold exteriors there were people so sympathetic to me in the village.

As it turned out, March 25, 1982, was a beautiful clear day in the remote Siberian village of Krivosheino; the temperature was a little over thirty degrees Fahrenheit at day time and there was no wind. As usual, the trees and huts were trimmed with snow, the smoke from the stoves circled above. As the police chief had promised me, everyone appeared on time and the procedure went quickly. He asked me to step into his office for a final talk, repeating the warning that I would never be allowed to leave the Soviet Union or be registered in Moscow.

"But the law is on my side," I insisted.

"You're more optimistic than I am," he replied. "If you have no one to go to, stay in the village," he suggested. "You won't be registered anywhere."

"We'll see," I muttered.

"I want to say in parting," he continued, "that I am very happy that fate brought us together. I personally respect you very much, but duty comes before everything else." He gave me his hand in farewell and said, "Who knows, maybe in fifteen years there will be a sign on your house: IDA NUDEL LIVED HERE."

I ran out because the bus was supposed to leave at any minute and if I missed it, I would have to spend another night in the village. And there was no way I would spend another night in exile! Mark and Naum were waiting anxiously for the bus. I waved my new passport as I ran up and the three of us piled onto the bus.

Pizer, however, refused to go on the bus. Although she had seen them on the street, she had never been inside one, and the noise of the motor frightened her. When persuasion failed and she continued to lie on the ground, I went on the bus alone and began to call her from inside. Clearly hearing my voice, but not understanding where it came from, she became agitated and then started to rise to her feet. Before she had time to realize what was happening, strong hands grabbed her and quickly carried her aboard, where her own bedding was spread over two seats. The familiar scent of her belongings calmed her somewhat, but when the bus started to move, she began to yelp hysterically.

I took her to me, this enormous hulk which weighed almost sixty pounds, and she put her front paws on my knees, and was silent for most of the several-hour bus ride to Tomsk, where we transferred to a plane for Moscow.

The plane was half empty and the airport authorities even let me take Pizer into the cabin. Exhausted from the excitement of leaving and the rattling of the bus, the dog lay down in the aisle at the tail of the plane, dozing or gazing around curiously. "What an intelligent and beautiful dog!" exclaimed the flight attendant. Pizer lazily wagged her tail in acknowledgment and patiently endured the rest of the journey to an uncertain future.

My Dears,

Irit von Esso from Kibbutz Gvaram sent me quite a book!—
The Doctor and the Soul *by Victor E. Frankl. It is perfect for my
mood when, weighed down by my terrible and senseless situation, I am
occasionally seized by doubts. Victor Frankl developed a
psychotherapeutic system by the name of logotherapy. Intuitively, I found
the correct formulation for survival, the very one advocated by Frankl.
I call it motivation, but he calls this human impulse the will-to-
meaning. Frankl asserts that if a person has a dream, he has a goal,
his desire to reach the goal will impel him to overcome the circumstances
in his way. Perhaps that is what Mama was trying to instill in me
when she said, "Never drop something in the middle." I am completely
under the influence of this book. I couldn't put it down and read it
straight through to the end, although I did not understand a lot of it.
Then I read it word by word, while compiling my own dictionary.
Afterward, I read it a third time, with my dictionary, which speeded up
the reading and afforded me great pleasure from the realization that I
myself had found the correct way. This is the way that I raise my
vegetables and chicks and puppies and all the details into which I put
my heart.*
We shall triumph.

Love,
Ida

CHAPTER 22

HAVING GROWN ACCUSTOMED TO THE RURAL QUIET AND ISO-
lation of Siberia, nocturnal Moscow overwhelmed me with its sea
of lights, endless streams of traffic and lively commotion. Surrounded by friends, I returned to my Moscow apartment, which
seemed alien, with unfamiliar furniture, curtains and smells. My
friends toasted my return with champagne but everyone's eyes
reflected the anxious presentiment that I would not be allowed to
live in that apartment. Soviet civil legislation guaranteed me the
right to keep the apartment in my absence and, within three days
after my arrival, to be registered and receive a residence permit to
live there again. I do not know why the KGB did not deprive me
of the apartment while I was in exile; evidently they were saving
it for my next bitter ordeal.

They refused to register me in Moscow and even claimed they
were doing so on the basis of the very law which guaranteed me
an immediate residence permit. At first I could not understand this
weird logic. How could they assert that precisely the law which
guarantees me a registration permit is the law that deprives me of
it?

I went to the library of the collegium of lawyers and asked if
I could see that law. The librarian was not permitted to give me
the actual document but she read it aloud and even reread it. Yes,
if I could only believe my ears, the authorities were obligated to
register me within three days. The librarian to whom I showed the
form for my release said, "Yes, they must register you because you

have a cooperative apartment and because the article according to which you were sentenced does not forbid registration in Moscow."

"In actual fact I am a political prisoner," I told her.

"What? A political?" She pursed her lips. "Then go to the police. The law has not been abolished, clear it up with them."

Several weeks had passed since my return to Moscow. Fortunately, I was not in financial straits because of the support of my sister and others from abroad. I had already met with foreign correspondents and briefly told my Siberian story. I was, however, lacking the most important thing for any Soviet citizen—a stamp in my passport which certified that I was registered to live in a certain location. Although I was living in my own apartment, I was doing so illegally. This precarious situation made my life tense and even risky. Without this little stamp I was automatically considered a criminal; and besides, there was my "criminal" past, my recently completed term for "hooliganism."

In complaining about the refusal to give me a permit, as usual, I worked methodically and consistently, starting from the lowest bureaucrat and working up to the highest.

My marathon march through the bureaucracy was quick. Time was working against me as the fall approached—clearly I could not continue indefinitely to remain illegally in my own apartment— and the prospect of remaining without a shelter in the chilly weather was alarming. To save time I delivered all the complaints to the offices myself. I often managed to talk things over with the next bureaucrat in the hierarchy and my complaint passed quickly through their departments. I made the rounds of all officials who had even the slightest connection to residence permits or Soviet legislation and its implementation. It turned out that neither the Presidium of the Supreme Soviet, which issues the laws, nor the procurator's office, nor the justice ministry has the least influence in the Soviet Union if the KGB is involved; the KGB simply ignores any laws that stand in its way.

I decided to turn to the last resort—the party, in particular to Albert Ivanov. My last conversation with Albert Ivanov had been in 1979, when I had called him from Siberia; now it was May 1982 and a lot of water had flowed under the bridge. Not everything had changed, however—Ivanov's secretary would not tell me when I could reach him. "Call again," she said, "maybe you'll be lucky and reach him." At first I was unsuccessful, although, as before, I spent hours by the phone.

I had one other number—that of a Central Committee worker I had never spoken to. I called him in the morning and asked him to listen to me but he refused. I then set my trap: "For many years I used to discuss various problems with Albert Ivanov and sometimes he helped me."

"Excellent," he said, "I'll give the phone to Albert Ivanovich, let him help you."

Over the wire I heard a broken voice, the voice of a very old man, "I'm listening."

"Please give the phone to Albert Ivanovich," I requested.

"I'm listening, Ida Yakovlevna," answered the very same voice. How could it be he; after all, we were born in the same year?

"Albert Ivanovich, I didn't recognize you, we haven't spoken for so many years that I forgot your voice."

"I recognized you immediately, Ida Yakovlevna. Where are you speaking from?"

"I'm calling from the waiting room of the Central Committee," I replied.

"Have you served your term?"

"Yes, of course, all four years."

"What?" he exclaimed. "Four years already rushed by!"

"I returned to Moscow but they won't register me at my own apartment," I stated.

"That means you're not allowed to be there."

"Why not? Indeed, I am permitted to live there; the law guarantees it, but the police and procurator's office don't give a damn about the law and obey only the KGB's orders."

"I hear that you haven't changed a bit."

"Why should I? Am I really wrong? I am demanding those rights which the Soviet Union, through signing international agreements, obligated itself to observe."

"No, even punishment did not change you, it's a pity!"

"What did you achieve during these years by your treatment of me? My name became known to millions of people all over the world. I received almost twelve thousand letters in Siberia from the four corners of the earth."

"That can't be, twelve thousand letters!"

"You know, don't you, Albert Ivanovich, that I never lie."

"I know," he admitted.

"In 1982 I was nominated for the Nobel Peace Prize."

"Who nominated you?" he asked.

"Wizo, a Jewish women's Zionist organization."

"I didn't know that. Well, Ida Yakovlevna," he said, "you have earned such respect. Phone me tomorrow at the same time; I'll give you an answer."

The rest of that day and the following morning I was not myself—after all, my fate was being decided. In the afternoon I took a walk in the woods with Pizer to a square where dogs were trained to obey various clever commands. We waited on line and boldly climbed up a high watch tower, but suddenly she became frightened because it was the first time that she had been so high above ground. Pizer lay down on the lattice floor of the tower and howled from fright. In the meantime a long line of people with their dogs formed below, down the length of the ladder, each one giving me advice more ridiculous than the next.

I was in a quandary and didn't know what to do. She kept howling her horrible cry, "Ay, ay," and I felt both ridiculous and embarrassed.

Finally some man climbed up the tower from the other side and said to me, "Put on her muzzle, I'll carry her down."

"I don't have a muzzle for her."

The crowd began to get indignant, "Lady, you don't know how to take care of your dog. The dog ought to be taken away from you."

Feeling empty, I stopped the squabble, and then said to the man who had come to my aid, "Don't be afraid, she won't bite. She never bit anyone in her life; she does not even know that she can attack a man." He looked carefully at the dog, somehow adroitly put his hands under her body, instantly swept her off the floor and carried her down below. She lay gently, trustingly and proudly in his arms—she loved to be carried. He descended very carefully and held her a little longer, showing her to the crowd. "What a beautiful dog and how brave!" he said jokingly.

She jumped from his arms and ran to me. She rubbed against my feet as if saying, "Don't get angry, such things happen to everyone!"

The next morning I was very tense; I went to the Central Committee and phoned Albert, who answered himself.

Hearing my voice he laughed like the devil over his victim, his hoarse voice adding a sinister tone. He suggested that I go to the reception room of the All-Union OVIR, the visa bureau. "They'll take you; tell them your name." My heart was filled with gloomy presentiments, but there was nothing I could do, I had to go. I phoned, however, to see when they had reception hours and it turned out to be the next day.

The neighbors began complaining that in my absence the dog was howling and barking. Of course she was frightened; sensing that I was under tremendous tension, she reacted nervously to the alien and anxious milieu.

I decided to take Pizer with me and tie her up near the OVIR office while I waited my turn. Although we rushed there by taxi, the waiting room was already packed. Moreover, there wasn't even a place to tie up the dog and the soldier on guard did not permit me to leave her in the hall. I tied her to a drain pipe and, full of fears for her and for myself, entered the waiting room.

"Your slip," asked the soldier. I had to sign up first, and got number 32.

"How long is the wait?" I asked him.

"Don't worry, they'll take everyone," he replied.

"I am worried," I said. "I left my dog on the street, tied to a drain pipe. If she gets scared and tugs, she'll break the pipe. Couldn't you let me go ahead of my turn?"

"No, I can't. Ask the other people."

I was very doubtful that people would give up their turn, but I said very loudly, "A few days ago I returned from exile. Could you let me go to the chief out of turn?"

At first there was silence, as they were probably stunned by my brazenness, but then they began to shout, "We're all from exile, we all came from far away. We don't permit it; guard, see that she does not go out of turn."

I lowered my head. Hadn't I gotten into conflicts with the KGB for their sake, so that they could emigrate in peace? I reminded myself that my conflicts were my personal problem and I should not expect gratitude or understanding from others. Had I started blaming my problems on those who don't even know about them, I would start hating them. While I was immersed in these thoughts, the door to the office opened and someone said loudly, "Nudel, come in."

I had already been in this office several times and had often heard the absurd accusations and fantastic explanations of the reasons why I had been refused an exit visa. In 1975, V. Anichkina, then a lieutenant, had tried to convince me that the period of restrictions on my emigration would end in January 1977. At the time it had seemed unbearably long to wait until 1977. Now it was May 23, 1982, and I was again standing there, facing Colonel Anichkina and General Rudolf Kuznetsov.

"What questions do you have?" asked General Kuznetsov.

"The police illegally refuse to register me in Moscow, and won't let me out of the Soviet Union."

"Appeal at your local police station," said the general.

"Your predecessors told me that I would receive a visa after January 1977. Now it's the end of May 1982."

"Appeal at your local police station," the general said again.

"What more do you need from me? How long will you suck my blood? According to the law, I ought to be registered in Moscow but I am kicked like a ball from place to place and illegally refused a residence permit."

"Appeal at your local police station," he reiterated, as if he didn't know any other words.

"You keep repeating the exact same sentence. When will I receive an exit visa, when will they register me?"

"Appeal at your local police station," he said once more in an even, toneless voice. He had a thin colorless face as if he never saw the sun, and his dull eyes were full of hatred. I had the feeling that in another minute he would pull out a knife from the top of his boot and thrust it into me, but he repeated his refrain in a dead voice.

"You are mocking me, aren't you? Did Albert Ivanov call you from the Central Committee so that you would tell me this important sentence?"

"Ida Yakovlevna," interrupted Anichkina, "you were told to appeal at your local police station where you were registered before your exile. Your question will be resolved there."

What was I killing myself for at this office if my case had

already been decided and the answer had been given to the police? Why did they have to get me into a frenzy if there already was an answer? I was crushed as I left the OVIR, but at least Pizer was still there. I untied her and walked through Moscow, because I did not have the spirit to raise my arm and hail a taxi. She ran ahead and looked inquisitively at me.

"Things are bad, Pizer. No doubt the police won't have anything good to say to me either." I left the dog in the apartment and went to the police.

"Where have you been, Ida Yakovlevna? I already sent a policeman after you," said the police chief, meeting me in the hall. "Come into my office. Read and sign here."

"What is it?" I asked.

"An order forbidding you to stay in Moscow. You must leave; if you don't vacate in seventy-two hours, I'll give you the final warning and if you violate it, you'll get a sentence. That's the law."

"How can you pronounce the word 'law' when you treat it like an old glove?"

"Will you sign?"

"Of course not. Your order is illegal; you are obliged to register me. How can you forbid me to be in Moscow when the law guarantees me the right to be in Moscow?"

He pressed a button and a policeman entered. "Two witnesses, please," he said.

Immediately two young men appeared. Without an explanation, he showed them where to sign and the order to expel me from Moscow gained the force of law.

"Take a copy for yourself, Ida Yakovlevna, you must leave the city. If you don't you'll receive another warning in seventy-two hours." I left, not knowing what to do or where to go.

"Pizer, let's go to the woods for a while."

She looked persistently into my eyes.

"Don't look at me like that or I'll burst out crying."

In my precarious situation, I had to find someone who would take Pizer for an indefinite period. Fortunately the refuseniks Inna Kitrossky and her husband, Naum Meiman, agreed to take the dog with them to their dacha while I set out to find a place where I could obtain a residence permit. While I was away on my search, a kindly relative took Pizer to the Meimans without my even managing to tell her what had happened to me.

*   *   *

While in exile I had already worked out a plan of action in case the police refused to give me a residence permit for Moscow. The first geographical place that I intended to try was Riga, Latvia, where Yosif Zalmanson, the father of Silva, Vulf and Izrail, lived. During the years of their imprisonment for their part in the hijacking attempt, I had developed close ties with their father and I counted on his help. Yosif responded warmly to my request but needed time to investigate.

When I was living in Siberia I had corresponded with several exiles. The dissident world was so small that each one knew the story of the others' conflicts with the KGB. Gabriel Superfin, had been active in helping Solzhenitsyn and had been arrested for anti-Soviet agitation. I would send him the letters I had received written in German, Italian and French, which he would translate and return to me. At my request my friend and proxy Evgeni Tsirlin visited him.

Gabriel had finished his term of exile earlier than I and had gone to live in Tartu, in the Baltic republic of Estonia. I sent him a telegram at the post office with a request for help. He replied telling me to come, explaining that he would leave his address for me at the central post office, general delivery, in my name, and he indicated the best dates for my arrival. Meantime Yosif Zalmanson reported that the Riga KGB categorically refused to register me; moreover, they asked him to convey to me that I could not be registered anywhere in the Baltic republics. But, it was tempting and certainly worth a try since Tartu was a cultural center, a university city and had a considerable Jewish population.

I arrived by bus in Tartu toward evening, deposited my heavy suitcase in the checkroom and rushed to the central post office. I wanted to take a cab but not even one stopped. Finally I went by foot and arrived at ten minutes after six, that is, ten minutes after the general delivery section closed. Every postal worker I asked to check whether there was a letter in my name just shrugged his shoulders and said, "It's impossible, all the boxes are closed; come tomorrow morning at ten o'clock."

They had no idea what the word "tomorrow" meant for me. I knew no one in the city, and lacking a stamp in my passport, I was an easy target for police harassment. Not knowing where to hide from the police during the night, I decided to walk around in the hopes of meeting a Jew who might know my story and not be afraid of helping me. Intently scrutinizing the faces of passersby, I finally stopped one, "Excuse me, please; I have a very unusual question—tell me, aren't you Jewish?"

"No," the man answered coldly, "you're wrong, I'm not."

No one answered in the affirmative; evidently my strange behavior and the question itself frightened them. I tried once more, approaching a young woman I was sure was Jewish and asking quietly, "Excuse me, aren't you Jewish?"

"No," she replied hastily and practically ran away.

I had never spent the night on the street and the thought of doing so was frightening. At the bus station I was told about a nearby hotel, and I made my way there, immersed in my sad thoughts and cursing Superfin for the idiotic situation in which I had landed. There were a few free places for women and the clerk gave me a blank, which I filled in, using my former registered address. The clerk asked for my passport, compared the data with the blank, turning over the pages in search of the residence permit. Her face fell and turned pale. "Lady," she said, "you're not registered anywhere."

"Yes," I answered frankly, "I came here in search of a residence permit, but my relatives were not home and I have to spend the night someplace. Just for the night and tomorrow morning I'll go to my relatives."

"Lady, you don't have a residence permit," she said in a threatening tone.

"Look at me, I'm not a thief or murderer. I came here to arrange for housing."

"Leave immediately or I'll call the police."

I took back my worthless passport, quickly left the hotel, and decided to go to the central telegraph office, where it is natural for people to stay a long time, perhaps even the whole night. Indeed, there were people there, and I even went up to two men who were waiting for phone calls and looked like Jews to me. I lost my sense of reality. Why should I inspire anyone's confidence, a middle-aged woman, poorly dressed in old-fashioned clothing, with an exhausted face and eyes blazing from mental anguish?

When everyone had left the telegraph office, the clerk on duty asked what I was waiting for. I lied, telling her that I had no relatives in town and was waiting for the first bus in the morning. At two in the morning she suggested that I leave because the telegraph office was closing for the night. In fact, she had no right to close the office but she wanted to sneak in a couple of hours of rest. I walked in the direction of the bus station, passing homeless people lying on the benches, but unlike me, they were not afraid of openly showing their condition. Noting that police patrol cars passed by from time to time, I decided not to lie on a street bench for fear of a policeman coming up and asking for my passport.

The bus station itself was closed in the evening, there were no intercity buses. Some people were talking near it, however, and I sensed instinctively that they also had problems concerning a passport stamp and did not want to attract the attention of the police. I drew closer and stood near but not with them because I was afraid. Having talked quietly, they slowly moved together and I decided to follow them. Trying to keep a little distance without falling behind, I followed them for some time until they came to the riverbank. They sat together, infrequently speaking, and I sat nearby. But when a man came up and sat down next to me I suddenly panicked, jumped up and dashed away before his hands reached out for me. It did not matter where I was going, as long as it was away from the darkness and fear. I finally stopped near a tree and saw that everything around was quiet and calm. I swore to myself that I would never, never again travel without being sure that someone would take me in for the night. Why hadn't I asked Superfin to send me his address by telegraph to general delivery in Moscow?

I climbed up from the low riverbank and walked toward the center of town; indeed, I soon recognized the spots I had passed several times in the evening. There was only one place to which I could go—back to the central telegraph office—and now the door was open again. I entered and quietly sat down at a table in the farthest corner of the room but the clerk recognized me. "You deceived me," she said. "You didn't leave on the first bus!" Indeed, it was now dawn and the first bus had already left town. I hate to tell even the slightest lie and at that moment, standing in front of the telegraph window and babbling some nonsense to that woman, I felt so humiliated and so unhappy that I almost burst out crying in front of her, but her haughty look and scornful smile stopped me.

"You deceived me," she repeated, and I silently left the room.

It was already light and the sight of a single woman walking hurriedly along the street no longer aroused any suspicion. I walked around in circles near the post office. This is some cultured city, I thought, the post office doesn't open until ten. A few more agonizing hours and I would receive the letter with Gabriel's address.

Near the post office I joined a small group of people waiting for it to open. Standing in line among lawful citizens, I felt calmer. The clerk gave me the envelope without even looking to see whether I was registered someplace in the Soviet Union.

Gabriel had left me his address and detailed instructions on how to get there, but when I reached the place no one answered my ring. I sat and watched the children playing in the yard for a while but there was still no answer when I returned. I rang the neighbor's bell, but they couldn't tell me anything and had no idea when he would return. Not wanting to give the KGB advance warning of my appearance, trying to be "invisible," I had not informed him about the exact date of my arrival.

I had to return to the bus station since I had paid for only one day at the baggage checkroom; but in case Gabriel returned, I left a note in his mailbox and another on his door to look in the mailbox. Back at the station, after paying at the checkroom, checking the bus schedule, and waiting a few hours, I returned to his apartment, but he still had not returned. Totally exhausted from my sleepless and nervous night, I decided to give up, take a bus out of town and then switch to a train to Moscow.

June 1982

Dear Ida,

    Fate has brought us in touch with many remarkable women, but I cannot include all their names in a letter. Some of them joined together in an organization called I WIN—Israeli Women in Defense of Ida Nudel. They are so well informed and identify so closely with your cause that they and we are like one big family.

    A man who has been a moving force in the campaign on your behalf is Peter Krauss. He helps us in so many ways, handling correspondence, planning activities, and encouraging us with his faith in our victory.

    I believe that you sense this and it must give you satisfaction and faith that the efforts of an enormous number of kindhearted people will bring us victory. You just have to be patient.

                    Love,
                    Lena, Leva and Yakov

CHAPTER 23

IN MOSCOW I ANXIOUSLY STEPPED ONTO THE TRAIN PLAT-
form. I was not worried that they would catch me there, because
for a long time I had not phoned anyone to tell of my whereabouts,
but I was still without a registration permit and I did not know
where to go or what to do. I couldn't keep hiding temporarily at
friends'. The homeless life was not for me; I am the kind of person
who cannot live without her own place.

My first task, however, was to get rid of my heavy suitcase.
Having put a change of underwear and a few items in my bag, I
dragged the suitcase to the checkroom where hundreds of people
were unhappily waiting in line.

"Go ahead, complain," said the attendant. "If you paid me
by the piece, not one of you would wait more than five minutes;
I'd scurry like a squirrel to make some money, but for eighty rubles
a month, I'm not going to run. Stand and wait. It's not my problem
that you're in a hurry."

I waited my turn but it was impossible to concentrate on my
problems. It was so stuffy in the basement and everybody was
cursing. It took me two hours to get rid of the suitcase and then I
had to decide where to go next. Despite my apprehension about
revealing my whereabouts, I decided to go to the post office to
check my mail at general delivery. Skimming it quickly, I noticed
several replies from the procurator's office and I looked them over
as I walked out of the building. Contemplating my sorry state of
affairs, I slowly walked the short distance toward the building with

the apartment which was legally mine. I had almost reached it when several young people briskly approached me. One of them asked, "Where is building 79, block 6?" As I pointed to the building, various strange sights assaulted my eyes: several on-duty policemen were running from all sides of the courtyard in our direction and police cars were rushing behind them, right on the sidewalk. While I was looking around, the people who had questioned me disappeared.

I was so overwhelmed that I did not even notice how I wound up surrounded by policemen and their cars. To think that they had removed uniformed policemen from various posts, equipped with weapons and the batons of traffic controllers and dispatched them in patrol cars in order to seize me, a small, lone woman whose only weapon was a ballpoint pen and reckless persistence and nothing more. All this to grab such a desperate criminal?

My God, would I really never leave this crazy country?

They yelled something to me but I did not hear and just stood in silent bewilderment. Someone gave me a push in the back, the police car almost drove into me and a strong hand again shoved me from behind.

"Citizen Nudel, you will receive a sentence for resisting the police."

"It looks like I will receive two terms, one for violating the prohibition against the appearance in Moscow of a dangerous criminal like me and the second for disobeying the police."

"You are disrupting our work; we are on patrol to preserve order in the city," said one of the policemen.

I came to my senses and said, "If you're busy with such important work, then what are you chasing after me for? You've got nothing to do and you're amusing yourselves."

The four of them surrounded me while their patrol cars crushed the grass on the lawn of the building in which I had lived. One of them said, "The operation is over, I'm driving to my post!"

Suddenly the crowd of policemen disappeared, leaving just the one. "You've been standing around enough, get into the car! I already warned you that you will be punished for resisting the police."

I got into the car on my own and in a few minutes we drove up to the district station, where I had been brought so many times in the past. They took me to the round-the-clock section and put me near a policeman. I began to feel ill; my heart was groaning and weeping. Massaging my left hand did not help nor did lying down on the bench. I took all my validol, a medicine for slight chest pains that I carried with me, but that, too, was ineffective.

"Give me some more validol, please!" I asked the policeman on duty.

"We don't have any medicine; if you're sick you ought to stay home!" was his answer. The policeman assigned to me said, "You can't lie down, get up and follow me!" He led me upstairs to the second floor to the door with the familiar sign, "Deputy Chief of Police, Major Zagladin, V.N." I entered but the policeman remained outside the door.

"Sit down, Ida Yakovlevna," said Zagladin.

"What does all this silly spectacle mean, please explain it to me."

"It's not a performance, Ida Yakovlevna, it's very serious. You violated the law and will be punished for it."

"You're the ones who violated the law; you were obligated to register me in three days; you mock not only me but also the law. Perhaps you are unable to read the laws?"

"I certainly can; I have a higher education and I am a lawyer."

"And you're not ashamed to say this? You insolently distorted the law and are proud of it. You're a lawyer, the guardian of legality! Doesn't it seem to you at times that this is some kind of crazy, absurd story, without any meaning or sense?"

"Ida Yakovlevna, if your departure depended on me personally, you would have left long ago. I regard you with great respect."

"Then why do you set the police on me as if you were snaring a wild beast?"

"I am at work, doing my duty. You violated the law. I warned you personally that you are prohibited from appearing in Moscow and in an area one hundred kilometers around the city."

"You violated the law in refusing me a registration permit. Your prohibition forbidding me to enter Moscow is illegal since I have the right to a permit."

"You may complain, but you are not allowed in Moscow now; there is a ban and you must obey it. I repeat, I warned you personally and you did not listen. Now you'll have to answer in court."

"And who will answer for the fact that you personally violated the law?"

"I am a soldier and follow the orders of my superiors."

He pressed a button and a policeman entered.

"Take her away."

I was brought down below, where I sat for a long time while hooligans, prostitutes, petty thieves and some criminals like me who had violated a ban on appearing in Moscow were brought in. Some were shoved into cells and others were seated next to me. Some were together with friends who brought them food and drink but I was completely alone and therefore went without either for twenty-four hours. Occasionally I was taken to the bathroom where I gulped some water from the faucet.

All night the phones rang and policeman came and went and they left me sitting in the same spot. Unable to get comfortable either sitting or lying on the bench, I kept shifting positions while imagining myself again at a trial and then in a criminal camp. I felt so sorry for myself that I began to pray to God to release me from this new ordeal; hadn't I suffered enough?

When morning finally arrived, the place became more lively. The police chief came and told me, "I summoned an investigator from the procurator's office who will draw up your case."

"Thanks," I replied and he silently turned and left.

In a few hours I was taken to an investigator, a young man under thirty, with an affable face. "Tell me about it," he suggested.

I was fed up with their cat-and-mouse games. What was the point of baring my soul and exposing my pain to alien, dirty hands? I therefore sat silently on the chair in front of the investigator, with the policeman who had been guarding me all along sitting behind me. The investigator looked over the papers the policeman had given him and asked, "Why did you come to Moscow?"

I pulled out a pile of letters and postcards from my bag and, selecting the replies from the procurator's office, I silently handed him the papers. "Read it and everything will be clear without my explanations," I replied.

After looking at everything carefully he said, "I don't understand anything, tell me in detail."

I told him about the absurd charge, the trial, exile, the refusal to give me a registration permit. Having sent the policeman out of the room, he listened attentively without interrupting me.

"Sit here for a while, I shall look at the order," he said. He returned later, holding a file of documents. "You're right, the law guarantees you the right to a residence permit and the police chief was obligated to register you immediately."

"He refused to, as did the department of the interior ministry; then the municipal, republic and union procurators upheld the refusal. There's no one left to complain to. The Presidium of the Supreme Soviet answered me that this question falls within the competence of the interior ministry. Because the police belong to the administrative authority, I can't bring a judicial complaint against them."

"You are right, but there is also a council of elders of the Moscow Council which in exceptional cases can solve the issue of a residence permit; send them a complaint. I wish you luck but you will have to leave Moscow even though your rights have been violated. How did they happen to grab you?"

"I think the postal worker where I received mail at general delivery phoned the police, who took everyone from the nearest patrol posts and dashed after me. The Soviet police performed as expected, with honor and glory."

"I'll order them to release you now," he stated. "After this you must go to the post office and let them see that you are free. Don't lose hope, and file a complaint."

Was he playing the simpleton with me or wasn't he with them? Why was I released?

Upon leaving the police station I slowly walked toward the subway. No, this was not a normal investigator; the KGB did not want to imprison me now because they had other plans: they would drive me from place to place, not permitting me to get registered, so that I would finally collapse, break down and submissively beg for a residence permit in Moscow.

I had to leave Moscow again, but before renewing my search for a city where I could get registered, I decided to see Pizer, at my friend Inna's dacha two hundred fifty miles from Moscow. I arrived at the village and found their home but no one was in. Strolling nearby, I began to call Pizer's name, counting on her excellent hearing. Indeed, in a short while I heard voices approaching and a dog's barking. I walked impatiently to meet them, but Pizer walked silently past me. My dog, who after even the shortest separation would give me a stormy welcome, kisses and howls of rapture, passed by me without even wagging her tail, and, what was worse, she acted as if I were an alien and repulsive being.

While I was greeting my friends and telling them briefly about my life, I kept watching Pizer's behavior. She showed me that she did not want to know me anymore and could not forgive the insult of my leaving. I addressed her with the tenderest words which in the past had thrilled her and made her obedient and quiet, but on that day she ignored me completely.

When Pizer was with me she usually slept on a little carpet on the floor near my bed. Normally, she lay down near my bed with her head facing the same direction as mine, but if she was very displeased with my behavior, she would put her head in the opposite direction. When she was really angry at me, she went as far away from me as possible, indicating by her whole manner how unjustly I had treated her. That night she slept near Inna and I was very sad that I had caused her such pain. I woke up several times during the night and quietly called her but she did not respond. In the morning she was lying on the door sill, showing me that she was still undecided—I'm not with you or with her, her proud and independent look said.

Unhappy with the state of affairs, I asked my friends to leave the two of us alone. They left, ordering her to remain with me, which she did, although very unwillingly. I sat on the porch steps and called her but she didn't respond.

"Come to me," I repeated the command. She stood near by, impudently looking me in the eye and ignoring me.

"Come to me, immediately!" I said in a harsh voice.

She unwillingly took a few steps in my direction. "Pizer!" I called very calmly, "Pizer!" She approached slowly and I went toward her to ease her struggle between love, custom and her still rankling pain at my betrayal. I walked up to her and put my hand on her collar, just in case she decided to run away. I cannot say that she obeyed joyfully—she lightly resisted while I slowly but firmly pushed her onto the porch where I sat down, hugged her and began to tell her my sad story from the moment when we parted, letting the tears flow down my cheeks. At first she did not want to listen and turned her face away, but gradually she forgave and began quietly to lick my tears and we made up. Unfortunately, our reunion was very brief, because in a few hours I sped off into total uncertainty.

*   *   *

After weighing all my options, I decided in August that my only chance was to use the invitation of Mark Nashpitz to try to get registered in Strunino. After completing his term of exile, Mark had settled in this city to the northeast of Moscow, outside the sixty-mile zone protecting the Soviet capital from criminal elements and "dangerous people" like Mark and me. Walking the streets of the city, I looked at the haggard, gloomy faces and imagined what my life would be like if I succeeded in getting registered there. It would be, in effect, a new difficult exile because the KGB and police would see to it that I did not leave the city.

Moscow, a mere two-hour train ride away, would tempt and draw me to it with the irresistible force of human companionship. Who knew, perhaps I would have to remain in the Soviet Union forever. I was the KGB's bait for the West and a symbol for the Jews. I had chosen my lot on my own, but who would have imagined that the ordeal would drag on for decades! Although I did not want to be locked up in that city of drunks and criminals, I could not live without that little stamp in my passport, and Mark had promised that he could get it for me.

Mark and I looked at the for-sale notices posted on the wall of a fence near the railroad station and examined all the places. A little house with one room, a kitchen, a tiny piece of land and a solitary tree seemed acceptable at an affordable price. The owner, who worked in the police station, said she could register me as soon as the following day if I decided to buy her house. In the morning Mark and I went to the woman, reached an agreement and set out together for the police station. How my heart fluttered when she took my passport and the forms and went into the passport section! Pale and tense, Mark and I waited anxiously until she returned with my passport.

"Everything's all right, and you thought it would take a lot of time," she said affably, clearly pleased that she had done us a favor. "We'll draw up the papers and in the meantime you can live in the house. If you need anything, come to the address where I live now."

"Well, what speed!" was all I succeeded to say, feeling both joyful and sad.

Mark went to his family, who were in Moscow, and I enjoyed my solitude, quiet and registration permit. On the morning of the fifth day after I had obtained the permit, the woman rushed in, looking very pale, her hands trembling.

"Where's Mark?" she asked, without even greeting me.

"Mark's in Moscow. Did something happen?"

"I won't sell the house. Give me your passport."

"No, I won't," I said firmly. "What happened?"

"Give me your passport!" she demanded.

I imagined myself for a moment without that stamp. "No, I won't give you my passport."

"I'm going to strike you out of the register anyway," she said, walking out.

"What happened?" I asked, following her, but she would not talk to me. I called Mark to inform him.

"Did you give her the passport?" he asked.

"No, of course not. But she's already struck me off the register at the police station, I'm sure."

"The hell with her, you have a permit in your passport and don't give it to anyone. I'll be back tomorrow morning to find out what happened."

At ten the next morning he told me the following: the evening before the woman had come to me, a chekist had come to her home and demanded that she immediately cancel my registration.

"Why should I? This woman is buying my home. You buy it and I'll register you," she told him.

"She is an enemy of the people, a Zionist, a criminal. She was just released from prison. Cancel her immediately," he demanded.

"But I have to sell the house and what difference does it make to me when she was released from prison? Almost everybody here has been released from prison!" she retorted, still resisting.

"Don't forget that your son is growing up. Now he's twelve, and then he'll be eighteen and we'll send him to Afghanistan. Give me the house registry book and I'll strike her off." The woman submissively gave him the book and the next morning came for my passport. She told Mark that she did not expect me to hand it over, but she had wanted to have another look at this awful woman, and having taken a look, she did not believe the chekist.

"Why are they so afraid of her? He was trembling all over when he spoke. What did she do—kill someone?"

Mark did not try to explain my difficult situation to the woman but just gave her some sausage to console her.

"Ida, you've got to get out of here quickly because any minute the police could come and take away your passport."

I myself realized that my rest was short-lived and had come to an end. At least fate had granted me a stamp in my passport and a few days' rest in preparation for new difficulties.

February 1983

My Dear Yakov,

For ten years I have been sending you birthday wishes by letter and it has been even longer than that since I have seen you. I didn't watch you grow up, I didn't see you become an adolescent, youth and a man, but I know that you are a sensitive, kind person who is always ready to help.

I am so eager to know everything about you, your friends and your interests. What profession are you choosing? Will you continue your studies or do you have other plans? Unfortunately, the difficult international situation has made me a hostage of cynical Soviet interests. It deprived me of much of my personal life but it has given me so much in the social sphere that even I sometimes look at my own life from an impersonal, detached point of view. Of course I want everything that a person should have! It's not easy, however, to escape one's fate, even a difficult one, and one must bear it with dignity. Our separation is lasting too long and many refuseniks all around have stopped believing that we shall be able to emigrate, but I believe and hope that we shall meet in the not distant future. We shall meet and rejoice together.

> *All my love and kisses on your birthday*
> *Ida*

CHAPTER 24

TIME WAS WORKING AGAINST ME IN MY SEARCH FOR A PLACE to reside legally. Autumn was approaching and in the cold weather it would be harder to travel. Moreover, my options were narrowing. My refusenik friends Isai and Grigori Goldshtein had inquired at the local KGB in Tbilisi concerning my chances of getting a residence permit there and had been told categorically, "The two of you are enough for us. Nudel will not be registered in Georgia or anyplace else in the Caucasus." I myself could not try the Ukraine, knowing how rabid the anti-Semitism was there. In short, I did not have a chance of being registered in any large city in the Soviet Union.

In my address book I had the name of a Jewish family in Bendery in the Moldavian republic, who had written to me in Siberia and sent me packages. I could not phone or write them in advance of my arrival because the correspondence of most Soviet citizens, not to mention refuseniks or dissidents, is opened. An elderly woman opened the door for me.

"I'm Ida Nudel. Can I see Anya or Mikhail Liberman?" I inquired.

"Ida." The woman began to tremble and cry. She hugged me and shouted, "Anya, Anya, look who's here, it's Ida Nudel!" Another woman dashed out of the room and we hugged. She offered me food, drink and a warm bath saying, "Go rest, I'll call Mikhail to come home immediately."

In the evening their friends the Royaks, another family of

refuseniks, came over to join in the happy excitement. I spent the first nights in the Libermans' tiny apartment, which was even too cramped for the family, and in two days I moved over to the Royaks'. They settled me on the couch, where the children had been sleeping, and moved the children into their small bedroom. They had electricity in the house but only cold water, and the toilet was outside. I became friendly with their youngest daughter, Leah, reading her stories and telling her about my special dog.

Mikhail Liberman, Slava Royak and I made the rounds of all the apartments for sale in the city. Only a person who lives in a given city, however, is entitled to buy there; my first step, therefore, was acquiring a residence permit, but in order to be registered in Bendery, I needed a stamp indicating that my previous residence permit had been canceled. I was afraid, however, of losing my fictitious registration in Strunino. Examining it, a policeman would not guess that I was some homeless wanderer. I decided not to return to Strunino until I had hopes of registering elsewhere.

Fortunately, a woman offered to help me get registered at her apartment. I therefore returned to Strunino and went to the police station.

"Please cancel my registration permit," I requested, handing the police officer my passport while my heart sank from fear.

She looked at the passport and then at me. "Oh, it's you! We canceled you in August."

"That was illegal, cancel it with today's date," I responded.

"Why today's date when we canceled you in our registry in August?"

"Cancel it with today's date," I said in such a way that she probably sensed that it came straight from my heart.

"What do I care," she said to herself, and she placed the date, October 26, 1982, on the stamp.

I immediately returned to Bendery without calling or seeing anyone. I was so tense I could not explain my problems to anyone. All I wanted was silence and solitude. The quiet train ride helped me regain my equilibrium, but only partially.

I sat motionless in the hall of the police station, silently praying for the success of the woman who had offered to help me. Slava was with me but he could not stand the waiting and kept walking outside and returning.

Finally the woman came out of the chief's office holding my

passport and a signed permit for registration. Quietly, I entered the office and silently handed over my passport and the permit. It was stamped and I went outside to rejoin Slava. Although I walked away, my feet wanted to fly, to escape quickly before my name was recognized.

"Thank God, I have a stamp in my passport and a registration permit," I said to Slava hurriedly and nervously. "Now I have to draw up papers quickly to buy a house and only then will I let myself believe that I have a place to live. I have to do everything very quickly, before the chekists catch on that I am already registered."

Slava tried to convince me that once I had a stamp the chekists could not do anything, but my bitter experience did not yet allow me to rejoice.

On the fifth day after I had obtained the permit, I arrived at a real estate office with the man who was selling me a house. The manager invited us in, but he was nervous and kept trying unsuccessfully to call someplace. Finally, after having spoken with someone over the phone, he said, "Give me your passport." He twisted and turned it, opening and closing it a few times. He was clearly stalling. Suddenly the door opened and three policemen came in.

"Citizen Nudel, come with us." One of them took my passport from the shaking hands of the office manager. The man who was selling me the house turned pale. Two policemen stood on both sides of me and a third, holding my passport, behind me. They obviously thought they had made a big catch.

"Get moving," commanded the one who was behind me. I began walking, with the policemen clinging to me. We passed through the hall in a tight cluster and swept out of the office to a police car standing on the sidewalk near the stairs. They probably thought I would run away from them!

"Get into the car! " they commanded.

I silently obeyed, sitting between the two policemen. The third sat in front, half turned toward me. Next to him was the driver. It was a picture familiar down to the last detail.

We piled into the police station in a tangle; one of them went ahead and I was shoved into a large room where a husky man was sitting behind a table. Although he was not that old, the big bags under his eyes suggested that either he drank a lot or was ill. I stood in the middle of the room, where the policeman had placed me.

"How did you manage to get registered in our city?" the chief asked after he had dismissed the two policemen. I decided instantly that I had to be patient and laconic.

"The usual way, like everyone, via the passport desk," I replied.

"No, you were not in the passport section!"

"You're wrong, I was."

"What does the room look like?" he asked.

While sitting in the waiting room I had caught a glimpse of the room where the head of the section was sitting. "An ordinary room; the desk is on the left."

"What was the woman who gave you the form for a residence permit wearing?"

"She was in something dark." I figured that she would not be at work in the police station in the fall in a bright dress.

"You did not appear in front of the head of the section; how did you manage to get registered?"

"I already told you everything."

"Why did you choose our city?" he suddenly demanded, standing up.

"There's a lot of food here, mountains of vegetables on the street. I came from Siberia, and after that, this is heaven on earth. Why not live in heaven?" I asked sincerely.

"Why did you pick our city?" he yelled this time, losing his temper.

"Is Bendery really a closed city? I didn't know."

"No, I didn't tell you that this is a closed city, but why did you come here?"

"What's the matter?" I asked. "I'm a citizen of the Soviet Union; my passport is on your table. According to the Soviet constitution, I have the right to live where I want to. Why do you keep on asking me why I chose your city? It's clean, green, well fed. Why shouldn't I live in it?"

"Your passport is counterfeit!"

"Look carefully; I was given it a few months ago in Siberia by your colleagues. I don't think the police hand out counterfeit passports."

"I'll let you rot in Siberia! Your passport is counterfeit!"

I looked at him silently, recalling a similar scene many years ago and I did exactly what I had done then. When he stopped to catch his breath, I told him firmly but quietly:

"Aren't you ashamed of yourself? You are the chief of police and have a pistol in your drawer, a button to call a guard and there are at least fifty policemen in the station. Why are you yelling at me! You hold my passport in your hands and you see that I have just been released."

He stormed toward the window, his back to me, and stood there silently for a few minutes.

"Come to me around seven in the evening with the woman at whose house you were registered," he said, without turning his head toward me. "Now go."

Outside, I told Slava, who was waiting for me, "This is completely fantastic. The chief said I should bring the woman whose house I'm registered at. Do you remember her address?"

"Yes," he replied, "we can warn her about everything."

It was dark when we finally located the home of the woman, who listened to our stormy and disjointed tale and understood everything at once.

"I'm not afraid of them, let's go together." On the way she coached me how to act. "Tell them that you'll pay me every month while you live in my house, but you did not give me any money yet. Say it like that and don't be afraid; if you don't panic, they won't be able to prove anything."

We arrived at the police station ten minutes ahead of time. That evening the chief was receiving people with complaints but the line quickly diminished. When one of the last two men entered the office, the remaining one said to us quietly, "It was terrible after you left. The police chief called in the head of the passport desk and threatened to fire her. He carried on so, that she burst out crying. She kept on saying that she did not register you."

The woman and I were called into the chief's office together. My eyes clouded over when I saw how many people were there. In addition to the chief there were seven men and one woman in the room, all dressed in black. We stood in front of them, where the policeman had placed us, at the end of the long room.

The police chief's face and voice were calm when he began to question us:

"Who registered Ida Yakovlevna, she herself or you?" he asked the apartment owner.

"She herself, I gave her my house registry book," the woman replied.

"For how long did you pay, Ida Yakovlevna?"

"I did not pay yet, I'll have to pay monthly, when I live there."

"Did you receive money for the residence permit?" he turned to the woman.

"No, she'll pay for lodging. I didn't take money for the permit."

"Did she take money from you, Ida Yakovlevna?"

"No, we agreed on a monthly payment."

The landlady said, "If you don't want her to be registered at my place, I'll cancel it tomorrow."

I was silent.

Suddenly the chief began to bellow at the woman, "I'll get you put in jail; tell me how much she paid you for the residence permit!"

"I did not take money from her. Why should I get into trouble with the police? What is she to me? She came in from the street and cried and begged me to register her. She had no place to live. If you don't want me to register her, I'll cancel her registration tomorrow."

All the people in black remained silent.

"You may go," he nodded to the woman. "But you remain, Ida Yakovlevna."

"You are all free to return to work," he said to his black horde. They marched out silently without looking at me. I remained standing in the same spot in the middle of the room.

Suddenly he asked me, "What will you do this evening?"

"That depends on whether I leave the police station or not!"

"You'll leave," he replied.

I immediately breathed a sigh of relief. That meant they had talked to Moscow and received a green light to register me in this city.

"Will you go to friends or to that woman where you are registered?" he asked me again.

"It's very dark now, and I don't know the city or how long I'll be in the police station. Most likely I'll go to friends."

He pressed one of the buttons on a telephone on the table

and said, "Duty officer, call a patrol car and take Nudel, Ida Ya-kovlevna, to her address."

I was so tired that day, so stretched beyond my emotional capacity that his action evoked no feelings.

"Thank you," I said when the door opened and a policeman announced that the car had arrived, "and goodbye."

"Relax, here is your passport, tomorrow you can draw up papers for the purchase of a home," he said, handing me my passport.

I found Slava and the woman waiting for me in the hall, and the police car took us through the dark city streets. "It's incomprehensible, but true," I later said to Slava. "This morning I was taken in perhaps the same car, but three policemen kept their eyes glued on me, thinking that I was a major criminal, and now in the evening this character takes a police car off the line of duty to take me to my address. What do you think?"

"I simply don't know what to think; I never had such an experience. You ought to know better than I."

The car brought us to the woman's house and she invited us in for tea and to stay the night in case the police came to check.

"No," I stated, "there won't be any inspections; that's illegal and the chief understood who he's dealing with. He won't make that kind of mistake. They will begin to ask the neighbors whether I live here or not but that will be the extent of it."

"I'm not afraid of them," she said.

Slava and I stayed a little longer to be polite, but we did not drink tea because we were in a hurry to get home after such a tense day.

I don't know why, but I usually make my decisions at night, after waking up suddenly. Warmly wrapped in a blanket, I analyze, compare situations and seek to discover the logic of it all. I woke up in the middle of the night, having rested despite the madness of the previous day. I couldn't believe it: I was registered. And besides, I was sure that there would be no obstacles to my purchasing a house.

What are you so happy about, you foolish woman, I chastised myself. This is not Siberia but it will be similar. I could leave town only by bus or train, both of which were guarded by the police. I could, of course, try to hitch a ride, but there was no assurance that I would not be picked up by chekists out to teach me a lesson.

Everyone would recognize my face, not just the policemen but also every informer. I could not leave town unnoticed and that is why I was left in Bendery. It was impossible to go anywhere by foot, and Moscow was thousands of miles away.

Did they leave me in Bendery because it was almost winter and I was homeless; did they have pity on me? I did not believe that! I realized that fate had once again smiled on me. No matter how difficult it was, I had to go on living.

Lying with my eyes closed on the couch in Slava's hospitable home, I could picture the fruit trees blooming in front of the house I had wanted to buy, but I did not dare phone the owner, he had been so frightened when the three strapping policemen had taken me away. Winter was approaching, however, and I needed shelter for me and for poor Pizer, who had been transferred from one person to another.

I soon phoned the man with the house I wanted and heard his affable voice. "Well, where have you been? You're alive; you didn't have any second thoughts?"

"No, I simply had some unpleasantness."

"Is everything all right now?" he asked.

"Yes, relatively speaking. Let's conclude the deal."

"Excellent," he answered, "come tomorrow morning at about ten to the same place where we met before."

"Fine." I had wasted several days in fears and doubts but now the entire bureaucratic side of the deal proceeded without any hitches, as if some invisible being were opening all the doors ahead of me. The price of the house was beyond my means, but fortunately my sister sent me money and I became the owner of a little garden and a small apartment with a large stove in the middle of the room, and whose only convenience was electricity. Although there had been a phone in the apartment, it was removed before my arrival and I was still dependent on pay phones. Again I had to fetch water and coal and stoke a coal stove. Again I had to run outside to the outhouse, which, like the Siberian one, was made of wooden planks that did not keep out either the cold wind or curious eyes. Of course this was not Siberia—the temperature did not go below minus fifteen Fahrenheit. But nevertheless, there was much in common.

Before it got too cold, I went to fetch Pizer. I was not afraid

to travel now—I had that invaluable residence permit in my passport and the chekists knew from bugged phone conversations that
I was going for my dog. When she arrived, Pizer ran happily around
the whole yard, chasing away a horde of cats eating near the chicken
coop, and then running back to me.

"Sit down, my auburn darling, let's talk." I extended my hand
to her and with a gracious, regal movement, she gave me her paw.
I told her we would live here and she listened carefully, catching
the nuances of my voice. When she heard a familiar word, she
perked up her ears and I knew then that she had understood.
"Everything around here is yours but that area over there is not.
It's better not to go on that path or the neighbors might object."
She looked into my eyes with a hypnotic stare. "And now—take
a walk." I let go of her paw, but she clung to me, as if saying,
"Don't be afraid, Ida, I am with you. We have gone through so
much together; we will handle this, too."

"You're right, we'll manage, but one thing worries me—how
long will we have to live here? Will it really be all our lives? I
certainly don't want that!"

I went around the yard with her, examining everything that
had to be done. It was completely cluttered—what kind of people
had lived here and tossed out so much garbage, broken beds and
chairs? I also looked over the inside of the apartment with a pro-
prietor's eyes. Everything had to be redone—the electric wires
were tied together by bits and pieces and hung in shreds here and
there, and the stove had to be checked.

I willingly set to work, but it took months before I was able
to establish the kind of order which enabled me to become somewhat reconciled to my new home.

In Bendery, I began to meet new people, some through my
friends and some on my own. My story was well known to many
Jews in the Soviet Union, for even though the Soviet regime did
not spare money and energy to jam the Voice of Israel, some information still managed to filter through. At the same time, my
sister was tireless. She begged and demanded from Soviet leaders
and prayed and appealed to people all over the world to help in
persuading her former motherland to open its jaws and spew me
out to Israel.

Jews, or at least my friends' acquaintances, were not afraid to be with me and I began to feel that there was some meaning to my life in this new backwoods.

"Let's start celebrating the Jewish holidays," I suggested to my new friends. "We can tell stories to the children and teach them songs and dances. It will add spice to our life." They yielded to my enthusiasm, perhaps out of respect for my gray hair! We were kept very busy with preparations—writing skits, rehearsing songs and poetry, sewing costumes and baking pies. On Hanukkah in 1982 we gathered for our celebration. The children were happily and noisily jumping around and the dog was barking when suddenly we heard the doorbell ring.

"The police, an inspection of documents," announced a voice.

"What's the matter?" I asked, a smile still lingering on my lips, as I opened the door.

"Everyone must present his documents," the policeman repeated.

I could not permit him to do this. The document check would not make any difference to the refuseniks because their names were already well known to the authorities, but it was unadvisable that the documents of those who had not yet decided to emigrate would land in the hands of the police.

"Why are you suddenly coming to check documents only in my apartment? It's because I'm a Jew, isn't it?"

There was an unwritten law in the Soviet Union that one does not mention someone's Jewishness. The word Jew has immediate associations of spy, traitor and enemy. The fact that I myself mentioned my Jewishness put the policeman in an embarrassing situation and he asked, "Who said anything about Jews?"

"You came here during our holiday, disturbed the peace and ruined our mood. Do you have a written order? Show it to us!"

Several people came to my aid and asked him why he had come when we were celebrating our holiday. "Look," they said, "here's my Soviet passport!"

Confused by our unconventional response, the policemen left. "In Moscow nothing would have helped," I told my friends when we closed the door. "In Moscow they would have burst in and dragged everyone away or, at the very least, recorded our names. Here they are not used to getting rebuffed."

Nevertheless, my guests were unhappy and whispered sadly among themselves. "Don't be afraid, there won't be any consequences," I assured them. No one listened to me, however, and the party mood turned funereal. People left the house separately, as if trying to show that they had dropped in casually and did not know one another.

On the street a few days later I met one of the women who had been at my house with all her children. Although she was coming directly toward me, she looked sternly ahead, not wanting to recognize me.

My life seemed to be going in circles again.

Sad or not, a person still has to fill his life somehow and give it meaning. The meaning and goal of my life was Israel: I passionately wanted to be there with my family and to be useful to my little country. It was difficult to try to work toward my goal in such isolation. I decided to try to meet as many local Jews as possible and to learn their moods and thoughts. When I saw a help-wanted ad for work in the fall and summer at an amusement park, it seemed like just what I needed. While I entertained the children with rides on wooden donkeys and camels, I would speak with their mothers and grandmothers and see whether they already planned to emigrate or what would hold them back if the opportunity suddenly presented itself.

The work at the park was leisurely during the week but hectic on weekends. I was the sole attendant responsible for three separate rides—it seemed like I myself was on a merry-go-round, constantly strapping children into one ride and freeing them from another. However, my reasoning for taking the job was proven correct. I did manage to meet and talk to many families, although I don't know how successful I was in my discussions.

My domestic tasks were taxing as well. In the garden that came with the house I had to weed, water and protect the plants from various dangers. Irritated by the cluttered yard, I gathered up the rags, bottles, remains of building material and other pieces of junk that had probably accumulated over decades. After dragging the heavy loads, my heart would beat like a drum. I fell asleep by swallowing various pills but would suddenly wake up at two or three at night from the pounding of my restless heart.

"Why are you doing this, Ida?" a neighbor asked when he saw me clutching my chest after carrying another heavy bucket. "Let it be messy, your health is more important!"

"I can't stand living in such dirt; anyhow, my heart has got to hammer, otherwise I'll forget that I'm alive." Perhaps the heavy labor was my salvation; at any rate, it provided an escape from the drumroll of my soul.

Pizer also suffered, perhaps in solidarity or perhaps because of the climate. In Siberia she had enjoyed the snow and long walks in the taiga and she had been a favorite in the village. Here, cut off by fences from the street and people, she was bored and unhappy. "You need to pair her off, otherwise she'll be even more unhappy," a man told me. A careful search led to a slightly cross-eyed but young fellow who had a good birthright. In another sixty-three days I became the owner of another seven little healthy and hungry collies, all of whom survived.

In the summer of 1983 I saw the fruits of my labor in the garden and my guests received bouquets of fresh lettuce, dill, parsley, celery and other greens. When autumn arrived I felt the longing for Moscow even more strongly but I was not sure of my status. I had been expelled for over a year and under threat of criminal prosecution forbidden to appear in Moscow or within the sixty-mile radius of the city.

I thought it might make sense to speak with the chief of the seventy-second precinct in Moscow, who had read me the expulsion order. After several days of hanging around the post office waiting for a phone line to Moscow, I finally got him at work.

"Oh, it's you. Where are you living?" he asked.

"I am registered and living in Bendery in Moldavia," I replied.

"How's the weather there?" he inquired.

"Excellent compared to Siberia. I am calling to find out whether there is a time limit to the order expelling me from Moscow or is it open-ended?"

"I don't know and I can't help," he answered.

I next tried to phone Mark Nashpitz since the law also affected him, but he, too, was unable to give me any more information and I remained in Bendery.

My Dear Ones,

I have answered everything in all your letters. Time flies but life in exile drags on slowly.

Yesterday I had a dream in which I saw myself climbing a snowy mountain; the snow was crumbling under my feet but I kept walking forward. There were some people behind me. We were almost at the top but the snow kept caving in under our feet. One more avalanche and I would fall down with the snow.

Suddenly I saw a dark spot. I stretched out my hand and grabbed it. It was a window frame and there were some people behind it. I cried, "Lena, Lena, faster!"

At the very summit of the mountain some people threw us a board which was bound with brown metal and had nails at the ends. I realized that the nails were to keep us from slipping. I quickly stood on the board and walked on it to the people. I did not see myself and don't know whether I crossed successfully or not. There was another avalanche. Both ends of the board lay precariously on a tiny protuberance, but they were still lying there. That's all. We shall overcome or we have done so already. In the meantime, goodbye for now. I await your letters. Hearty greetings to all our friends.

Ida

CHAPTER 25

On a winter day in 1984 the post office summoned me for a call from Lev Blitshtein, who asked whether I could come to Moscow between February 12 and 15. Since our phones were tapped, we tried to reveal as little as possible, but I knew that if Lev had contacted me, he had an important reason and I promised to try to get to Moscow. First, I had to find a place for Pizer. This proved to be no problem when the Libermans kindly agreed to take her for a week. The rest of my preparations, however, were not as easy. The day after I bought a plane ticket for Moscow, a policeman appeared at my door to summon me to the station.

"Please bring me a written notice," I told him. "After all, you know that is how the police summon people."

He left and returned a little later with a notice indicating the time and purpose of the summons: "For a conversation with the police chief."

I had no choice but to obey. On the way I left Pizer at the Royaks' and informed them of my summons.

The police chief greeted me politely. "Ida Yakovlevna, we haven't seen each other for a long time, how are you doing?"

"Fine, thank you. Why did you summon me here?" I demanded.

His expression turned harsh and he asked, "You want to go someplace?"

"Am I really under surveillance? I didn't know anything about it; I didn't sign any papers and did not promise to inform on my-self."

"No, you are not under surveillance."

"Then I don't understand why you are asking such a ques-tion."

"Look, Ida Yakovlevna, you are an unusual citizen. You just finished serving your sentence. Of course the police force observes those who were in trouble with the law. I am warning you not to leave this city. I will personally have to answer for this."

"Give it to me in writing that I may not leave the city."

"I hope you understand me and that my word is sufficient."

"I shall protest against your illegal demand; I am a free per-son," I declared and left the office.

I picked up Pizer from the Royaks'. She was happy to see me, but turned sad when she looked at my face. "Something happened to you again," her attentive gaze knew. Hoping to calm myself down and figure out what to do next, I took her for a stroll.

"Let's go for a little walk, my auburn beauty."

Still suffering from my Siberian tribulations, I did not want to get into trouble again with the regime, but I saw no other way out. If I silently accepted their restrictions, they would simply crush me. Although my chances for gaining satisfaction were almost nil, I decided to turn to the procurator's office. At least if a conflict developed later on, I could refer to the fact that I had warned the procurator's office that my rights had been violated and that the procurator, in fact, had sanctioned such an offense.

I had met the procurator the previous fall after the police had broken up our Hanukkah celebration. Mikhail Liberman, Slava Royak and I had complained to the procurator's office about the police's violation of our civil rights and infringement of our national rights. The chief procurator of the city declared that we did not have the right to assemble on Jewish national holidays and warned us that if we did not stop our activity, he would charge us with the establishment of an unregistered religious community, and as the leader of such, I could then be held criminally responsible.

"Do you know what we did?" Mikhail had asked him.

"What did you do?"

"We sang songs and danced," Slava had replied.

"You sang Zionist anti-Soviet songs," he said. "Don't forget, Nudel, that you have recently served a sentence."

"Is that a threat? Fortunately, it's not up to you whether I receive a new term or not. That depends on relations between America and the Soviet Union and you know that as well as I."

Standing before this same procurator once again, I was sure he would support the police.

"Leave a complaint and I'll investigate it."

"When will you give me an answer?"

"In a month or so. We'll call you when your complaint has been considered."

"Please do it quickly, if possible. Can I count on a written reply?"

"Of course," he promised. I never received any reply from him.

That evening, as I returned home after having dropped off the dog at the Libermans', I noticed a car with its headlights off across the street from my house. I went up to it and saw three men inside. Deciding that they must be watching me, I went outside several times during the night and saw that the car remained in the same place.

In the morning the taxi arrived on time and I set out for the airport with the other car following right behind. The two cars arrived together at the terminal. Inside it was difficult for me to guess what the chekists were up to; not only was the waiting room full of people but also my heavy bag slowed me down. In any case, it was not likely that a car with three chekists and a driver had guarded my house all night and accompanied me all that distance just to make sure that I successfully boarded the plane.

Finally it was my turn to check in at the airline counter. The clerk who took my passport started to tremble when he read my name, his hands shaking as if he had Parkinson's disease. Stalling for time, he inanely kept turning over my passport and ticket while looking all around.

"Give me back my ticket and passport!" I demanded.

He silently kept leafing through my passport.

"Give me my ticket and passport!" I repeated loudly. "What is going on?"

His hand trembled as he slowly extended his hand to me with my ticket. His dilemma was painfully clear: he could not leave his post but his anxious nods to some invisible person were ineffective.

The people on line began to raise a commotion. "What's taking you so long? Look how many people are waiting, work faster!"

The clerk held out my passport, but he did not want to let it out of his hands.

I pulled it toward me, but his trembling hand held it tightly. The crowd behind me was hollering; boarding for the Moscow flight had already been announced.

Without waiting for the police or further instructions, he let go of the passport. I wondered what would happen next.

I phoned Lev Blitshtein in Moscow to tell him about the situation. While I was speaking a man remained glued to the glass door of the telephone booth.

The line for boarding the Moscow flight moved slowly and I noticed a lot of policemen standing around the crowded security checkpoint. When my turn came to present my ticket and passport, I saw the clerk look at a list, then turn her head to the side and nod to someone. A sharp peremptory command rang out, "There's the woman, take her!" Turning my head in the same direction as the attendant, I saw that the order came from a young man in a brown leather jacket who pointed an umbrella at me—how picturesque! The area quickly emptied out and a policeman appeared on each side of me. The clerk gave one of the policemen my passport and ticket. The man with the umbrella went through a side door.

"Citizen, follow me!" said the policeman.

"First of all, explain what is going on here!" I demanded.

"Citizen, you are causing problems," stated the policeman.

"Why did you detain me? Give me back my passport and ticket," I demanded.

Some people were hurried through the security checkpoint so that they wouldn't hear what I was saying.

"Why did you detain me—because I am a Jew and want to leave your country? Because I'm a Jew I'm not allowed to travel around the country? Tell me and the other people what you are doing!" I accused.

"Citizen, follow me, you are obstructing the operation of the airport and we shall punish you!" The policeman took me by the shoulders and began to push me toward a door behind which a chekist was hiding.

"Get your hands off me, don't you know that the law prohibits you from touching me!"

He jumped away, clearly unsure what to do. Was he allowed to beat me or not? They stalled until the plane departed at 6:05 and the building emptied out. Only one policeman remained with me.

"We'll return your money for the ticket," he said. "Go to the cashier, here is your ticket and passport."

"Why should I lose fifty percent of the cost? I lost twenty-five rubles which I paid for the taxi and I ruined my nerves and health. Doesn't that count for something?"

"Sit here and I'll be right back!"

The policeman returned, bringing me the money. I had missed my plane and no one would sell me another ticket. I silently took the money and left.

It did not seem like anyone was following me so I decided to try to travel to Odessa and from there to Moscow. Tired from dragging around my heavy bag, I took a taxi from the crowded bus station to the train station. The dispatcher announced that the train standing on the tracks would leave for Odessa in a minute. I started rushing to the ticket booth because I did not yet have a ticket. The ticket seller instructed me, "You won't make it, get on the train immediately!" Without a ticket I ran and barely managed to jump into the car before the train pulled out. Exhausted from the ordeal of the morning, I sat huddled in a corner of the bench. When the conductor entered the car, I took ten rubles out of my bag to cover the ticket and the penalty for not having bought the ticket at the station. The conductor, however, paid absolutely no attention to me and went by without even asking for my ticket. At least I had gotten lucky here, I thought. I did not have the strength to explain things to the conductor.

When a strange man entered the compartment, I knew instinctively that he was a chekist, and I changed my place so that I could look over the passengers more easily. Yes, I was under guard—I spotted another man and a woman, too, reading a book in the oddest manner, without turning the pages. I wondered why they were traveling with me instead of sending me back to Bendery.

From the train station I phoned David Shekhter, a young refusenik, and asked him to help me fly to Moscow.

"Wait for me next to the telephone booth; I'll come in fifteen minutes," he said.

"Remember I'm under guard."

"I'll be there soon, just wait."

David hurried over and was not discouraged by my entourage. "We'll slip away from them; I was born here and know every alleyway," he said, taking my heavy bag. "Don't stay behind."

I felt more cheerful once I had gotten rid of my burden. We walked rapidly down some side streets, then turned and suddenly turned again in the opposite direction. "Now run fast, keep up with me, we'll get away from them now," he said, hurrying with long strides. I kept up with all my might, as if my chest pains, aches and ulcers did not exist.

"Phew," David said, when we had passed an iron fence. "I think we got away." Just then we saw the smiling mug of a man running toward us and David started cursing. "No, you won't succeed; now the Odessa KGB is after you and they know the city just as well as I do; they have Japanese walkie-talkies and patrol cars. What do you think they want from you?" he asked.

"I don't think they want anything; I suspect they are practicing surveillance and control techniques. They have to pass some examination or do some work under supervision. And I am their guinea pig."

"It can't be; there are so many people and cars. That's a lot of expense for such work," he mused.

"Who worries about money? They have to account for their work, for 'foiling the intended action of Ida Nudel.' I'm sure they receive a citation or some other reward."

"Are you serious?"

"Not only am I serious; I'm sure I'm right." I then asked, "David, perhaps you know someone who could buy a ticket for me in advance?"

"Yes, of course; you rest and I'll get it."

"Where does this person work?"

"In the central ticket office."

"Does she herself sell tickets?"

"Yes, at the cash register."

"That's no good. She'll put down the number of her machine and will get into trouble; they could even drive her from her job. Is she Jewish?"

"Yes."

"Then she'll get fired for sure. Tomorrow I'll try again myself, but for today, please take me to the Nepomnyashchy family."

A car with four men in it stood outside the entrance to my Odessa friends' home for the whole night. The next morning I didn't have the energy to continue my marathon. Managing to stir only after midday, I traveled to the airport, secretly hoping that there would be no ticket to Moscow and I could return to Bendery to rest from the last three nerve-racking days. This is indeed what happened and I returned home, accompanied by a crowd of chekists; two even rode with me in the bus. If all this had not happened to me, I would never have believed that it was real, or possible. What was it that I possibly could have done in Moscow that made it worthwhile to post four chekists and a car to follow every step of mine, not to mention the additional people who were drawn into this idiotic game? Every one of the men who were constantly chasing me seemed to be talking to his own armpit as he yelled into the walkie-talkie nestled there, "I'm following the target." At the same time someone on the other end was listening to his armpit, following and keeping track. I would have no rest until I could escape from these mindless savages.

My life dragged on monotonously, filled with work in the garden, letters to my sister in Israel and to the prison zones. My attempts to influence the Jews in Bendery had been frustrated by the police's disrupting our Hanukkah celebration. The circle of three families in Bendery who were not afraid to associate with me was so small that it was also difficult to keep relations on an even keel with them. I wrote dozens of letters a week in order to maintain contact with the outside world. I began to hate both letter writing and my writing desk. As in Siberia, I spent a lot of time with Pizer, talking and playing with her. I also did a lot of reading—everything that I could get hold of in English. A lot of time and energy was taken by the lack of conveniences in my life. I had to drag in coal, stoke the stove, tend the vegetable garden.

Sometimes I got a brief visit of a few hours when someone would come to talk or unburden his soul, write a complaint or consult on some matter. I would get so worked up from the conversations and the contact with people that it would take a few days to return to my normal self.

CHAPTER 26

December 1983

My Dear Ones!
I haven't heard from Lena for a while. How is your correspondence with Jane Fonda going? I know of Jane only from the film They Shoot Horses, Don't They? *It's probably about fifteen years since I saw that film, but even now I still remember some scenes as if I had seen it yesterday. Both the subject matter and the acting were striking, particularly young Jane. Since then I have only read about her films. From what I understand, her films always touch on a serious social problem; therefore she must be very understanding of my story. She has a vivid and strong personality and she, too, rebels against indifference. People really admire her here. The authorities are interested in her and she could travel to Bendery. Please see that she gets a copy of the movie which I made with Zhenya Tsirlin. She will understand that I am not a primitive criminal, alcoholic or hooligan as the authorities claim but a normal person who openly and loudly declares her ideals and defends them. Because she is a sensitive person she will feel my sincerity and directness and will trust me. My English is poor but I can express the most important things. It would be wonderful if Jane succeeded in breaking through my isolation, even for a short time. Given my personality and my goals, it is a terrible ordeal to be cut off from my normal surroundings*

*for so many years! Please send her the film. It will give me
the opportunity to speak with Jane before we meet; I do
believe that we shall meet. Keep me informed; it's very, very
important.*

*Love and kisses,
Ida*

February 1984

My Dear Ones!
*I received your letter describing Jane's meeting with Dobrynin
[Soviet ambassador to the U.S.]. Bendery is a completely open
city; there is no point in their intimidating her. There are no
tourists here either because they did not construct a suitable
hotel or because there are several military garrisons near the
Romanian border.*

*Please tell Jane that she has nothing to worry about. If the
authorities permit her to come, then they will guarantee her a
successful trip. She should know that the Soviet regime is
interested in her good will. Whether they permit her or not
depends on her perseverence. If she repeats her request
several times, they will give in, believe me. Tell Jane I hope she
is persistent; she will receive an entry visa. It would be
marvelous if she comes! This little city would be so happy. Our
life here is so emotionally deprived. The intelligentsia languishes
terribly: the capital of the republic is fifty miles away and only
someone with a car or relatives in Kishinev can manage to
attend a play or concert. Usually, however, those who thirst for a
play or concert do not own cars. As for me, I don't move
anywhere, even in this little town, without my guard. They
probably do that in order to frighten the townspeople from
associating with me.*

*I am planning and dreaming about meeting Jane. What a
shame that one of her films is not showing now.*

*For some reason your letters take a month to creep to me,
whereas other people get mail in twelve days. What are my*

tormentors learning from them, what are they examining and sniffing out?

Goodbye until the next letter.

Love and kisses,
Ida

April 1984

My Dear Ones!

What joy! She is coming! I can't believe it! She won! What a remarkable woman! I told Slava about it and he agreed to help me and to take care of the dog at his house on the day that Jane arrives. I am so excited. In the past few days I have been breaking my teeth practicing new words in English. I have no experience speaking the language. I turned to local teachers a long time ago but they were afraid of getting into trouble. Only one agreed but I am making little progress with her.

I wonder if they'll let me meet her? Please write more often and tell me everything you know about her upcoming visit. Everything!

Love and kisses,
Ida

April 1984

My Dear Ones,

We met! I must tell you how it happened. Lena, they delivered your telegram two days late; how clever you were to phone Slava and inform him and me that Jane was arriving on April 26.

I woke up at four in the morning of that marvelous day and took the first bus to Kishinev. It seemed like no one was following me but when I got off the bus, I noticed a car parked brazenly on the sidewalk. The Kishinev chekists "welcomed" me and accompanied me around the city. I did not know whether that meant they wanted to disrupt the meeting or not. In trying to slip away I jumped onto a bus that was starting to

move, but a hefty fellow jumped right after me. The bus was
very crowded and he reported on his activities almost in my ear.
It made me nauseous to hear his abominable "I'm following the
target." I tried to get rid of my guard several more times but
was unsuccessful. These pressures were too much for me.

I decided to go to the hotel where I had agreed to meet Slava
at midday. Exactly at twelve o'clock the tails left me alone. I felt
immediately that no one was breathing down my neck. Slava
and I sped to the airport; we knew the number of the flight and
arrival time from Lena's call. We were ten minutes late but it
turned out that the flight had been canceled. A flight from
Moscow had arrived an hour earlier. We then rushed to the hotel
—luckily there is only one Intourist Hotel in Kishinev.

I asked a foreigner to inquire at the registration desk whether
there was a Jane Fonda at the hotel. They told him she had
arrived. I couldn't believe that they actually revealed information
in the U.S.S.R.

After circling around the hotel for a while, Slava and I decided
we had to try something. Fortunately, Lena had mentioned that
a Marshall Grossman was with Jane. I went to the registration
desk and stated authoritatively that I had to see Marshall
Grossman, who was staying in the hotel.

"What is your connection with this person?" asked the clerk.

"He's a relative," I replied.

"Sit down and wait until he comes down. We don't call
anyone."

"But I don't know what he looks like!"

"What, you can't recognize your relative?" she asked.

"I never saw him. He lives in America and I live here."

"I won't look for him for you."

"Please give me his phone number."

"No, we don't give out such information. By the way, there he
is."

"Which one?"

She hesitated. "The tallest man."

"Marshall," I shouted. "I'm Ida."

An enormous man rushed to me, doubled over and lifted me
in a hug. "I can't believe we're together," he kept repeating.
"How did you find us? We wanted to visit you tomorrow. I was
about to arrange the trip. Let's go upstairs quickly. Jane will be

so happy. She didn't think you would find us. Meet Steve Rivers; the three of us came together.''

While we were oohing and aahing and laughing happily, Steve went up to tell Jane. When Marshall and I reached her room, we heard her excited voice from behind the door, "One minute, I just got out of the bath!"

In a few minutes the door opened and Jane stepped out into the hall. "Where is she?" Jane asked in confusion as Marshall partially concealed me. He moved away slightly and Jane exclaimed, "Such a great country is afraid of such a small woman?" We hugged, and the rest—walking, eating, talking— remains for me till today a thick haze. Slava and I left in time to make the last train back to Bendery. It's difficult for me to say how many hours I slept that night or whether I slept at all.

The authorities not only permitted Jane to spend a day in Bendery but even provided her with a rented car, an English-speaking driver and guide, a hitherto unheard of luxury in Moldavia. My guests arrived at my house at noon on a gray, rainy day. As if the rain had washed them away, the street for once was empty of KGB and police cars. Jane was modestly dressed in a brownish-beige long wool coat with a brown shawl draped over her shoulders. A transparent raincoat covered her from head to toe. Her hair was tied back simply like mine and she wore dark-framed glasses and no makup. As we talked she studied my movements, following me into the kitchen, and imitating some of my gestures. I was so excited I really can't say whether the guests understood my weak English but I know they saw my situation clearly and understood what I was going through.

It was too rainy to go touring around the town, but Jane suggested sending a telegram in order to arrange a meeting with the communist party leader Chernenko on her return to Moscow. We went to the post office and asked the clerk to help us send a telegram as quickly as possible. The tiny room on the second floor contained a table and a chair. Several propaganda posters and a map of the city hung on the wall.

Steve decided to take a picture of Jane sitting near the table, but as soon as he clicked the camera some woman clerk began to scream, "They're spies, they're photographing a map of the city. They'll know everything about us!"

I translated and Jane became terribly upset. "I don't know how this happened and I didn't believe that such a thing could happen. This is real spy-mania."

Various officials ran up to us and began demanding one after the other, "Who let you in here? How did you get here? What are you doing here?"

"What are you women so panicked about?" I answered. "It's not the fifteenth century that you have to get into such a flutter. If there are foreigners in this town, that means that the KGB gave them permission."

The sounds of the familiar name gave them an idea and someone went to call the authorities. While we were squabbling, unequivocal instructions apparently arrived from the KGB. It was clear from the women's conduct that they had been ordered not to make a scandal, to behave correctly and to accept the telegram addressed to Chernenko.

We said goodbye in the evening. Jane, Marshall and Steve traveled back to Kishinev and I sat down on a bench in my garden with Pizer lying near my feet. What did her visit mean? Was it merely a publicity stunt on the part of the regime or might it mean something more momentous about my future?

Love,
Ida

My Dear Ones!

　　The Passover holiday begins in a few hours. I have cleaned the apartment, cut some magnificent yellow tulips, and Pizer and I are ready to greet the holiday.

　　It took me a long time to recover from the last time when they threw me off the bus. Externally it appeared as if I did not react to the incident but my soul cried for a long time and I could not calm down. I dropped everything—I had no desire to read or write and even the garden did not give me any pleasure. Even though it was springtime and all living things were rejoicing, I was unable to enjoy life. Each year it becomes harder and harder for me to overcome stressful situations. I am growing more distrustful and skeptical about people. This KGB experiment on me is continuing much too long. I pray that I will not be consumed by a terrible feeling of disillusionment. I do believe I shall hold up mentally and not give in.

　　It is difficult, however, to live in solitude; there is no one to share my pain. The people who come to me primarily want to unburden their pain; one's own pain is always the hardest. I sympathize with them. Sometimes I, too, complain at the injustice of society and the stupidity of neighbors or friends.

　　This letter has turned out very gloomy.

　　In a few minutes it will be Passover. Be well.

Love and kisses,
Ida

CHAPTER 27

ONE NIGHT IN EARLY MAY 1986 IT BECAME DIFFICULT FOR ME to breathe. In the middle of the night I had to open the window wide, but it became even worse. All my bones ached. I had felt something like this before but could not recall when. It was particularly painful in the area of my kidneys. I suddenly remembered that I had felt this way when I had been poisoned at Krivosheino. But why did I have this sensation now? Had I eaten or drunk something yesterday? Had the chekists poisoned me again?

During the whole day of May 3 I felt nauseous, my mouth was dry and I wanted to drink all the time. My head ached with an unfamiliar pain. In the evening I finally connected it with the foreign news reports over the past several days that had been filtering through jamming noise: an atomic reactor had exploded somewhere in the Soviet Union and a cloud of radioactive fallout was circling above the earth. Neither the Soviet nor foreign broadcasts explained what to do or how to protect yourself; we were left alone.

On the night of May 9, I again felt nausea, pain in my bones, dryness in the throat and a headache. This time I knew what it meant. Western radio broadcasts reported that besides those who lived right near the Chernobyl reactor, people in Kiev, about sixty miles away, were also suffering. Bendery, almost six hundred miles from Chernobyl, was outside the most acute danger zone and I wondered whether I could help any acquaintances in Kiev. I called Lyuba Murzhenko, the wife of one of the non-Jews arrested in the

Leningrad hijacking case, and asked whether she would like to come to Bendery for a while. Lyuba was very happy to receive my invitation and informed me that she would bring another mother and a total of five children.

Figuring that my neighbors would not be pleased about such a crowd of children, I decided to "legalize" the situation with the police. The police chief received me immediately. "Ida Yakovlevna, at your service; you know that I regard you with the greatest respect. Yes, of course the police would not object if you take in so many children," he said. "We shall have to register all those who stay with you." The neighbors also supported my decision. It took another two weeks for them to arrive because Kiev was seized by panic, making departure difficult.

When the children arrived, they were pale and nervous. The crowd of people left no room for me in the house. In the summer it was warm and easy to sleep out in the open, but we would have to make different arrangements in the fall.

I don't know how the people who lived near Chernobyl felt but I, living far from the explosion, felt its negative effects. The leaves on the trees became brownish and it made me wonder what would happen to us. My dog was also very sad and lay around drinking a lot. Rumors circulated about how to protect yourself, resulting in many people drinking iodine, alcohol, vodka or dry wine. They also ate large quantities of the contaminated greens which had just appeared in the market.

As if to torture us, the harvests were fantastic that summer. The cherries in my yard were beautifully large and red but I forbade the children to pick the tempting fruit. Nevertheless, when the adults were not around, climbing one on top of the other, they would pick the magnificent but dangerous fruits.

Other troubles came directly from nature. I remember the incredibly hot day of August 31, 1986. I was alone in the house, as the Kievans had gone away for a few days. The sun did more than bake and burn; it looked as if it wanted to destroy. Toward evening a wind started blowing, chasing clouds across the sky. At night I twisted and turned for a long time before I finally fell asleep. I woke up suddenly at the sound of a tremendous roar; it seemed as if a heavy truck had lost control and was rushing at me. I jumped up and ran to the window. It was thundering and raining cats and dogs; the darkness was illuminated by flashes of lightning. Dogs were barking madly, frightened chickens were cackling and people were screaming. I had no idea what was happening.

All of a sudden my little house began to rise and fall as if it were rocking at sea. At first the waves were broad—perhaps three or four of them. The wooden boards, closely nailed together, bent strangely under foot, then the walls and ceiling also started bending.

Afterward the broad waves were replaced by shorter, more intense ones. Each second they became more frequent and shorter and soon every living and inanimate thing was shaking with a slight tremor in dissonance with our internal rhythm. A mysterious approaching rumble added to the eerie feeling that paralyzed my muscles and brain. The entire apartment was in motion: lamps were rocking and ringing, pieces of plaster snowed onto the floor.

I was standing dazed in my nightgown in the middle of the room when the noise and tremors suddenly stopped. I managed to jump up, grab my coat and run out of the house, screaming to Pizer, "Follow me!"

The neighbors, similarly garbed in their nightclothes, gathered in the courtyard. The mixed sound of crying children, hysterical women and howling animals was incredible.

"Ida, don't go into the house," a neighbor yelled to me. "It's going to start again!" Before he finished speaking, everything began to shake again, but much more quietly. All night we heard the sirens of ambulances and police cars. In the morning we found out that the earthquake had measured six on the Richter scale. We were fortunate that it had been short. According to official reports, it lasted less than a minute, but to me it seemed like eternity.

My house withstood the ordeal. Although there were some large cracks and some corners had crumbled, my apartment was intact. That's what it means to live in a house that was built a hundred years ago of clay with walls three feet thick.

When autumn came I was called one day to the police and told that all out-of-towners had to return to their original place of registration.

"But the radiation there is high," I objected.

"Everything is clean. If it were not possible to live there, no one would have returned. We are warning you that we shall not extend the temporary permit; everyone must go back."

I returned from the police with the sad news. Both mothers

decided not to return to Kiev for the time being because their relatives reported that radiation was still very high. My Moscow friends collected a hundred rubles for each child and this enabled the mothers to travel elsewhere, delaying their return to Kiev for several months.

In October the noisy herd left my home and everything became quiet again. I returned to my own bed, writing desk and books and letters, the externally imposed life of a hermit. I was exhausted from the stormy events of the past months—the Chernobyl catastrophe, the crowd of people in my house, the earthquake, my completely disorganized daily life and my hopelessly gloomy personal prospects. I felt at that time that I had lost my long war with the diabolic machine which destroys entire nations. I was only a drop in the ocean of the communists' victims, but my rebellion against the devil had not been meaningless after all. Possibly, I thought to myself, it was a drop of lava which, joining with millions of others like it, would someday spew out thunder and fire and destroy this monstrosity which so vehemently consumed human lives. Yes, my sacrifice had not been in vain, but still—how could I go on living in such a way?

The year 1986 marked the fifteenth year of my struggle against the Soviet system, including eight long years in exile, four in Siberia, four away from Moscow. Moreover, the international situation was not at all promising. U.S.–Soviet relations had not improved in the 1980's and emigration from the U.S.S.R had dwindled to a trickle. After 1980 only a selected few lucky individuals had received exit visas. What chance did I have—a symbol for both friends and enemies?

My sister bore the brunt of my despair. "Ida, take yourself in hand! I insist!" she pleaded into the receiver from Israel. "Pull yourself together; everything possible is being done for you. Believe me, things are at a serious stage now."

I had not become reconciled or resigned. The living must go on—but how? I tried reading books but I couldn't. I crumpled the leaves in my little garden but still could not relax. There was no one to whom I could bare my soul, no one who could understand and share my despair. Although people were living all around me, I was totally alone.

I opened the Bible in Hebrew and transformed all my despair and pain into persistence. Word by word I built up my vocabulary.

I spent a whole day on the first page and the next morning started it again. Each day I began with the first page of the Bible until I remembered all the words. I pictured myself first as a shepherd, then as a warrior, an anonymous participant in the history of my people. The associations returned me to reality, to the desert which I myself was crossing.

To my surprise I was summoned one winter day for a telephone call from Moscow. I couldn't imagine who it could be. It turned out that my dissident friend Bella Koval had been talking on the phone with Andrei Sakharov and Elena Bonner, whose telephone was suddenly reconnected. Sakharov asked her to give me their telephone number. What a change! Only a few months ago, I had faithfully ordered a phone conversation with them every three days only to be given the usual excuse, "No one appeared at the summons." I persisted, complained and ordered again. This went on for almost a month and a half until other events crowded out my idea of having a phone conversation with them.

Now I could speak to them. We spoke for ten minutes and no one interrupted or disconnected us. What was going on? Was it freedom of expression? Now it was possible to talk with the still disgraced Sakharov! He told me they had been permitted to return to Moscow and he asked that I meet them upon their return on December 21, 1986. I was eager to do so, but would I succeed where I failed before in traveling there? I decided to send telegrams to the interior ministers and procurators of the Soviet Union and of Moldavia. The constitution guaranteed me the right of free movement throughout the country, the Sakharovs also promised to send a telegram to the interior minister upholding my rights. I was almost certain that in the current atmosphere of "freedom," when Andrei Sakharov had his eyes on me, the chekists would not throw me off the bus as they had in the past.

A clerk sold me an airplane ticket although after I handed her my passport, the woman at the ticket office left the room, probably to call the KGB for instructions. I bought a ticket for the day flight so that I could phone the Sakharovs if things did not go well. No one stopped me when I got on the bus and, in fact, there was not even one policeman that I could notice at the station. I made it safely to the airport but decided to phone Moscow just in case and spoke with Vladimir Kislik, a fellow refusenik who had suffered through many prison experiences.

"Volodya, I'm at the airport and passed the first checkpoint. There are a lot of policemen in the building; perhaps it has nothing to do with me, but nevertheless, if I don't call at three o'clock Moscow time, that means they took me off the plane. Please phone Sakharov right away and tell him about my call, okay?"

"I'll do as you wish, but I'm sure you'll make it to Moscow. Right now they do not want a big fuss, especially as Sakharov is involved."

I really did fly to Moscow. How many phone conversations and telegrams, how much money, time and agitation had been wasted on such a simple action!

At the Sakharovs' old Moscow apartment everything was just as it had been eight years before. The furniture was unchanged, conversations took place in the kitchen over tea and good food. We, however, were not only older, we had changed much after experiencing suffering. It was impossible to look at Andrei Dmitrievich without cursing his tormentors. I saw a very old man in front of me; even his voice had become hoarse and deeper. I wanted to ask, "What have they done to you!" but I kept silent. Our meeting, though, was a happy one; it was so good to sit with friends and talk about people and issues close to our hearts.

After my successful visit with the Sakharovs in Moscow, living in Bendery became even more unbearable. My Moscow apartment had been waiting for me since my exile in 1978. As if the KGB had read my thoughts, they now decided to take the apartment away, thus depriving me of any hope of returning. In my absence and without consulting me, a Soviet court, in violation of the law, delivered a verdict depriving me of the right to an apartment in Moscow. It wrung my heart when I unexpectedly received this court ruling among various other letters, but what could I do? I could only do what millions of other Soviet citizens did—curse "the most humane system," which does not even recognize its own laws. I remained silent.

In February 1987, I received a letter from Vladimir Kislik, who wrote that as his situation was now relatively normal, he was willing to help me; in particular he was concerned about my regaining a residence permit for Moscow. Although I harbored no hopes, I sent Vladimir all the relevant papers. He then informed me that he had consulted with a lawyer without telling him about my problems with the KGB; he had just given the official version, that I was an ordinary Soviet hooligan. The lawyer confirmed that the apartment had been illegally taken from me and he consented to take the case, feeling confident he could win it.

Vladimir hurried me along so that I would not miss the deadline to appeal and a date was set for a preliminary hearing. In addition to the plaintiff, the defendant and the woman judge, an unidentified "someone" showed up for the hearing. Hearing the plaintiff's complaint and the replies of the defendant, this someone questioned the judge about the legislation concerning residence permits. She confirmed the fact that in my case the law guaranteed a residence permit in Moscow. Saying, "I understand," the someone got up and left the room.

A hearing was set for two months later but just before that date, Vladimir and I received a notice from the court that the hearing had been postponed. I had neither illusions nor faith in Soviet law. I knew that if the KGB said no, so would the court. Vladimir, however, waited for the hearing, for which a new date had been set.

My life in the meantime followed the general course of liberalizing developments in the country. Tails no longer crowded around me, cars did not chase me down the streets and no one guarded my house anymore. I often phoned the Sakharovs in Moscow from the local telephone booth—the cheapest intercity call in the world! I would drop in a fifteen kopeck coin and dial their number; when someone answered on the other end, the coin would go down and we could talk for hours since the meter went off at the first sounds of a voice. I discovered this once when, having spoken on the phone, I pressed on the coin return button and coins began spilling out. When I later told the Sakharovs, they were distressed, realizing that it meant their freedom was only an illusion: the KGB was still listening in and watching them. They were in the same cage as before, only now it was slightly gilded.

One day Vladimir Kislik unexpectedly sent a telegram asking me to call him back. He had received a notice that the court would consider my suit on restoring my rights to a residence permit in

Moscow on October 2, 1987. "I think you should come to Moscow at that time," he said.

I think I shall never in my life get rid of that particular anxiety which I feel when I come to an airport, train or bus station. Only those who have been forcefully ejected even once from such places would recognize this feeling. My situation had changed, however, since the Sakharovs' return from exile and I felt that their name somehow protected me. I thus did not have any trouble appearing in Moscow on the eve of the court hearing. I went straight to the apartment of Judith Ratner. She and her husband Leonid Bialy were also refuseniks. I strolled around the city in the morning and when I returned to Judith's apartment, she opened the door and said, in a quiet voice, "Ida, sit down, please, I have something to tell you."

Frightened by her manner, I stared and asked, "What happened, tell me right away, is it something in Israel?"

"You have a visa!" she said quietly.

"It can't be. I don't believe it!"

"You have a visa," she repeated, and her face, I thought, revealed her envy.

"No, they want me to leave Moscow! Who said that I have a visa?" I asked, beginning to tremble from excitement.

"Slava just called from Bendery. The police are looking for you, but Slava refused to give them your address in Moscow. Then they asked him to tell you to come back immediately; you have a visa."

"Do you believe it?" I asked.

"I think it's true," replied Judith.

"How can I find out whether it's true or whether they just want to trick me into leaving Moscow?"

"Call the OVIR, perhaps they know something," Judith suggested.

I phoned immediately. "This is Nudel speaking; I was told that the Bendery police are looking for me."

"Hold on a minute," said a male voice.

"Ida Yakovlevna, this is Rudolf Kuznetsov speaking, you do have a visa; return immediately to Moldavia."

"I don't believe it."

"This is Kuznetsov, the chief of the All-Union OVIR. You

must remember me. I repeat, you have a visa. Go back to Moldavia immediately, today. They'll explain everything to you in Kishinev."

"Is it really true? Really?"

"It's true," he said. "Return to Moldavia immediately."

"Thank you, thank you!" I mumbled and immediately pictured the face of this Kuznetsov, labeled a sadist and bloodsucker by thousands of refuseniks. I bit my tongue and hung up the receiver. How could I forget, even for a moment, the tears and pain, mine and others, linked to this person? How did my tongue twist to thank him?

Still doubting, I said slowly, "It seems like I really have a visa. I am actually beginning to believe it. He spoke to me so politely! I must call Lena immediately." My request for a call to Israel was taken right away.

I immediately phoned Sakharov and exclaimed, "Andrei Dmitrievich, I have a visa; two minutes ago Kuznetsov himself told me so and to return to Moldavia immediately."

Elena Bonner took the receiver, "Ida, how happy we are for you; finally your suffering is over. We are so happy, Ida. Everyone here including Mama sends you congratulations."

I put down the receiver and immediately got a call from the international telephone service.

"Did you order a call to Israel?" someone asked.

"Yes, certainly."

"Don't hang up; I'll connect you."

"Just think," I said to Judith, "the KGB took care of everything, even the telephone call."

There in my distant motherland, which in my dreams I had flown to so often and for so painfully long a time, my sister answered, speaking in Hebrew before she realized that it was me.

"Lena, I have a visa, I just found out five minutes ago from Kuznetsov. I believe that it's for real. I have a visa."

She broke into loud sobs. Through her crying she called, "Leva, Ida has a visa."

Leva's voice came over the wire, "Well, dear, finally! Congratulations and come quickly."

Lena again took the receiver and I told her all the details; then we said goodbye and I promised to call frequently.

It's impossible to describe the commotion that followed. Right away I called various people to share my good fortune. When I called Vladimir Kislik, he wanted to tell me about the hearing but I had already forgotten about it and everything else that had been so vitally important just five minutes before. Vladimir considered it his duty, however, to report that the hearing had not taken place; the defendant had not appeared and the hearing had been delayed until October 20.

"That was to be expected. Perhaps that's why they chose this day to inform me of the visa?"

I felt like I was beginning to go crazy; the news had completely overwhelmed me. Someone else in my place would have pranced around the room and jumped from joy, but I smiled and quietly sat in an armchair. Is it really true? I asked myself. Is it?

The phone rang incessantly. People began to call from abroad—Israel, the U.S., England, France, Australia, again Israel and again and again. As soon as I replaced the receiver, the phone would ring.

I did not return to Moldavia that day or the next because Yom Kippur began that evening. I had waited for this hour for sixteen years; they could wait two days for me. On this holy day I would not budge.

The silence of Yom Kippur began and the whole next day was quiet and calm. I completely accepted the fact that my life had taken another turn and a new life was awaiting me. This would now be my third life on this earth. The first I had lived as an ordinary Soviet citizen, the second as a fighter for the right of my people to emigrate to Israel. In the third I would live as a simple Israeli.

The preparations for my departure proceeded smoothly, as if everything had been planned and thought out in advance. Tickets for the flight to Kishinev were waiting for me at the Aeroflot office. From the Kishinev airport I rushed by taxi to the Moldavian interior ministry. Although it was only ten minutes before the midday closing, the reception room supervisor listened to my incoherent words and suggested that I go to the building where visas are issued.

"I don't have very much time and it's just a few minutes before the lunch break," I said nervously.

"You'll have to wait; they'll take you after lunch."

In fact, the head of the Moldavian OVIR received me during

the break and declared, "You must leave the Soviet Union by October 20."

"I won't be able to. I have a private apartment and a person who owns property can't leave. Besides, I'm taking my dog with me and it takes a month to get permission from the veterinary service."

"What other problems do you have?" he asked.

"I don't know; I never left before," I replied.

He summoned an assistant and handed me a list of documents which I had to present in order to receive a visa. "Let us know about all your difficulties. I am personally responsible for your departure. You must leave the Soviet Union no later than October 20."

"If I can manage it," I murmured, almost to myself.

In Bendery, acquaintances saw my beaming face and sincerely sharing my joy vigorously shook my hand. Some said, "If even you received an exit visa, then we, too, can apply to leave."

As soon as I put the key into the lock of my front door, Pizer began to howl joyfully. Her patience was exhausted while I was opening the outside door and, unable to restrain herself, she decided to break the door in her excitement to greet me after our long separation.

Usually reticent about showing my feelings, I had trained the dog to be like me, but now, when no one saw me, I showered my tumultuous joy on her. "Pizer, we're leaving! We're going away forever! And you're going with me," I cried, circling with her in dance, singing a song of my own invention.

I had barely managed to celebrate with her when Slava arrived and again related how everything had happened. "Ida, you can't imagine how I envy you," he said. "You had powerful patrons. What will happen to us? I have three children!"

"Slava, you must be an activist," I told him for the millionth time.

"How can I be an activist when I have three children?" he responded.

"For the sake of your children you must be so!"

The next day I became the happy owner of three large suitcases which Slava had seen in a local store. I made a list of the things and books which I wanted to take with me and proceeded to dispense with the rest of my possessions. Books, personal items and domestic articles began flying around the apartment as if they were alive. Each corner was meant for someone else. One corner, for example, was for Malva Landa, a Jewish woman who devoted many years of her life to a struggle against the Soviet system and had often suffered at the hands of the KGB. I divided up among friends the books which I had carefully collected during the years of exile, works of Eric Fromm, Viktor E. Frankl, Sigmund Freud, Martin Buber, Elie Wiesel and the history of the Jewish people. I had not realized that I was such a hoarder.

Time flew by. One morning my neighbor impatiently knocked on my door and shouted that the head of the republic OVIR was on the phone. As I ran to answer it, the horrible thought flashed through my mind that my visa had been canceled.

"Ida Yakovlevna, are you willing to fly with Dr. Armand Hammer aboard his private plane on October 15?"

"I'm going to Israel," I replied.

"Are you willing to fly with Doctor Armand Hammer to Israel?"

I realized instantly that if I'm with Hammer, they won't search me; the chekists won't have a last chance to scoff at me. "Yes, but I don't have my documents yet. Today is October 8."

"We'll help you with everything, just don't get upset," he said.

How polite he was and how they were hurrying!

Finally the day arrived. It was raining but I walked in an unbuttoned coat without an umbrella. I could not think of anything but my visa.

My body began to shake when the OVIR chief opened the middle drawer of his desk and took out a small sheet of greenish paper. I knew that that was it, the magical key to freedom. I stretched out my hand toward the paper, but he was not yet ready to hand it to me. I lacked the mettle to lower my hand without the visa and I remained sitting with my outstretched, trembling hand; it was my last moment of weakness. I did all the rest calmly and coolly—I took the visa, checked the stamp, dates, my name —as if not my own fate, but someone else's was lying trembling in my hand.

"Don't worry, Ida Yakovlevna, I personally will be present at the airport. If any problems arise, we shall settle them on the spot," said the head of the republic OVIR. "I congratulate you, your dream has finally come true."

Everything seemed to be happening in a dream, a naive fantasy; just a few months ago I had been thrown off a bus when I had tried to go to Moscow. My suspicious mind would sometimes ask whether this was not some Satanic game that the KGB was playing with me.

Three days before my departure I arrived in Moscow with all my possessions, a few suitcases and my dog. During those three days I made a final visit to familial graves and I parted with my friends, with many as it turned out forever. It was painful thinking of those with whom I had shared my agonizing but glorious path. What still awaited them in this country? Which way was the Soviet Union turning now? How would it deal with those who kept pressing for change, risking health and life itself?

On the morning of that marvelous day, October 15, 1987, a small cortege of cars, headed by Dr. Armand Hammer's, drove up to the special entrance to Moscow International Airport. All my things were on the other side of the main building on the runway. I wanted nothing more than to be on the plane, that piece of non-Soviet territory! The waiting was agonizing.

We had reached the moment of parting, when the traveler is already far away in his thoughts and sees the present through the fog of the future. That very moment, when there is no longer anything to say, is the real parting. It is always silent.

What am I feeling now, I asked myself. Nothing that a person who is leaving forever ought to feel—not a drop of regret about the past nor an ounce of anxiety about the future.

Finally we were called for inspection. My assumption had been correct—the customs check was merely symbolic.

"Aren't you taking foreign currency with you?" asked the customs inspector. Like any Soviet emigrant I was entitled to buy and take out $143 in American currency. I showed her this money and the official bank receipt for it.

"Do you have any valuable or antique objects?"

"Of course not," I replied, and I was telling the truth. Although I had no costly jewels or antiques, my suitcase contained documents and records of the history of another political prisoner, Leonid Lubman, yet another senselessly tormented soul, another broken life.

We quickly passed through passport control—Dr. Hammer and his wife, Frances, Richard Jacobs, the young vice president of

Occidental Petroleum and I, with Pizer tightly clutching my leg. In my pocket I felt the reassuring presence of the two religious symbols that had been sent to me in Siberia.

The flight to Israel was similar to one of the fairy tales from my childhood. Dr. Hammer's magic carpet airplane was a Boeing converted into a comfortable apartment for its owners, who lived in it while traveling. Unhappy about being in the plane, Pizer ran around the cabin, sniffing for a way out. Neither the dog food nor the kindness of the crew helped. She stood near the closed hatch, drawing in air and whining.

Dr. Hammer and his wife retired to the bedroom, the crew occupied their posts and I was left in the cabin with Rick Jacobs. Enjoying my conversation with him, I did not notice how the time passed. The pilot came into the cabin of the plane and shook my hand, saying, "I congratulate you, Ida, we have just left the borders of the U.S.S.R. and are flying over Turkey. Now you are really a free person."

Although the flight from Moscow to Tel Aviv took three and a half hours, it seemed only some minutes later when the pilot announced, "We are approaching Israel; in five minutes we'll be arriving at Ben-Gurion Airport. The crew and I congratulate Ida Nudel on her return to her homeland." Armand Hammer and his wife came out of the bedroom, glasses and a bottle of champagne appeared on the table, and we drank a toast to the *return*.

The dog settled down the very second the plane touched ground. Calmly wagging her tail, she made the rounds of the passengers and affably touched each one's hand with her moist, warm nose. We all began laughing, amazed at her conduct.

"She understands everything," said the pilot.

During the long, tortured years of waiting, I had often imagined my return home, and now it was only seconds away. The engines had stopped roaring, but the door was still closed. When it finally opened, the first people I saw were Lena, Leva and Yakov, whom I had not seen for sixteen years. Those years seemed to have flown by in a minute and at the same time to have crawled like eternity. The plane quickly filled with friends and I went from one embrace to another. The faces of Lena and Leva shone with the warm glow of unlimited and sincere joy; their eyes gave off such warmth that I could feel it physically. I remembered my nephew Yakov as a lively, curious nine-year-old and now I saw a young man. I painfully searched his bearded face, shaded by dark glasses, for recognizable features, but there was no time for leisurely contemplation. People were shaking my hand, hugging and kissing me, familiar faces flickered in front of me but I did not have time to identify one person before I landed in the embrace of another.

"Ida, thousands of Israelis came to meet you," I heard my sister say. "Jane Fonda flew in specially with friends to greet you," she added and then I saw Jane's shining face right in front of me.

My face was burning and my eyes sparkling; it seemed as if I were melting in the fire of superhuman joy, but they did not let me melt. Forcing me to return to reality, a strong hand guided me toward one and then another direction, identifying people. In a dense crowd we proceeded into a sparkling hall filled with many people; I saw smiles and cameras flashing everywhere like magic lights. Although people were talking to me and I was answering, I was so excited that I heard neither their voices nor my own words. In my honor people were singing songs, delivering speeches, floodlights were lit and cameras were clicking, people were smiling and waving their hands and flags.

I had returned Home.

Although it was late in the evening—the holiday of Simchas Torah had ended a few hours earlier—thousands of Israelis gathered at the airport, young and old, members of government and ordinary citizens, religious believers and atheists, to celebrate the festival promised by our prophets—the return Home! It was a great joy, honor and responsibility to symbolize the Return. The celebration took place not only in Israel; people all over the world who had made our celebration possible rejoiced in unison with us. My heart was full of triumph and victory, and though I did rejoice, my memory preserved the suffering and tears.

"Ida, come to the phone, Secretary of State George Shultz wants to speak with you." Shultz had once said to Lena, "Only among the Jews would a sister—not a mother or wife—fight so devotedly and desperately for the freedom of her sister." Over the phone I heard Shultz's excited voice, "Ida, we are happy for you, you are a free person." I remember that I just smiled in reply, forgetting that he could not see my face. "Ida, your release is a great victory," he continued. "Soon your other friends will also receive exit visas. Many people will be able to leave the Soviet

Union. It is a great victory." His words were encouraging and his voice inspired confidence.

"Ida, come to the phone, speak to President Ronald Reagan," and someone took my hand. In a panic I felt as if I had forgotten my English. Simply beyond the bounds of my emotional capacity, I don't remember what the President said or whether I answered him in Russian or English.

Late at night the guests left my sister's small apartment. My sister kissed me good night like a mother kissing her little daughter. The next day I would begin a new, third life—life at Home.

EPILOGUE

IT IS SO DIFFICULT WHEN THOUSANDS OF EYES LOOK AT YOU with love and admiration. When people surround me on the street and offer their hands in a sincere burst of joy, I experience mixed emotions. Watch yourself, Ida, I tell myself, the force of such love can be destructive!

My dream came true and I am home. I was fifty-seven when I arrived and I had to start life anew. Like a child I had to learn to speak and to understand how that society operates.

"Ida, tell us how you survived, how you managed not to give in and how you defeated them," people asked me.

"Oh, how I want to get away from the past, the sooner the better. I can get stuck between my past and the future I am seeking for myself."

"What do you want to do in Israel?" people wanted to know.

"I don't know yet. I know only what I don't want," I reply. "I don't want to belong to Russia anymore. I want to forget and erase it from my memory."

"That's impossible," say sober-minded friends. "It will always be with you—the language, habits and the fifty-seven years which belong to it, too."

"Is this how you imagined Israel? Weren't you disappointed?" people inquire.

"No, when I see how beautiful the country is, I love it even more."

"Times are very difficult now, Ida, perhaps more difficult than ever before," I am told. "Our state faces not only an external threat but a crisis of self-definition."

"I have been in difficult situations before; I shall find my place in this struggle, too. I must find it. I promise that I will."
May 1988–July 1989
Israel

INDEX